THE NORTON/GROVE
HANDBOOKS IN MUSIC

Analysis

THE NORTON/GROVE
HANDBOOKS IN MUSIC

Analysis

by
Ian Bent

with a Glossary
by
William Drabkin

W. W. NORTON & COMPANY
NEW YORK   LONDON

Parts of this material first published in
The New Grove Dictionary of Music and Musicians®,
edited by Stanley Sadie, 1980

The New Grove and *The New Grove Dictionary of Music and Musicians*
are registered trademarks of Macmillan Publishers Limited, London

First published in the UK 1987 by
THE MACMILLAN PRESS LTD
Houndmills, Basingstoke, Hampshire RG21 2XS
and London
Companies and representatives throughout the world

British Library Cataloguing in Publication Data
Bent, Ian
Analysis. — (The New Grove handbooks in music)
1. Musical analysis
I. Title   II. Drabkin, William   III.
The new Grove dictionary of music and musicians
781   MT6

ISBN 0-333-41731-3 (hardback)
ISBN 0-333-41732-1 (paperback)

First American edition 1987 by
W. W. NORTON & COMPANY
500 Fifth Avenue, New York NY 10110

ISBN   0-393-02447-4

Contents

Abbreviations

AcM	*Acta musicologica*
AMw	*Archiv für Musikwissenschaft*
AMZ	*Allgemeine musikalische Zeitung*
AnMc	*Analecta musicologica*
anon.	anonymous(ly)
appx	appendix
BB	*Bayreuther Blätter*
BJb	*Bach-Jahrbuch*
BMw	*Beiträge zur Musikwissenschaft*
BWV	Bach-Werke-Verzeichnis [Schmieder, catalogue of J. S. Bach's works]
c	circa [about]
cf	confer [compare]
chap.	chapter
CHum	*Computers and the Humanities*
CMc	*Current Musicology*
Conn.	Connecticut
Cz.	Czech
DC	District of Columbia
diss.	dissertation
DJbM	*Deutsches Jahrbuch der Musikwissenschaft*
ed.	editor, edited (by)
edn.	edition
e.g.	exempli gratia [for example]
EM	*Ethnomusicology*
Eng.	English
esp.	especially
etc	et cetera [and so on]
ex., exx.	example, examples
f, ff	following page, following pages
f., ff.	folio, folios
fig.	figure [illustration]
fl	floruit [he/she flourished]
Fr.	French
Ger.	German
GfMKB	*Gesellschaft für Musikforschung Kongressbericht*

Grove 1(–5)	G. Grove, ed.: *A Dictionary of Music and Musicians*, 2nd–5th edns. as *Grove's Dictionary of Music and Musicians*
Grove 6	S. Sadie, ed.: *The New Grove Dictionary of Music and Musicians*
H	Hoboken catalogue [Haydn]
HMT	H. H. Eggebrecht, ed.: *Handwörterbuch der musikalischen Terminologie*
HV	*Hudební věda*
ibid	ibidem [in the same place]
i.e.	id est [that is]
IMSCR	*International Musicological Society Congress Report*
IMusSCR	*International Musical Society Congress Report*
incl.	includes, including
Ind.	Indiana
IRASM	*International Review of the Aesthetics and Sociology of Music*
It.	Italian
ITO	*In Theory Only*
JAMS	*Journal of the American Musicological Society*
JASI	*Journal of the Arnold Schoenberg Institute*
JbMP	*Jahrbuch der Musikbibliothek Peters*
Jg.	Jahrgang [year of publication/volume]
JIFMC	*Journal of the International Folk Music Council*
JMT	*Journal of Music Theory*
JMus	*Journal of Musicology*
JRME	*Journal of Research in Music Education*
K	Köchel catalogue [Mozart; no. after / is from 6th edn.]
KJb	*Kirchenmusikalisches Jahrbuch*

Mass.	Massachusetts	RdM	Revue de musicologie
Mf	Die Musikforschung	ReM	La revue musicale
MGG	F. Blume, ed.: Die Musik in Geschichte und Gegenwart	repr.	reprinted
		repubd	republished
MIT	Massachusetts Institute of Technology	rev.	revision, revised (by/for)
		RiemannL 12	·W. Gurlitt, ed.: Riemanns Musik Lexikon, suppls. to 12th edn. by C. Dahlhaus
Mj	Musique en jeu		
MJb	Mozart-Jahrbuch des Zentralinstituts für Mozartforschung		
		RIM	Rivista italiana di musicologia
ML	Music and Letters	SIMG	Sammelbände der Internationalen Musik-Gesellschaft
MMR	The Monthly Musical Record		
MQ	The Musical Quarterly	SM	Studia musicologia Academiae scientiarum hungaricae
MR	The Music Review		
MT	The Musical Times		
MTS	Music Theory Spectrum	SMw	Studien zur Musikwissenschaft
MusA	Music Analysis	SMz	Schweizerische Musikzeitung/Revue musicale suisse
MZ	Muzikološki zbornik		
		SovM	Sovetskaya muzïka
		Sp.	Spanish
no.	number	STMf	Svensk tidskrift för musikforskning
NRMI	Nuova rivista musicale italiana		
NY	New York State		
NZM	Neue Zeitschrift für Musik	TP	Theory and Practice
		trans.	translation, translated by
ÖMz	Österreichische Musikzeitschrift	TVNM	Tijdschrift van de Vereniging voor Nederlandse muziekgeschiedenis
op., opp.	opus, opera		
orig.	original(ly)		
		U.	University
p., pp.	page, pages	UCLA	University of California, Los Angeles
Penn.	Pennsylvania		
pl.	plate	unpubd	unpublished
PNM	Perspectives of New Music	USA	United States of America
PRMA	Proceedings of the Royal Musical Association		
		vol.	volume
pubd	published		
R	photographic reprint	ZfM	Zeitschrift für Musik
RBM	Revue belge de musicologie	ZMw	Zeitschrift für Musikwissenschaft

Preface

This book is a revision and expansion of the article 'Analysis' in *The New Grove Dictionary of Music and Musicians* (London, 1980). The historical section (now Chapters II and III) has been extended to include developments since 1975. It has also been substantially amplified at a number of points, notably to include discussion of Renaissance diminution theory and of figured-bass and harmonic theory. The consideration of several theorists has been enlarged, as has been the treatment of 19th-century theory in particular. The section on analytical method (Chapter IV) now has a separate discussion of set-theory analysis, as is only right for what has proved itself a major new contribution to the world of analysis. Errors have been corrected, thanks in large part to the care taken by reviewers of the original article. The bibliography has not only been updated, expanded and corrected but has been rearranged in a form more appropriate to a book, in alphabetical order with cross-references.

The largest addition is the glossary, which furnishes definitions of truly analytical terms in a wide range of 20th-century methods (see p.109). Some of the terms have brief entries in *The New Grove*; these have been expanded or rewritten, not only in the light of reviewers' comments and recent trends but also in the hope that the glossary may be used as a practical tool both for analysts and for readers of analytical texts. The glossary is supported by 28 music examples, and 12 figures have been added to the book.

For all these changes, the book retains the underlying perceptions of the article, particularly as regards the nature of analysis and its relationships to its contiguous disciplines.

This preface gives the author of the original article the opportunity at last to acknowledge the great help in drafting given to him in the mid-1970s by his now co-author, at a time when they were fellow editors in the *Grove* office.

Ian Bent
William Drabkin
December 1986

CHAPTER I

Musical Analysis in Perspective

Musical analysis is the resolution of a musical structure into relatively simpler constituent elements, and the investigation of the functions of those elements within that structure. In such a process the 'structure' may be part of a work, a work in its entirety, a group or even a repertory of works, in a written or oral tradition. The distinction often drawn between formal analysis and stylistic analysis is a pragmatic one, but is unnecessary in theoretical terms. Both fall within the above definition, since on the one hand any musical complex, no matter how small or large, may be deemed a 'style'; and on the other hand, all the comparative processes that characterize stylistic analysis are inherent in the basic analytical activity of resolving structure into elements.

A more general definition of the term as implied in common parlance might be: that part of the study of music which takes as its starting-point the music itself, rather than external factors.

1. The Place of Analysis in the Study of Music

The phrase 'musical analysis', taken in a general sense, embraces a large number of diverse activities. Some of these are mutually exclusive: they represent fundamentally different views of the nature of music, music's role in human life, and the role of the human intellect with regard to music. These differences of view render the field of analysis difficult to define within its own boundaries. (Such a definition is the concern of Chapters II–III and of Chapter IV, §1.) More difficult still, in some ways, is to define where precisely analysis lies within the study of music. Underlying all aspects of analysis as an activity is the fundamental point of contact between mind and musical sound, namely musical perception.

The concerns of analysis as a whole can be said to have much in common on the one hand with those of musical aesthetics and on the other with those of compositional theory. The three regions of study might be thought of as occupying positions along an axis which has at one extreme the placing of music within philosophical schemes and at the other the giving of technical instruction in the craft of composition.

Analysis in Perspective

The analyst, like the aesthetician, is in part concerned with the nature of the musical work: with what it is, or embodies, or signifies; with how it has come to be; with its effects or implications; with its relevance to, or value for, its recipients. Where they differ is in the centres of focus of their studies: the analyst concentrates his attention on a musical structure (whether a chord, a phrase, a work, the output of a composer or court etc), and seeks to define its constituent elements and explain how they operate; but the aesthetician focusses on the nature of music *per se* and its place among the arts, in life and reality. That the two supply information to each other is undoubted: the analyst provides a fund of material which the aesthetician may adduce as evidence in forming his conclusions, and the analyst's definition of the specific furnishes a continual monitoring service for the aesthetician's definition of the general; conversely, the aesthetician's insights provide problems for the analyst to solve, condition his approach and method, and ultimately furnish the means of exposing his hidden assumptions. Their activities may overlap so that they often find themselves doing similar things. Nonetheless, they have two essential differences: first, that analysis tends to strive towards the status of a natural science, whereas aesthetics is a branch of philosophy, the significance of this being that it sets up a one-way flow whereby analysis supplies evidence in answer to the empirical questions of aesthetics (and the extent to which it fails to do this effectively is a measure of the scientific achievement of analysis so far); and second, that the analyst's ultimate concern is with the place of a musical structure within the totality of musical structures, whereas the aesthetician's is with the place of musical structures within the system of reality.

Similarly, the analyst and the theorist of musical composition (*Satztechnik*; *Kompositionslehre*) have a common interest in the laws of musical construction. Many would deny a separation of any kind and would argue that analysis was a subgroup of musical theory. But that is an attitude that springs from particular social and educational conditions. While important contributions have been made to analysis by teachers of composition, others have been made by performers, instrumental teachers, critics and historians. Analysis may serve as a tool for teaching, though it may in that case instruct the performer or the listener at least as often as the composer; but it may equally well be a private activity – a procedure for discovering. Musical analysis is no more implicitly a part of pedagogical theory than is chemical analysis; nor is it implicitly a part of the acquisition of compositional techniques. On the contrary, the statements of musical theorists can form primary material for the analyst's investigations by providing criteria against which relevant music may be examined.

Of greater significance is the fact that analytical procedures can be applied to styles of performance and interpretation as well as to those of composition. But the point at which composition ceases and interpretation begins is rarely incisive. Most Western analysis takes a score as its subject matter and implicitly assumes it to be a finalized presentation of musical ideas. If it is true that the notated form in which a medieval, Renaissance or Baroque work survives is an incomplete record, it is even more to the point that for the analyst of ethnomusicological material recorded on tape a score is only an intermediary device which in no way marks off 'composer' from 'performer'. It provides a

2

coarse communication of the detail recorded on tape, much of which he will have to analyse by ear or with electronic measuring equipment. Analytical techniques can be applied to aurally perceived material in any cultural tradition of performances.

Briefly, then, analysis is concerned with musical structure, however it arises and is recorded, not merely with composition. Moreover, within the subject matter that analysis and compositional theory have in common, the former is by definition concerned with resolution and explanation, so that its reverse procedure – synthesis – is no more than a means of verification; the latter is concerned directly with the generation of music, and analytical method is only a means of discovery. Again, the fields overlap but with essential differences of subject, of aim and of method.

* * *

A rather different relationship exists between musical analysis and musical history. To the historian, analysis may appear as a tool for historical inquiry. He uses it to detect relationships between 'styles', and thus to establish chains of causality which operate along the dimension of time and are anchored in time by verifiable factual information. He may, for example, observe features in common between the styles of two composers (or groups of composers) and inquire by internal analytical methods and external factual ones whether this represents an influence of one upon the other; or, in reverse order, seek common features of style when he knows of factual links. Conversely, he may detect features out of common between pieces normally associated for one reason or another, and proceed to distinguish by comparative analysis distinct traditions or categories. Again, he may use an analytical classification of features as a means of establishing a chronology of events.

In turn, the analyst may view historical method as a tool for analytical inquiry. His subject matter is rather like sections cut through history. When under analysis they are timeless, or 'synchronic'; they embody internal relationships which the analyst seeks to uncover. But factual information, concerning events in time, may for example determine which of several possible structures is the most viable, or explain causally the presence of some element which is incongruous in analytical terms. Comparative analysis of two or more separate phenomena (whether separated chronologically, geographically, socially or intellectually) only really activates the dimension of time – becoming 'dia-chronic' – when historical information relating the phenomena is correlated with the analytical findings. Historical and analytical inquiry are thus locked together in mutual dependency, with all things in common as to subject matter and with completely complementary methods of working.

* * *

One further proximity needs to be accounted for: that of analysis and criticism. Criticism is inseparable on the one hand from aesthetics and on the other from analysis. Within criticism there has been constant debate as to the extent to which it is a descriptive or a judicial activity. The 'descriptive' critic tries to do

3

either or both of two things: to portray in words his own inner response – to depict his responding feelings – to a piece of music or a performance, or to think his way into the composer's or performer's mind and expound the vision that he then perceives. The 'judicial' critic evaluates what he experiences by certain standards. These standards may at one extreme be dogmatic canons of beauty, of truth or of taste – pre-set values against which everything is tested; or, at the other extreme, values that form during the experience, governed by an underlying belief that a composer or performer must do whatever he is attempting to do in the clearest and most effective way. This last approach suggests the way that most modern musical criticism works: by trying to deduce the artistic conception that lies behind what the critic experiences, and by evaluating the effectiveness with which the conception is realized, not to mention the extent to which the conception itself answers its prior demands (an 'occasion' for a commissioned work, a dramatic starting-point for a stage work, the work itself as presented by the composer for a performance).

In none of the above does criticism differ categorically from analysis: there is a latent debate within analysis as to whether the analyst's function is descriptive or judicial. There is perhaps a difference of degree. In general, analysis is more concerned with describing than with judging. Most analysis arrives ultimately at the point that the judicial critic has reached when he has perceived to his own satisfaction the artistic 'conception', and is about to present judgment. In this sense, analysis goes less far than criticism, and it does so essentially because it aspires to objectivity and considers judgment to be subjective. But this in turn suggests the other difference between analysis and criticism, namely that the latter stresses the intuitive response of the critic, relies upon his wealth of experience, uses his ability to relate present response to prior experience, and takes these two things as data and method, whereas analysis tends to use as its data definable elements: phrase-units, harmonies, dynamic levels, measured time, bowings and tonguings, and other technical phenomena. Again this is a difference only of degree: a critic's response is often highly informed and made in the light of technical knowledge; and the analyst's definable elements (a phrase, a motif etc) are often defined by subjective conditions. To say that analysis consists of technical operations and criticism of human responses is thus an oversimplification.

Finally, whereas criticism works always through the medium of words (perhaps with music examples and illustrations) analysis may work through graphic display or annotated score, or even through musical sound rather than through words.

2. The Nature of Musical Analysis

The primary impulse of analysis is an empirical one: to get to grips with something on its own terms rather than in terms of other things. Its starting-point is a phenomenon itself as it does not necessarily rely on external factors (such as biographical facts, political events, social conditions, educational methods and all the other elements that make up the environment of that phenomenon). But like all artistic media, music presents a problem, inherent in the nature of its material. Music is not tangible and measurable as is a liquid or a solid for chemical analysis. The subject of a musical analysis has to be determined; whether it is the score itself, or at least the sound-image that the score projects; or the sound-image in the composer's mind at the moment of composition; or an interpretative performance; or the listener's temporal experience of a performance. All these categories are possible subjects for analysis. There is no agreement among analysts that one is more 'correct' than others – only that the score (when available) provides a reference point from which the analyst reaches out towards one sound-image or another, a 'neutral level' (to use the language of semiotics) which furnishes links between the creative activity and aesthetic experience.

Analysis is the means of answering directly the question 'How does it work?'. Its central activity is comparison. By comparison it determines the structural elements and discovers the functions of those elements. Comparison is common to all kinds of musical analysis – feature analysis, formal analysis, functional analysis, information-theory analysis, Schenkerian analysis, semiotic analysis, style analysis and so on: comparison of unit with unit, whether within a single work, or between two works, or between the work and an abstract 'model' such as sonata form or a recognized style. The central analytical act is thus the test for identity. And out of this arises the measurement of amount of difference, or degree of similarity. These two operations serve together to illuminate the three fundamental form-building processes: recurrence, contrast and variation.

This is a highly 'purified' portrayal of analysis, impartial, objective, yielding the answer 'It works this way . . .' rather than 'It works well' or 'It works badly'. In reality the analyst works with the preconceptions of his culture, age and personality. Thus the preoccupation which the 19th century had with the nature of 'genius' led to the phrasing of the initial question not as 'How does it work?' but as 'What makes this great?', and this has remained the initial question for some analytical traditions late in the 20th century. Since the 'scientific', comparative method was predominant over evaluation in such traditions, and since only works of genius possessed the quality of structural coherence, it followed that comparison of a work with an idealized model of structure or process produced a measure of its greatness.

This is only one example of many. The history of musical analysis that follows inevitably recounts the application of intellectual outlooks from successive ages to musical material: the principles of rhetoric, the concepts of organism and evolution, the subconscious mind, monism, probability theory, structuralism and so forth. Ultimately, the very existence of an observer – the scientist, the analyst – pre-empts the possibility of total objectivity. No single method or approach reveals the truth about music above all others, yet each age has felt that it is moving towards the authentic method.

5

CHAPTER II

History to 1900

1. Early History

Analysis, as a pursuit in its own right, came to be established only in the late 19th century; its emergence as an approach and method can be traced back to the 1750s. However, it existed as a scholarly tool, albeit an auxiliary one, from the Middle Ages onwards. The precursors of modern analysis can be seen within at least two branches of musical theory: the study of modal systems, and the theory of musical rhetoric. Where, in either of these branches, a theorist cited a piece of music as illustrating a point of technique or structure, only a small amount of discussion was necessary before he was using what would now be called the analytical approach.

In a sense, the classificatory work carried out by the Carolingian clergy in compiling tonaries was analytical: it involved determining the mode of every antiphon in a repertory of chant, and then subclassifying the modal groups according to their variable endings ('psalm tone differences'). Such theorists as Wilhelm of Hirsau, Hermannus Contractus and Johannes Afflighemensis in the 11th century cited antiphons with brief modal discussion, as did later theorists such as Marchetto da Padova and Gaffurius. Their discussions were essentially analysis in the service of performance. Renaissance theorists such as Pietro Aaron and Heinrich Glarean discussed the modality of polyphonic compositions by Josquin.

Such citations of individual works were all concerned with matters of technique and substance. It was only with the development of musical rhetoric that the idea of 'form' entered musical theory. The literature of ancient classical Greek and Roman rhetoric was rediscovered with the finding of Quintilian's *Institutio oratoria* in 1416. But the application of the ideas of classical oratory has been traced back as far as the Notre Dame polyphony of the early 13th century, and its direct impact is clear in late 15th-century music. It was with Listenius (*Musica*, 1537; Eng. trans., 1975) that *musica poetica* – musical rhetoric – was introduced into musical theory. Dressler (1563–4) alluded to a formal organization of music that would adopt the divisions of an oration into *exordium* ('opening'), *medium* and *finis*. Pontio (1588) discussed the standards for composing motets, masses, madrigals, psalms and other genres, and similar discussions occur in Cerone (1613), Praetorius (1618), Mattheson (1739) and Scheibe (1737–40).

A plan similar to Dressler's appeared in Burmeister (1606). Burmeister had already proposed (1599, 1601) that musical 'figures' could be treated as analogous to rhetorical figures, and it was he who first set out a full formal analysis of a piece of music. It was Burmeister, too, who gave the first definition of analysis (1606, pp.71f):

> Analysis of a composition is the resolution of that composition into a particular mode and a particular species of counterpoint [*antiphonorum genus*], and into its affections or periods.... Analysis consists of five parts: 1. Determination of mode; 2. of species of tonality; 3. of counterpoint; 4. Consideration of quality; 5. Resolution of the composition into affections or periods.

He then discussed each of the parts of analysis in detail, and followed this by his analysis of Lassus's five-voice motet *In me transierunt*. He defined the mode as authentic Phrygian, and discussed the total range of the piece and the individual vocal ranges. He defined the tonality as 'diatonic' ('because its intervals are usually formed by tone–tone–semitone'), the species of counterpoint as 'broken' (*fractum*: 'many notes are connected together in unequal value'), the quality as *diazeugmenorum* (signifying the use of $b\natural$, c', d', e' over middle a, rather than $b\flat$, c', d'). Burmeister then proceeded to the fifth stage (pp.73f):

> Furthermore, the work can be divided up very comfortably into nine periods, of which Period 1 comprises the *Exordium*, which is elaborated with two kinds of ornament: *fuga realis* [regular imitation] and *hypallage* [imitation by contrary motion]. The seven middle periods are the *Corpus* of the work, just like (if comparison be allowed with a kindred art) the *Confirmation* in oratory. Of these, the first [Period 2]

1. Orlande de Lassus: motet 'In me transierunt', bars 16–23, with annotations showing the analysis of J. Burmeister (1606), 64, 74

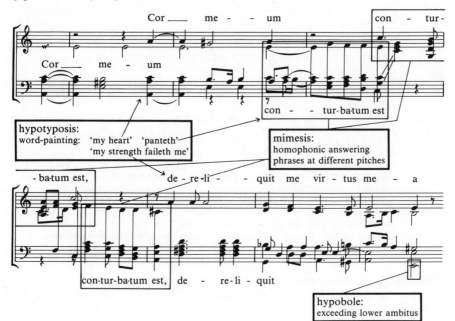

is ornamented with *hypotyposis* [word-painting], *climax* [repetition of a figure one step higher or lower] and *anadiplosis* [homophonic passages in multiple restatements at different pitches]. The second [Period 3] is ornamented in like manner, but has *anaphora* [pseudo-imitation of a figure, but not in all the voices] added to it. The third [Period 4] has *hypotyposis* and *mimesis* [homophonic phrases from different sub-choruses, answering each other at higher or lower pitches]. The fourth [Period 5] divides into two sub-choruses, and has *pathopoeia* [a semitone chromatic step expressive of sadness (on the words 'dolor meus' in Tenor I and Bassus)]. The fifth [Period 6] has *fuga realis*, the sixth [Period 7] *anadiplosis* and *noemate* [homophonic passages], the seventh [Period 8] *noemate* and *mimesis*. Period 9, the final one, is like the Epilogue in oratory. The piece ends with a principal cadence [with Tenor I falling to *E* and the Altus ascending to the octave above it].

Passages from this motet are cited elsewhere in Burmeister's treatise to illustrate rhetorical devices, thus giving a very full exegesis of the work. Fig.1 shows his analysis applied to Period 4.

Six years later Lippius (1612) discussed rhetoric as the basis of the *forma*, or structure of a composition. Throughout the Renaissance and Baroque periods the principles of rhetoric were prescriptive: they provided routine techniques for the process of composition rather than descriptive techniques for analysis. But they played an important part in the growing awareness of formal structure during these eras, and in particular of the function of contrast and the links between contrasted sections, out of which the analytical faculty was eventually to develop. Mattheson (1739) enumerated six parts of a well-developed composition such as an aria (p.236):

> *Exordium*, the introduction and beginning of a melody, in which its purpose and entire intention must be shown, so that the listener is prepared and his attention is aroused. . . .
>
> *Narratio* is a report or a narration in which the meaning and nature of the discourse is suggested. It is found immediately at the entrance of the voice – or the most important concerted [instrumental] part, and is related to the Exordium . . . by means of a suitable association [with the musical idea found in the Exordium].
>
> *Propositio* briefly contains the meaning and purpose of the musical speech, and is simple or compound . . . Such propositions have their place immediately after the first phrase of melody, when actually the bass takes the lead and presents the material both briefly and simply. Then the voice begins its *propositio variata*, joins with the bass, and thus creates a compound proposition.
>
> *Confirmatio* is the artistic strengthening of the proposition and is usually found in melodies by imaginative and unexpected repetitions, by which is not to be understood the normal Reprise. What we mean here are agreeable vocal passages repeated several times with all kinds of nice changes of decorated additions.
>
> *Confutatio* is the resolution of objections [i.e. contrasted or opposing musical ideas]. In melody it may be expressed either by tied notes or by the introduction and rejection of passages which appear strange.
>
> *Peroratio*, finally, is the end or conclusion of our musical oration, and must above all else be especially expressive. And this is not found just in the outcome or continuation of the melody itself, but particularly in the postlude, be it either for the bass line or for a strong accompaniment; whether or not one has heard the Ritornello before. It is customary that the aria concludes with the same material as it began; so that our Exordium also serves as a Peroratio.

Mattheson then went on to apply this sectionalization to an aria by Marcello, complete with discussion and music examples (pp.237ff), introducing other technical terms as he did so.

So far, this discussion has been occupied with principal developments up to 1750 in the analysis of structural organization. However, if a full appreciation is to be gained of the groundwork of analytical theory, then three other traditions of musical theory must be touched upon at this point: the art of embellishment, the technique of figured bass and the theory of harmony. None of these is itself centred upon analysis, but each bears on it.

The tradition of embellishment manuals, stretching from Ganassi (*Opera intitulata Fontegara*, 1535) to Virgiliano (*Il dolcimelo*, c1600) and then on to the 17th-century vocal and instrumental tutors, was primarily concerned with teaching graces and *passaggi* to performers. This was done by means of tables of ornaments, extended practical examples and formulated rules. In these manuals is established the fundamental concept of 'diminution'. This concept has two aspects to it: (1) the subdivision of a few long note values into many shorter values; and (2) the application to an 'essential' melodic line of a layer of less essential linear material. In both aspects, a hierarchy is created, and in both the possibility exists of the hierarchy becoming multi-layered as an already embellished line is subjected to further embellishment. On the face of it this was the purely transient affair of the virtuoso performer. In reality much 16th-century music contained elements of embellishment as it was written down; and the modern style of 17th-century *seconda prattica* subsumed ornamentation within its notated exterior. The compositional notion of inventing (or adopting) a basic structure and then elaborating it, which goes back at least to the 9th century and was developed as *contrapunctus diminutus* by 14th-century theorists (see Leech-Wilkinson, 1983), was crystallized in this instructional tradition and was absorbed deep into European musical consciousness. Nowhere was this truer than in the *stile antico* lineage, which led from Diruta (*Il primo libro*, 1580) through Berardi (*Ragionamenti musicale*, 1681; *Miscellanea musicale*, 1689) and Fux (*Gradus ad Parnassum*, 1725) right into the heart of the 19th century. It should not be forgotten that Beethoven was steeped in this tradition and to the end of his life remained profoundly influenced by his lessons from Albrechtsberger. This tradition was to be of incalculable importance to the theories of Heinrich Schenker at the beginning of the 20th century.

The teaching of figured bass was similarly performer-orientated. The line of treatises stretched from Agazzari (*Del sonare sopra 'l basso*, 1607) into the 18th century. It tended to foster the concept on which it was founded: that of the chord as an indivisible unit. It evolved a new categorization of consonance and dissonance which, like the concept of diminution, was absorbed profoundly into the main stream of musical thought. However, it masked the concept of 'root' by concentrating on the actual bass line.

Unquestionably the most influential music theorist of the 18th century was Jean-Philippe Rameau (1683–1764). Rameau was not himself concerned with analysis of form and large-scale structure. His theory of harmony nonetheless had latent significance for future analysts. Rameau 'conceptualized those principles of tonality which were so thoroughly revolutionizing harmony in the early eighteenth century' (Gossett in Rameau: *Traité*, Eng. trans., 1971, p.xxi). He asserted the primacy of harmony over melody. At the heart of his theory are the three 'primary consonances', the octave, 5th and major 3rd, and the fact

9

that they are contained within and generated by the single note. (This he saw first through mathematical subdivision of string lengths, as had Zarlino before him, and later through the observed overtone structure of a sounding body, or *corps sonore*.) He saw the octave as the 'replica' (*réplique*) of its source (ibid, p.8). From these observations, he posited the notion of transposing the natural order of sounds in a harmony, thus isolating the principle of 'inversion' (*renversement*): 'inversion is basic to all the diversity possible in harmony' (ibid, p.13). The principle of 'implication' (*sous-entendre*) allows that sounds may be heard in a chord while not existing in their own right. Inversion, replication and implication together yield the notion of 'root' (a concept which had already been grasped by Lippius, 1612, and Baryphonus, *Pleiades musicae*, 1615, 2/1630) and thus also the series of such roots, some present and some implied, that underlies a harmonic progression containing inverted chords. This series of notes he termed 'fundamental bass' (*basse fondamentale*).

What did this theory have to offer to analysis? First, it offered explanations for chordal structures, consonant and dissonant, thereby providing tools for chordal analysis. Second, it presented a highly centralized view of tonality, comprising a very few elements which could occur in a rich variety of ways. Together with the rules for the operation of 'fundamental bass', this paved the way for a reductionist approach to musical structure. Finally, by giving acoustical primacy to the major triad it offered the prospect of scientific verifiability to analytical systems.

Rameau's exact contemporary, Johann David Heinichen (1683–1729), was almost as prophetic in certain respects. His *Der General-Bass in der Composition* (1728) was written towards the end of the figured-bass tradition and brought that tradition into contact with the theory of composition. Heinichen came close to formulating a theory of chord-progression. Of particular interest to the analyst is his notion of 'fundamental notes' (*Fundamentalnoten*), by which he denoted the principal notes in a melody line after inessential notes have been stripped away.

The direct heir of the two lines of theory which descended from Rameau and Heinichen was Johann Philipp Kirnberger (1721–83). His theory of melodic construction is discussed in §2 below. Worth noting in addition are three harmonic analyses of pieces (two of them entire) which are associated with him. The first is an analysis of his own E minor fugue, which he appended to vol.i (1771) of *Die Kunst des reinen Satzes in der Musik* in order to demonstrate how to 'detect the true harmony as conceived by the composer', distinguishing it from passing notes, in complex situations. 'Once beginners have acquired skill in the accurate analysis of harmony in this piece, we recommend to all of them that they also study the works of great masters in a similarly thorough way' (Eng. trans., pp.266 and 270ff). This analysis is laid out on five staves, the top two presenting the fugue entire. The fifth staff shows the fundamental bass as Kirnberger derived it, the fourth shows the inessential dissonances, and the third presents a figured bass for the composition, so as to show the inversions of chords.

Die wahren Grundsätze zum Gebrauch der Harmonie (1773), published over Kirnberger's name, was probably written by his pupil Johann Abraham Peter

64

2. From J. P. Kirnberger [J. A. P. Schulz]: 'Die wahren Grundsätze zum Gebrauch der Harmonie' (1773), 64

Schulz (1747–1800) under his supervision. Appended to this work are harmonic analyses of two works from Bach's *Das wohltemperirte Clavier*: the Fugue in B minor from book 1 (selected because of its apparent insolubility) and the first part of the Prelude in A minor from book 2. The latter is rather simpler, but the analysis of the B minor Fugue (see fig.2) is laid out on two pairs of staves (the top pair presenting the fugue in finished form), with two further individual staves below. The third and fourth staves give a figured bass (using the bass of the fugue where appropriate) with chords over it which simplify by removing all inessential dissonances. The fifth staff gives the fundamental bass, with figures which retain the essential dissonances. Finally, the sixth staff gives the fundamental bass with only the fundamental chords recorded in its figuring – i.e. only triads and chords of the 7th, in accordance with Rameau's principles.

Schulz (or Kirnberger) made a most significant remark in connection with this analysis: 'we maintain that all music which cannot be reduced to a natural progression of both fundamental chords according to our principles is composed unintelligibly, hence incorrectly and contrary to the strict style of composition' (*JMT*, xxiii, 1979, p.208).

11

2. 1750–1840: Phrase Structure and Formal Model

The origins of musical analysis as one now thinks of it lie in early 18th-century philosophy and are linked with the origins of the aesthetic attitude itself. For it was in the 18th century, and particularly with the English philosophers and essayists, that the idea came to the surface of contemplating beauty without self-interest – that is, without motive of personal improvement or utility. This new attitude was termed, by one of its earliest protagonists, Lord Shaftesbury (1671–1713), 'disinterested attention'. It embodied a mode of interest that went no further than the object being contemplated, and was engrossed in the contemplation itself. Leibniz, at about the same time, had evolved a concept of perception as an activity in itself rather than as a processing of sense-impressions. This active concept of perception was important in the work of Alexander Baumgarten (1714–62), who coined the word 'aesthetics'. It was during this period that the notion of 'fine art' as such, divorced from context and social function, arose.

In Shaftesbury's equation of disinterested attention with 'love of truth, proportion, order and symmetry in things without' lies the germ of formal theory as it was developed in Germany during the second half of the 18th century. His declaration that *'the Beautiful, the Fair, the Comely, were never in the Matter, but in the Art and Design; never in the Body it-self, but in the Form or forming Power'* (*Characteristicks of Men, Manners, Opinions, Times*, 1711, ii, 405) drew attention to the outward form as the object of contemplation rather than content. Such an attitude came through in, for example, Kirnberger's *Der allezeit fertige Polonoisen- und Menuettencomponist* (1757), one of a number of publications that laid down a fixed chord scheme for dances, and supplied several motifs for each bar from which one was to be selected by throwing dice.

However, it was not in the field of analysis or of criticism, as one might expect, that these perceptually based ideas were fully articulated in music for the first time. It was in composition teaching: in particular in the writings of the theorist H. C. Koch (1749–1816). The most significant aspects of Koch's important work, *Versuch einer Anleitung zur Composition* (1782–93), were the twin subjects of phrase structure and formal model.

Koch's exposition of melodic phrase structure was of the profoundest importance for musical theory, ultimately also for analysis, and it led directly to Riemann's theory of dynamic and agogic. The exposition is in Part ii of the *Versuch* (section 2, subsection 3 'On the construction of melodic sections', and subsection 4 'On the combining of melodic sections, or the construction of periods'), occupying in all some 500 pages. It follows immediately on a discussion of rhythm and metre, and establishes a hierarchical framework in which two-bar 'segments' or 'incises' (*vollkommene Einschnitte*) combine in pairs to form four-bar 'phrases' (*Sätze*) which in turn combine to make 'periods' (*Perioden*). Koch then laid down rules as to how this framework might be modified without loss of balance. Chapter 3 of subsection 4 contains three studies 'Of the use of melodic extension'. The first is by repetition of all or part of a phrase; here Koch conveyed the idea of function within a phrase rather than melodic material, speaking often of 'the repetition of a bar' when the content of that bar is different on second statement. The second is multiplication of phrases and cadential figures. The third is the highly significant concept whereby a two-bar or four-bar phrase-unit may be embedded within an existing melody. Koch explained with each extension device (*Verlängerungsmittel*) how it could be used without upsetting the general effect of symmetry. Thus for example he stated that 'When a phrase contains one-bar units of which the first is repeated, then the second must also be repeated', because if not 'the unequal handling of these small units stands out as an unpleasant effect' (ii, 63f).

Chapter 3 of subsection 3 describes processes of melodic compression effected by the telescoping of two phrase-units to form a single unit. In this chapter he used a bar-numbering system that shows the bar at the point of telescoping as having two functions. Fig.3 shows the telescoping of two four-bar phrases into a seven-bar period, with the suppressed bar (*Tacterstickung*) marked with a square (ii, 455).

Koch's principle of phrase extension had its forerunners in the five-volume *Anfangsgründe zur musikalischen Setzkunst* (1752–68) of Joseph Riepel (1709–82) and in Kirnberger's *Die Kunst des reinen Satzes in der Musik* (1771–9). In his second volume (1755) Riepel had discussed the construction of eight-bar phrases in two four-bar units, designating each according to its type of cadence as *Grundabsatz*, *Aenderungsabsatz* or *Aenderungscadenz* (pp.36ff). He went on (pp.54ff) to discuss repetition and phrase extension (*Ausdähnung*) and interpolation (*Einschiebsel*). Koch's use of graphic signs can be traced back to Riepel, who used the square, crosses and letters to designate constructional devices. In his fourth volume (1765) Riepel considered melodic 'figures' (*Figuren*) not in the

3. From H. C. Koch: 'Versuch einer Anleitung zur Composition' (1782–93), ii, 454–5

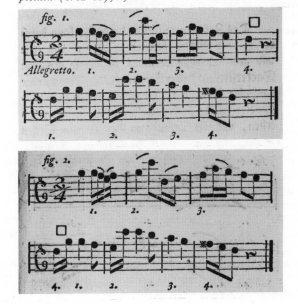

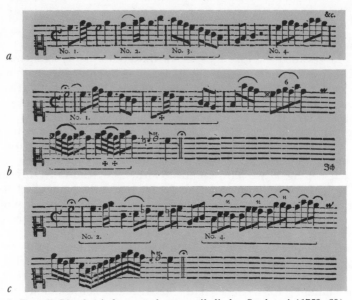

4. From J. Riepel: 'Anfangsgründe zur musikalischen Setzkunst' (1752–68),
iv, 81–2

rhetorical Baroque sense but as units of formal construction. He presented the
first five bars of an aria, marking the four musical figures by brackets and
numbers (see fig.4*a*). He then took no.1 and showed how it might be repeated
sequentially at the interval of a 3rd (marking the repetition with a single cross;
see fig.4*b*), then in subsequent illustrations at the 2nd and the 5th. He then
worked a sequential extension of no.2 which continued with no.4 (see fig.4*c*),
and so on (pp.81ff). The examples are still very much in the style of Baroque
melodic construction, but Koch described Riepel's work as 'the first ray of light'
(ii, 11).

Kirnberger was probably influenced by Riepel in his writings. He had apparently been a pupil of J. S. Bach, and certainly sought to disseminate Bach's
methods; and in turn he was the musical adviser to the great Swiss aesthetician
Johann Georg Sulzer (1720–79). In the second volume of his *Die Kunst des reinen
Satzes in der Musik*, Part 1 (1776), he employed a range of terminology for
melodic structures which provides a halfway-point between Riepel and Koch.
Each large-scale section of a piece, called *Haupttheil*, was subdivided into several
units, each called *Periode* or *Abschnitt*. This was itself subdivided into several
units, each known as *Satz* or *Rhythmus*. This in turn is subdivided into several of
the smallest unit of all, each known as *Cäsur* or *Glied*. The term *Einschnitt* equated
sometimes with *Satz*, sometimes with *Cäsur*. Kirnberger offered rules (ii/1,
140–51; also briefly i (1771), 96; Eng. trans., pp.407–16, 114) on the construction of all these units, especially as to their length, rhythmic patterning and
cadence-forms. In stating that the number of bars constituting a *Satz* should
normally be a multiple of four, or at least of two, he made special allowance for
interpolation. A one-bar unit, a repetition of the previous bar, could be inserted
(ii/2, 143; Eng. trans., p.409) without disturbing the feel of the unit. Moreover,

14

5. From J. P. Kirnberger: 'Die Kunst des reinen Satzes in der Musik'
(1771–9), ii/1, 147

the *Satz* could be extended by the elongation of the value of one or more of its
main notes. This might result even in five-, seven- or nine-bar *Sätze*. Fig.5 shows
his graphing of a succession of three five-bar units by bar number and slur
marks.

Koch's processes of extension and compression show his concern with symmetry and proportion on the small scale. Subsection 4 also presents the construction of compositions in ascending order of magnitude, from 'the combining
of melodic sections into periods of the smallest size, or the organization of small
compositions' (chap.2; iii, 39–152; Eng. trans., pp.78–128) involving the combination of four melodic sections 'of which two have a cadence in the home key'
(p.57), 'of which one has a cadence in a related key' (p.81), and 'in which only
a single closing phrase occurs' (p.111), and the combination of 'more than four
sections in small compositions' (p.128) to 'the combination of melodic sections
into periods of greater length, or the organization of larger compositions'
(chap.4; iii, 231–430; Eng. trans., pp.165–248). In this way Koch drew all the
musical elements of a composition into mutual relationship – for music is 'that
art which expresses feelings through the relationships between notes' (i, 4).

It is in these two chapters that the other important aspect of Koch's work
comes to the fore: that of the formal model. In this respect he cited as his
authority Sulzer, in whose *Allgemeine Theorie der schönen Künste* (1771–4) the idea
of 'layout' (*Anlage*) or model is put forward. Such a model sets down a plan for
a work and the most salient features. The artist, following this model, is then to
proceed to the 'execution' (*Ausführung*) or completion of design and finally to
the 'elaboration' (*Ausarbeitung*) of the work in all its details. Accordingly, within
the discussion of smaller forms (iii, 39ff) Koch provided the plan and characteristic details of the gavotte, bourrée, polonaise, anglaise, minuet and march,
concluding with the chorale and figured melody. He described, for example,
the gavotte as 'a dance piece of lively and pleasant character' much used in
theatrical dance. Its features are '(1) an even time signature which is usually in
2/2 and not too fast; (2) that each phrase begins with a two-crotchet upbeat; (3)
that it has even-numbered rhythmic units with a detectable phrase division at
each second bar; (4) that it comprises two sections, each of eight bars'.

All these models were offered as generative: from them compositions could be
created, almost mechanically – 'almost', because Koch held 'the view that
'living expression' (*lebendiger Ausdruck*) was essential to the artist ('the poet who
abandons expression, image, figure, and becomes a dictionary-user, is in error',
i, 6). They form part of an instruction manual which proceeds from harmony
to counterpoint and then to melody and form. Yet they are important, too, in
the history of analysis, because they separate 'norm' from individuality, im-

plicitly stating what was 'expected' and thereby defining liberty. Moreover, although most of Koch's abundant music examples were specially written for the book (in the contemporary style of Graun, Benda, and early Haydn and Mozart), appended to his discussion of the combination of four melodic sections is a brief analysis (iii, 58ff) of the minuet from Haydn's Divertimento in G (ʜII:1). The criteria for his analysis are particularly interesting: 'This little minuet', he began, 'has the most complete unity'. He followed the philosophical dictate, transmitted by Sulzer (under 'Einheit'), that 'wholeness ... and beauty consist of diversity bound together in unity'. Sulzer described unity with reference to a clock: 'if only one of its mechanical parts is removed then it is no longer a whole [*Ganzes*] but only a part of something else'. In his analysis Koch identified the first four bars as the 'sole principal idea', repeated to form a closing phrase. The opening of the second half, also repeated as a closing phrase, 'while different from the preceding sections, is actually no less than the self-same phrase used in another way; for it is stated in contrary motion, and by means of a thorough deviation which results from this becomes bound together through greater diversity'.

Not only is the 'model' an important tool for formal analysis, later to be used by Prout, Riemann and Leichtentritt, but also the Sulzerian process of model–execution–elaboration is itself an important concept of artistic creation which later acquired its analytical counterpart in the theory of layers (*Schichten*). In addition, Koch took up the terminology that he had inherited from Riepel, Sulzer and Kirnberger, itself derived from grammar and rhetoric, and shaped it into an efficient tool for the description of structure. For him, melody was 'speech in sound' (*Tonrede*), comprising grammar and punctuation. He sought to establish a 'natural law' of musical utterance (*Tonsprache*) which he called the 'logic of the phrase'. In this logic the smallest sense-unit, called 'incomplete segment' (*unvollkommener Einschnitt*), normally occupied one bar, the 'complete segment' (*vollkommener Einschnitt*, itself divisible into two *Cäsuren* in Sulzer's definition of *Einschnitt*) two bars. Such segments combine to form the 'phrase' (*Satz*), defined as either 'opening phrase' (*Absatz*) or 'closing phrase' (*Schluss-Satz*). Phrases form a 'period' (*Periode*). All three principal words are grammatical constructs: *Einschnitt* as phrase, *Satz* as clause, and *Periode* as sentence, the third of these divisible, according to Koch, into 'subject' (i.e. first four bars, *enger Satz*) and 'predicate' (latter four bars).

A set of comparable technical terms was established in French some 30 years later by the Czech composer and theorist Antoine Reicha (1770–1836), a friend of Beethoven, who had produced a treatise in 1803, *Practische Beispiele*, containing models of forms and genres, and who spent the last 28 years of his life as a teacher in Paris. In his *Traité de mélodie* (1814, 2/1832) he used 'dessin' to denote the smallest unit of construction (equivalent to *Einschnitt*), and likened it to an *idée*; two or three *dessins* normally make up a *rythme* (equivalent to *Satz* – Sulzer spoke of *Rhythmus* as being widely used for a subdivision of the period), repetition or multiplication of which (the second of a pair being called the *compagnon*) produces the *période*. A composition made up of several *périodes* is a *coupe*: that of two or three *périodes* is a *petite coupe binaire* or *ternaire*, and that of two or three *parties*, each comprising several *périodes*, is a *grande coupe binaire* or *ternaire*.

The *dessin* is punctuated by a quarter-cadence (*quart de cadence*), the *rythme* by a *demi-cadence*, the *période* by a *trois-quarts de cadence* (if repeated) or by a *cadence parfaite*. Koch's division into grammar and punctuation is mirrored in this view, as is his fundamental concept of hierarchical phrase structure – for Reicha spoke of *la symétrie* (p.9): 'A good melody . . . needs (1) to be divided into equal and like units [*membres* – in German, *Glied* was used in the same generic way]; (2) to have its units forming points of repose [*repos*] of greater or lesser strength which are located at equal distances; that is, symmetrically placed'. He then gave an eight-bar rhythmic scheme (*mouvement*), and said of it:

> Symmetry exists because (1) each division is into two bars; (2) after each division there is a repose which separates one from another; (3) all the divisions are equal within the scheme; (4) the points of repose, or cadences, are placed at equal distances – that is, the weaker repose occurs in the second and sixth bar, the stronger in the fourth and eighth: in short, there is in this scheme a regular plan, and it is this alone that fixes the attention.

Rythme implies not rhythmic patterning at the level of detail but rather control over the number of bars in related units, coordination (p.13). It is thus more an equalizing force than a unit as such, and reveals a sense of rhythm at a higher level, at the level of formal disposition.

Koch's principles of phrase extension and compression also have their equivalents. Reicha said that the four-bar *rythme* was 'commonly called the *Rythme carré*' (p.21), and that in practice the 'grands maîtres' avoid monotony by using *rythmes* of 2, 3, 5, 6 and 8 bars as well. Thus *rythmes* may be extended by using the device of *écho*, whereby an internal unit is repeated, or compressed by using suppression (*supposition* – not to be confused with Rameau's use of this term) of a bar (pp.20ff). (It is worth noting that Meude-Monpas' *Dictionnaire de la musique* (1787) states of the term *phrase* that 'it is only in the last 30 years that French composers have acknowledged the absolute necessity of rendering phrases as *quarrées*'.)

Dessin has much in common with Riepel's *Figur*, and implies melodic character. Like Koch's *Einschnitt* it exists at more than one level. Thus Reicha took the theme of the last movement of Mozart's String Quartet к458, 'The Hunt', divided it into two *membres* (i.e. *rythmes*), each comprising two *dessins* of two bars' duration. Three of the four *dessins* are melodically distinct (his nos.1, 2 and 3), and Reicha broke each of these further into two sub-units, numbering five of them (nos.4–8) and still calling them *dessins*. All this is illustrated in his music example B[5], of which the first section is shown in fig.6 (overleaf). The theme is represented first as a set of numbered sub-units, and then graphically with brackets and labels. Reicha termed this analytical process *décomposition du thème* (or *motif*) (pp.61f). Moreover he went on, like Riepel, to explore in the next 19 examples which of these two-bar and one-bar *dessins* lend themselves to repetition and sequential restatement.

Perhaps the most striking aspect of Reicha's melody treatise is its citation of so many examples from actual music (he listed the composers in his preface). All these examples are submitted to segmentation and discussion. This in itself represents a significant shift from the compositional to the analytical standpoint – Reicha remarked in the preface to the *Traité de mélodie* that 'It is with music

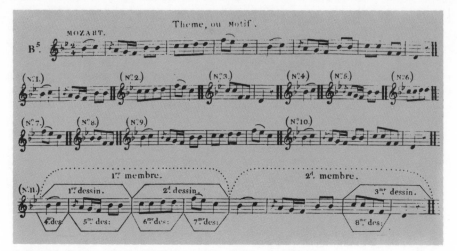

6. From A. Reicha: 'Traité de mélodie' (1814, 2/1832), Planches, 46

as with geometry: in the former it is necessary to prove everything by music examples, just as it is with the latter by geometric figures'. Such a shift is emphasized by the inclusion of six extended analyses of works by Haydn (pp.40f and ex.D[4]), Mozart (p.43, E[4]), Cimarosa (pp.43ff, F[4]), Sacchini (pp.45ff, G[4]), Zingarelli (pp.47f, Q[4]) and Piccinni (pp.49ff, R[4]). Each piece is presented as a continuous melodic line annotated with brackets, labels and comments, and a page or two of discussion in the text.

Fig.7 shows the first page of the last of these analyses, with one of Reicha's footnotes. The aria by Piccinni is divided graphically into two *parties* and 16 *rythmes*. These *rythmes* are, in the 1832 edition, labelled from a. to p., their lengths are indicated and the types of cadence defined. In the text Reicha said of *rythme* 'f.' that it 'ought to be divisible into two equal parts, each of four bars, but it lacks a bar between bars 3 and 4'. It is clear that he was not describing *supposition* here: his 'ought to' implies adverse criticism. In contrast to his purpose in analysing Mozart, Reicha set himself the task of explaining here why a piece which violates the principles of rhythm, which is 'vague, uncertain', in which 'the vocal phrases do not link well together, appear isolated and exhibit no symmetry', should have gained the approbation of 'an enlightened public'. He deduced that there are two aspects to a melody: *rhythmé* and *non rythmé*; and that a composition that excels in only one may still have charm. He praised the 'colour' of the piece, its 'sweet, natural and simple harmony', its 'nuances of loud and soft', and its use of instrumental timbre. Finally he suggested that the nature and prosody of the French language may be the cause of rhythmic defect.

Reicha's *Traité de haute composition musicale* (1824–6) is devoted to counterpoint, harmony, canon and fugue. Book 6, however, is a manual of form, and 26 pages of it are taken up with a segmental analysis of the first part of Mozart's overture to *Le nozze di Figaro*, after which Reicha composed additional sections to show ways in which Mozart might have developed its musical ideas (pp.236ff). He then gave analyses of three whole movements. He used struc-

18

Cette Cadence parfaite dans cet air fait qu'on croit que les 5 mesures qui la suivent doivent appartenir à une toute autre Période, tandis qu'elles appartiennent nécessairement à la Période précédente; ces 5 mesures paraissent après cette cadence parfaite tout-à-fait superflues, parce que la 1ᵉ partie de cet air serait parfaitement bien terminée avec cette cadence. On ne peut jamais alonger une Période après une cadence parfaite mélodique et harmonique.

7. From A. Reicha: 'Traité de mélodie' (1814, 2/1832), Planches, 34

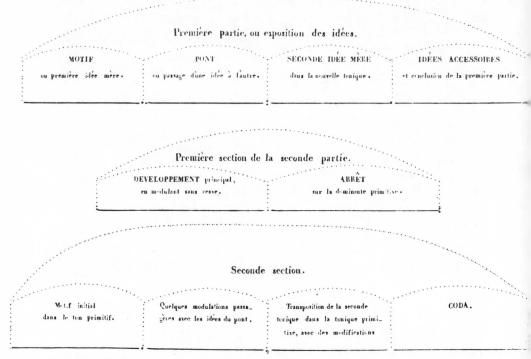

Première partie, ou exposition des idées.

MOTIF	PONT	SECONDE IDÉE MÈRE	IDÉES ACCESSOIRES
ou première idée mère.	ou passage d'une idée à l'autre.	dans la nouvelle tonique.	et conclusion de la première partie.

Première section de la seconde partie.

DÉVELOPPEMENT principal,	ARRÊT
en modulant sans cesse.	sur la dominante primitive.

Seconde section.

Motif initial	Quelques modulations passa_	Transposition de la seconde	CODA.
dans le ton primitif.	gères avec les idées du pont.	tonique dans la tonique primi_ tive, avec des modifications	

8. From A. Reicha: 'Traité de haute composition musicale' (1824–6), ii, 300

tural diagrams in his section on large-scale binary and ternary forms. Fig.8 shows the diagram for the *grande coupe binaire* (ii, 300): punctuation signs are used to denote cadence types, dotted phrase marks to indicate sections (*idée mère* signifies thematic material, and *motif* the principal thematic material).

Between the treatises of Koch and Reicha came a work that gave an unprecedented amount of space and range of thought to analysis. J.-J. de Momigny (1762–1842) in his *Cours complet d'harmonie et de composition* (1803–6) devoted no fewer than 144 pages, including analytical plates, to an analysis of the first movement of Mozart's String Quartet in D minor K421/417b. He provided a double analysis, examining both phrase structure and expressive content. Momigny's phrase-structure analysis is based on the novel rhythmic concept that musical units proceed from upbeat (*levé*) to downbeat (*frappé*) and never vice versa. He termed his smallest sense-unit, made up of two successive notes, upbeat and downbeat, the *cadence* or *proposition musicale*. These two notes are in the relationship of *antécédent* and *conséquent*. In the opening bars of the movement by Mozart (see fig.9), two *cadences mélodiques* pair off in antecedent–consequent relationship to form a *cadence harmonique*, two of these forming a *hémistiche*, two *hémistiches* forming a *vers*, and two *vers* forming a *période*. Momigny's concept does not, however, insist on hierarchy by pairs, and allows for as many as six or eight *vers* to make up a *période* in certain contexts. The *périodes* form further into *reprises* and are designated according to function within their *reprise* as 'de début', 'intermédiaire', 'de verve', 'mélodieuse' or

20

9. From J.-J. de
Momigny: 'Cours
complet d'harmonie
et de composition'
(1803–6), iii, 109–10

21

'complémentaire'. (In other contexts Momigny used other terms from versification also to designate structural units of intermediate size: *distiche, strophe* and *stance*.)

In this phrase-structure analysis Momigny laid the basis for a view of music that was to become important at the end of the 19th century: of music as a succession of spans of tension. In his expressive analysis, on the other hand, he was looking back to the *Affektenlehre* of the 18th century. His method was to determine the *caractère* of the work under analysis, to select a verbal text that had the same character, and to set the text to the principal melodic material of the work so that melodic repetition was mirrored by verbal repetition, fluctuations of musical mood by fluctuations of textual meaning. He constructed a poetic parallel with the music, offering through it an interpretation of both form and content.

The plates for the analysis, reminiscent of those by Kirnberger and Schulz (see §1 and fig.2), present the music laid out on ten parallel staves; the top four show the quartet in conventional score, the fifth staff presents the melodic line (and notes printed small here reveal the beginnings of melodic reduction technique) with its *cadences* marked, the sixth and seventh staves provide a harmonic reduction of the texture with harmonic *cadences* marked, the eighth and ninth staves present the principal melodic material with poetic text underlàid (in this case a dramatic scene between Dido and Aeneas, with notes from the first violin assigned to Dido and from the cello assigned to Aeneas) and with simple piano accompaniment, and the tenth staff shows the roots of the prevailing harmony as a fundamental bass (see fig.9).

Momigny's other extended analysis is of the first movement of Haydn's 'Drumroll' Symphony, no.103. This spans 24 pages of text combined with 47 pages of annotated full score. The text first investigates the substance of the movement, proceeding period by period, examining the thematic material and its deployment, its use of contrasting dynamics and timbres, stressing the achievement of variety in unity; it then builds a poetic analogue to the music in the form of a village community terrorized by a fearful storm and eventually chastened in the eyes of God. This latter 'pictorial and poetic analysis' belongs to an 18th-century tradition of exploring the borderland between words and music – a tradition exemplified by Klopstock and Lessing, of which the most celebrated product was Heinrich Wilhelm von Gerstenberg's double adaptation of C. P. E. Bach's C minor Fantasy, first to the words of Hamlet's monologue 'To be, or not to be' and then to those of Socrates' monologue as he takes hemlock (see Helm, 1972). Indeed, Momigny's writings suggest that there was a veritable school of such activity in Paris at this time. André-Joseph Grétry was a skilled exponent of this group, which Momigny called 'les parodistes'.

Momigny's two analyses from 1803–6 are monumental achievements. So too was another extended analysis, which occupied 21 columns of the Leipzig *Allgemeine musikalische Zeitung*, published in two instalments in July 1810: E. T. A. Hoffmann's analytical review of the score and parts of Beethoven's Fifth Symphony, complete with copious music examples. Together these three mighty analyses form the head-waters of the broadening stream of 19th-century analysis. Superficially, Hoffmann's review has much in common with those of

Momigny. Both deal in detail with matters of structure, both use highly technical language, both offer rich descriptive imagery. Hoffmann's pictorial language, however, belongs (as one would expect) to the world of Romantic literature, speaking of 'foreboding, indescribable longing' and a 'wonderful realm of spirits', and of the work being held together 'in a fantastic way ... like an ingenious rhapsody'. His technical description, which freely uses such terms as *Hauptgedanke*, *Zwischensatz* and *Figur*, sees the music not in fixed format, through a series of periodic frames, but in free format, as a seamless continuity powered by motifs. It adumbrates the organicist view of musical structure (see §3 below), as for example (Eng. trans., p.163):

> it is particularly the intimate relationship of the individual themes to one another which produces the unity that firmly maintains a single feeling in the listener's heart. ... it becomes clearer to the musician when he discovers a common bass pattern in two different phrases, or when the connecting of two movements makes it obvious. A more profound relationship, however, which cannot be described in such terms, is often communicated from the heart to the heart. It is this relationship which prevails among the themes of both Allegro movements and the Menuett and magnificently proclaims the self-possessed genius of the master.

At one point Hoffmann's text sets out five forms of the Menuett theme so that the reader can see the transformations.

Extended examples of 'analysation' were given also by J. B. Logier (1777–1846) – the German inventor of the 'Chiroplast' (a mechanism devised to train pianists' hand movements and fingering) who lived most of his life in Ireland – in his *System der Musik-Wissenschaft und der praktischen Komposition* (1827). Logier (who, in this title, seems to have coined the term *Musikwissenschaft*) offered analyses (Eng. trans., pp.294–320) of a concerto grosso by Corelli and the Adagio of Haydn's Quartet in G op.76 no.1 examined under eight distinct headings: key – time – fundamental basses – modulation and fundamental 7ths – dissonances – passing notes, auxiliary notes and secondary harmony – periods – sections and imitation. The scheme constitutes a wider base for analysis than hitherto, yet has something of the mechanical nature of Burmeister's rhetorical scheme. More interesting are Logier's instructions as to

10. From J. B. Logier: 'System der Musik-Wissenschaft und der praktischen Composition' (1827; Eng. trans. 1827, rev. 1888), 278

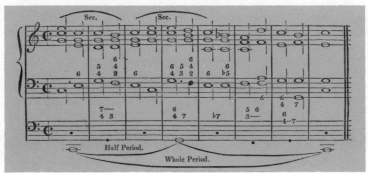

'How to construct melodies' (Eng. trans., pp.276ff), in which the student proceeds in four stages, first laying down an abstract bass line of three notes (*C–G–C*) which frames the period and divides it into two half-periods, then constructing a 'fundamental bass' over it, then overlaying this with the 'inverted bass' (i.e. the sounding bass line) and finally building a superstructure of melody and inner parts. The result looks graphically not unlike a Schenkerian reduction (see fig.10, p.23).

A different type of reduction occurs in Czerny's *School of Practical Composition* (?1849). Carl Czerny (1791–1857) stripped away the surface figuration ('the moving figure') from several compositions, leaving only the underlying harmonies ('the ground-harmony'), presented in block chords. He did this for Chopin's Etude op.10 no.1 (see fig.11), for the first prelude in book 1 of Bach's *Das wohltemperirte Clavier* and for the introduction to a sonata by Clementi; he also reduced a study by Cramer to its basic part-writing ('the ground-melody').

Czerny's *School* rests, as does Reicha's *Traité*, on citation of authority. (That is not surprising, since Czerny had previously translated Reicha's *Cours de composition* and two *Traités* as *Vollständiges Lehrbuch der musikalischen Komposition*, 1834.) All the music examples are attributed (they represent the next generation, of Beethoven, Hummel, Rossini, Méhul etc), and many analyses of whole compositions are included. It is unique in being the first independent manual of form and instrumentation. It takes for granted a grounding in harmony and counterpoint, and concerns itself exclusively with the development of ideas and the formation of compositions 'from the most simple Theme to the Grand Symphony, and from the shortest Song to the Opera and Oratorio' (i, p.iii). It

11. From C. Czerny: *'School of Practical Composition'* (?1849), 92–3

is a veritable compendium of musical forms, including exotic dances (such as the bolero, fandango, tarantella and Russian national dances) and vocal forms (such as the *romance, preghiera* and ballad), as well as the constituent movements of a sonata, genres such as the quartet, quintet and sextet, and many other forms.

Another theorist of the time concerned with form was J. B. H. Birnbach (1793–1879), whose *Der vollkommene Komponist* was published between 1832 and 1846, but to whom the first use of the phrase 'second theme' is credited in 1827 (Berlin – *Allgemeine musikalische Zeitung*, iv).

The work done in the area of harmonic theory by Rameau and others in the 18th century was taken further in the first half of the 19th century. By far the most visionary steps were taken at the beginning of the century by Momigny. Over a period of 18 years, he formulated a theory of long-term tonality which enabled him to imply, for example, that the first movement of the Mozart D minor String Quartet in its entirety modulates (in the modern sense) a mere eight times, and that other extended passages normally regarded as modulating several times never leave the home key. While writing the *Cours complet* (1803–6) he evolved an expanded notion of tonality whereby a key comprised not only its seven diatonic notes but also the five flanking notes on the sharp and flat sides and a further five on the double-sharp and double-flat sides (relatively speaking), to produce a tonal space of 27 notes. Finally, in *La seule vraie théorie de la musique* (1821) that space is divided into diatonic genus, chromatic genus and enharmonic genus. By this formulation (derived from classical Greek music theory), most conventionally accepted modulation is classed as movement within this expanded tonal space–movement between areas called 'octa-chordes'. Such local movement within the tonal space is termed *modulation* (or *modulation négative*), whereas movement outside that space is termed *transition* (or *modulation positive*).

Between these two publications of Momigny, another theory of tonality was being formulated which, if less visionary, was much more widely used and acknowledged. This was the four-volume *Versuch einer geordneten Theorie der Tonsetzkunst* (1817–21) by Gottfried Weber (1779–1839). This work went through three German editions; and its American-English edition (under the name of Godfrey Weber), translated by James Warner (1842), went through some six impressions and was revised in 1851 by John Bishop of Cheltenham (the translator of Czerny and editor of Reicha). In §53 Weber set out a new method of designating chord types. This uses Gothic letters in upper and lower case, with superscript circle, '7' and crossed-'7', to designate major, minor and diminished triads, dominant 7th, secondary 7th, half-diminished 7th, and major triad with major 7th. Then in §151 there are roman numerals, large and small (actually small-capital), with the same superscript symbols, to denote chord types as located on degrees of the scale within a given key (see fig.12). The two 'modes of designation', as described in §153, can be combined by prefixing an upper- and lower-case italic letter and colon to the roman numeral as an index of the prevailing key, thus: $C: IV^7$ = dominant 7th on the fourth degree of C major.

Weber (who incidentally was involved in a celebrated public controversy

Fundamental harmonies of each major key.

I and I^7,

II " II^7,

III " III^7,

IV " IV^7,

V " V^7,

VI " VI^7,

$^{\circ}$VII " $^{\circ}$VII^7.

Fundamental harmonies of each minor key.

I

$^{\circ}$II and $^{\circ}$II^7,

IV " IV^7,

V " V^7,

VI " VI^7,

$^{\circ}$VII.

12. From G. Weber: 'Versuch einer geordneten Theorie der Tonsetzkunst' (1817–21; Eng. trans., rev. 2/1851 ed. J. Bishop), i, 287

over the analysis of the opening bars of Mozart's 'Dissonance' Quartet к465 – see Vertrees, 1974) claimed originality for these symbol-systems and complained of piracy by contemporary writers. The combined system just outlined provided the basis for Schenker's designation of fundamental harmonic steps (*Stufen*), and has become widely used in 20th-century theoretical writings.

Some 30 years later, Johann Christian Lobe (1797–1881), in his *Lehrbuch der musikalischen Komposition* (1850–67), used a similar system of designation but rather cruder, thus: *C:* 3 = (minor) triad on the third degree of C major; *a:*5̇ = dominant 7th on the fifth degree of A minor; *h:* 2̊ = chord of the 9th on the second degree of B minor. Lobe's discussion of harmony is centred around the notion of harmonic step (*Stufe*). It makes a distinction between progressions which are diatonic (*leitereigen*) and those which are modulatory (*ausweichend*); and the concept of the altered (*alterirt*) chord allows chords with foreign harmony notes to be viewed as diatonic in certain contexts, thus increasing the power of the harmonic step greatly (i, 242f). Lobe, it should be said, claims credit for only part of this thinking – thinking which looks forward to the harmonic theories of Schenker and Schoenberg.

Lobe's *Lehrbuch* was still in progress when, only three years after the appearance of its first volume, Simon Sechter (1788–1867) published the first volume of his composition treatise, *Die Grundsätze der musikalischen Komposition* (1853–4). Sechter's harmonic system took over the concept of fundamental bass originated by Rameau and transmitted via Heinichen, Kirnberger and Schulz. Sechter developed a theory of chord progression based on correct succession of 'fundamental notes' and the 'underlying harmonies' (*Grundharmonien*) which they project. Like Lobe, Sechter used the notion of *Stufe*, and he defined notes as either *leitereigen* or *leiterfremd* (literally 'alien to the scale'). 'Beneath every chromatic progression lies a diatonic one'; most chromatic harmony can be read as diatonic harmony with chromatic inflection; and most 'apparently modulatory passages in reality retain their allegiance' to the tonic. Fundamental notes must be diatonic to a major or minor scale, whatever goes on over them, but a subordinate *Stufe* of one key may become the tonic of a new key, thereby permitting transition from key to key. Some chords are described as 'representing' a fundamental that they do not contain (*Stellvertreter*: '[root] representatives'). Other chords are seen as belonging to two key areas (*Zwitterakkorde*: 'hybrid chords'). Sechter's theory marks a major step in coming to terms with 19th-century developments in harmonic language; it influenced many generations of musicians, of whom Schoenberg is perhaps the most prominent example. Its view of chromaticism laid a basis on which theorists in the 1880s and 1890s could analyse the harmonic language of Wagner.

Sechter's third volume (1854) speaks of 'rhythmic sketches', and makes use of two noteworthy graphic devices. The first sets out the harmonic structure of an entire piece in terms of fundamentals whose durations are undifferentiated but which are marked off into phrases (*Abschnitte*) by commas (shades of Mattheson). The second presents a fully rhythmicized succession of fundamentals with two rows of numerals immediately beneath the staff. These numerals denote for each fundamental in turn the *Stufe* which it forms of either or both of two prevailing key areas. This graphic technique was adopted and elaborated by several analysts, notably in the quest for a theoretical formulation of the harmony of Richard Wagner: fig.13, from an analysis by Carl Mayrberger, is a good example.

13. *From C. Mayrberger: 'Die Harmonik Richard Wagner's', BB, iv (1881), 176*

3. *1840–1900: Organic Growth and the Teaching of Form*

Czerny's attitude towards form was highly determinate: 'the composition must . . . belong to a species already in existence; consequently, in *this* respect, no originality is, in general, necessary' (i, 1). His understanding of *'form* and *construction'* is itself quite specific (i, 6):

> 1st [A work's] extent and proper duration.
> 2ly The requisite modulations, partly into established keys, and partly also into arbitrary and extraneous ones, as well as the places where they are introduced.
> 3ly The rhythm (the proportion or symmetry) both of the whole, and also of the individual parts and periods of a piece.
> 4ly The manner in which a principal or an accessory melody is brought in at the proper place, and where it must alternate with such passages as form either a continuation, a moving figure, or a bridge to the following.
> 5ly The conduct and development of a principal or accessory idea.
> 6ly The structure and proper succession of the different component parts of the piece, answerable to the species of composition which the author has had in view, as expressed in the title.
> There are . . . a tolerable number of different forms in music. These, however, are reducible to a far lesser number of each principal form, and are totally different in their structure from one another.

A. B. Marx (1795–1866), in his *Die Lehre von der musikalischen Komposition* (1837–47), was less procrustean. 'The number of forms is unlimited', he said, and there are ultimately no laws dictating what form a particular composition should take. For Marx, form was 'the way in which the content of a work – the composer's conception, feeling, idea – outwardly acquires shape'. A better term for it, he suggested, might have been 'the externalization of content'. Nonetheless, the student-composer cannot learn composition through inspiration and idea alone. He needs the models of previous composers as an intermediate stage on the road towards free composition. Thus 'it is possible to *derive* certain *principal forms*, and also certain composite or *compound forms* which are made up of these or variations of them; and only by creating these distinctions does it become possible to comprehend and master the immeasurable array of [formal] moulds [*Gestalten*]' (ii, 5). For Marx, 'form' was almost synonymous with 'whole' (*Ganzes*) (ii, 4f):

> Every work of art must have its form. For every work of art has of necessity its beginning and its end, hence its extent. It is made up in different ways of sections of different type and number. The generic term for all these features is the *form* of a work of art. . . . There are as many forms as works of art.

Marx acknowledged that there were similarities in form between pieces, but denied strongly that forms were, as a result, 'routines' through which composers worked. Content was not really separable from form. Even so, the very appearance of similarities suggests that 'there must be some rationale underlying these moulds, some concept which is of broader significance, greater strength and longer duration' (ii, 7). Thus Marx denied form as 'convention' and proposed for it an epistemological basis. Forms are patterns abstracted from past practice, rather than conscious guidelines; they represent deep-seated principles of organization which analysis uncovers.

This idea is close to the ideas of the aesthetician A. W. Schlegel (1767–1845) concerning the relationship between art and nature: beneath the consciously moulded work of art must lie an unconsciously moulded work of nature. Nature 'is an intelligence . . . [It should be understood] not as a mass of products but as itself a producing [force]' (*Vorlesungen über schöne Literatur und Kunst*, i, 1801–2). Very much abreast of the Romantic philosophy of his day, Marx believed in the originality of the artist, in genius as a special endowment, in the developing 'idea' as all-important, in rules as existing to be broken. Marx was also influenced by the outlook of the Swiss educationist Heinrich Pestalozzi (1746–1827), who saw the law of man's development as essentially 'organic' – not as a combination of circumstances but as an inner growth process. All processes have a starting-point, they germinate and grow, and at all points are harmonious and whole. At that starting-point Marx placed the *Motiv*, a tiny unit of two or more notes which serves as 'the seed or sprout of the phrase out of which it grows' (i, 27).

Marx's first discussion of sonata form (*Sonatenform* – he was probably the first to use that term for the internal scheme of one movement) differs significantly from that of Czerny. Marx offered (ii, 498ff) a page of formal instruction on sonata form in the major key followed by twice as much indicating ways in which the 'ground-form' may be deviated from, stressing always that the spirit (*Geist*) of the composer may lead him in some other direction, and citing specific cases in Mozart and Beethoven. He pointed only to the unique balance of the key scheme, spelling it out in a highly original fashion, and recommended the composer to keep its advantages carefully in mind. This discussion was superseded when Marx issued the third volume of his compositional manual in 1845. There he devoted close on 100 pages to the topic, treating each of the principal sections of sonata form in turn, the design of each subject group (*Hauptsatz, Seitensatz, Schlusssatz*), the linkages between groups, the internal construction into antecedent and consequent, the use of motifs, ideas and cells. Significantly, he used the Beethoven piano sonatas as his exemplification throughout this discussion. Volume iii is itself a manual of musical forms which starts with simple forms, including variations, proceeds to rondo forms, to sonata form and thence to hybrid forms such as sonata-rondo, multi-movement structures and the fantasy, and concludes with vocal genres.

Marx's most significant analytical writing is contained in his *Ludwig van Beethoven: Leben und Schaffen*, which was first published in 1859 and continued to be reissued into the 1900s yet was never translated. This is a biography of the oeuvre rather than of the man – a sequence of analyses through which the development of Beethoven's art is traced. It contains extended analyses of all the symphonies, *Fidelio*, the *Missa solemnis* and several of the quartets. Many other works receive briefer analytical treatment. It is in this book that the concept of developing idea is exploited most fully, especially in the chapter 'The Sinfonia Eroica and Ideal Music' (i, 275), which expounds the aesthetic basis of 'idea'. The chapter on the Ninth Symphony (ii, 260) shows Marx's idealistic analytical technique at its best. His introduction to the performance of Beethoven's piano sonatas (1863) is alleged to be an outgrowth of this book. As well as giving advice on executant matters, it supplies brief analyses of most of the sonatas, motivic and descriptive.

Marx's chapter on the 'Eroica' refers to Berlioz's essay on that symphony. Berlioz wrote a series of articles on the symphonies in the *Revue et gazette musicale de Paris* between April 1837 and March 1838 that forms the first study of an entire genre of Beethoven's work. The articles, later published together in *A travers chants* (1862), constitute an essay in criticism, yet they have a technical content whose clear terminology, derived from Momigny and Reicha, is masked by Edwin Evans's English translation (1913–18).

Marx was a professional writing for professionals. In the early 19th century the amateur musician writing for the music lover emerged. Among the German amateur writers, one of the best was Ernst von Elterlein (apparently a pseudonym for Ernst Gottschald), whose studies of the Beethoven symphonies (1854) and piano sonatas (1856) were widely circulated. Von Elterlein did not describe his activities as 'analytical'; to him they were 'explanations' (*Erläuterungen*), based on a dilute form of Marx's idealism.

Perhaps the most distinguished representative of the amateur analytical tradition was the Russian civil servant Wilhelm von Lenz (1809–83). His *Beethoven et ses trois styles* (1852) is a vivid and fertile study of the development of Beethoven's musical style, based on the threefold classification of the works first proposed by Fétis (1835), and using the piano sonatas as its centre of focus. Keen observation and sharp judgment lie behind the flowery surface; metaphor is used as a powerful analytical tool.

In 1841–2 Marx had engaged in public dispute with the critic G. W. Fink over methods of teaching composition, showing himself fully aware of the philosophical basis of his position (see Marx, 1841; see also Eicke, 1966). Marx's *Die Lehre von der musikalischen Komposition* went through six editions during his life and eventually underwent revision by Hugo Riemann (1849–1919) between 1887 and 1890 (i, rev. 9/1887; ii, rev. 7/1890; iv, rev. 5/1888). An English translation of the fourth edition was issued in 1852. The work was used in theory teaching well into the 20th century, and profoundly influenced generations of musicians. Riemann's own *Katechismus der Kompositionslehre* appeared in 1889, and the bulk of his powerful theory of rhythm in his *Musikalische Dynamik und Agogik* (1884) and *System der musikalischen Rhythmik und Metrik* (1903), and was summarized in the *Vademecum der Phrasierung* (1900, 8/1912 as *Handbuch der Phrasierung*).

A forerunner of Riemann had been Moritz Hauptmann (1792–1868), whose work was conditioned by Hegelian philosophy, and who did much to introduce the idea that music theory should be systematic and founded on logical principles. He formulated (1853) a theory of harmony and rhythm based on what he claimed to be universals. His theory of rhythm, like that of Momigny, took a two-element pattern as its basic unit and explained all units comprising more than two elements as intersections of two-element units. In Hegelian terms, a two-element unit was the 'thesis', a three-element unit the 'antithesis' and a four-element unit the 'synthesis' in the metrical system. Hauptmann's basic unit, unlike Momigny's, was made up of downbeat followed by upbeat, and it was Mathis Lussy (1828–1910) who in his study of the anacrusis (1903) took up Momigny's *levé–frappé* pattern and developed the theory further. From this Riemann proceeded to develop a full theory based on the indivisible unit of the *Motiv*. Underlying the theory is the idea of a single unit of energy (*Lebenskraft*) passing through phases of growth, peak and decay. Musical form is constructed of many such units overlapping and interacting to produce extended and compressed spans of energy, these interactions occurring against a 'background' of absolutely regular hierarchically built-up patterns. (For Riemann's method see also Chapter IV, §5.)

In 1844 Lobe published his forward-looking *Compositions-Lehre*, which he described as a 'comprehensive theory of thematic development and of modern instrumental forms'. In this he rejected contrapuntal and fugal training as a basis for composition, believing that once schooled in this way the composer's creative ideas would always tend to come in that guise for free instrumental genres. Lobe's four-volume treatise, *Lehrbuch der musikalischen Komposition* (briefly discussed in §2 above), which has separate volumes on instrumentation and opera, was first published in 1850–67 (the first volume went through six editions), with translations into French and Russian but strangely not into English; it makes extensive use of graphic analyses, contracting the musical texture to a single 'principal melodic strand' (*Hauptmelodiefaden*). In this he went far beyond Reicha (1814), for he systematically reduced the full texture to its essential material, setting out guidelines for such reduction and then reversing the process to show how a composer should work from initial melodic ideas to the finished score by a sequence of established 'procedures' of expansion and elaboration. Lobe's brief *Katechismus der Compositionslehre* (1862), which went through eight editions, and his enormously popular *Katechismus der Musik* (1851), which was still being issued over a century later, show how widely distributed and influential his work must have been.

In 1852 E. F. E. Richter produced his manual of musical form and analysis, influenced by Kirnberger and Weber, and in 1853–4 the immensely influential Simon Sechter published his composition treatise (see §2 above). In 1885 Salomon Jadassohn produced volume iia of his composition treatise, entitled *Die Formen in den Werken der Tonkunst* ('analysed and graded as a course of study'). In 1887 the American writer A. J. Goodrich published his *Complete Musical Analysis*, and the American teacher Percy Goetschius (1853–1943) produced a succession of books on musical form, of which his *Models of the Principal Musical Forms* (1895) was the first. Between 1893 and 1897 the English theorist Ebenezer Prout (1835–1909) produced his *Musical Form* and *Applied Forms*. He expressed himself indebted to Riemann for the fundamental principles of rhythm, and in particular the study of motifs, and admitted that both volumes had involved intensive study of 'large German treatises'. The first volume proceeds from motif to 'phrase' and 'sentence', and then to simple binary and ternary forms, the second from dance forms to sonata form and vocal music, including a chapter on 'cyclic forms' which deals with the symphonic poem. In 1908 Stewart Macpherson produced his *Form in Music*, which has been the standard manual for English music students for much of the 20th century.

Hugo Leichtentritt (1874–1951) completed his *Musikalische Formenlehre* in 1911, later to become the first part of a more extended study (translated into

English in 1951) including chapters on 'Aesthetic ideas as the basis of musical styles and forms' and 'Logic and coherence in music'. It also has detailed analyses of works, notably the 45-page study of Bruckner's Eighth Symphony and the chapter devoted to Schoenberg's piano pieces opp.11 and 19. It was with Prout and Leichtentritt that *Formenlehre* became a branch of the discipline of musical analysis rather than a prescriptive training for composers, and hence entered the field of musicology (see Chapter IV, §4).

4. Historical Awareness in the 19th Century

The use of analysis to serve an interest in musical objects themselves, rather than to supply models for the study of composition, reflected a new spirit of historical awareness which arose with Romanticism. It was not a dispassionate 'scientific' interest in the past, but a desire to enter into the past, to discover its essence. This spirit (exhibited in Thibaut's *Über Reinheit der Tonkunst*, 1825, concerning music from Palestrina to Handel), in confluence with the Romantic image of 'genius', resulted in a new type of monograph, biographical and historical. Early examples were Baini's study of Palestrina, *Memorie storico-critiche della vita e delle opere di Giovanni Pierluigi da Palestrina* (1828), Winterfeld's of Palestrina (1832) and Giovanni Gabrieli (1834), Ulïbïshev's of Mozart (1843), Jahn's of Mozart (1856–9) and Spitta's of Bach (1873–80).

Even before these, Forkel's *Über Johann Sebastian Bachs Leben, Kunst und Kunstwerke* (1802), while including nothing that could be termed formal analysis as such, contained an extended characterization of Bach's music as a whole – in short, a stylistic analysis. J. N. Forkel (1749–1818), like A. B. Marx, was much influenced by the concept of 'organism' in contemporary philosophy and education; to seek the depths of 'Bach's transcendent genius' (Eng. trans., 1920, p.xxix) in the totality of his work rather than in individual compositions was consistent with this – 'The butterfly method, a sip here and there, is of little use' (p.147). Forkel stressed the presence of two indispensable factors in Bach's creative make-up: 'genius and indefatigable application' (p.152). It was an educational as well as a musical embodiment of organism that led Forkel to say that '[genius] enabled him to develop out of a given subject a whole family of related and contrasted themes, of every form and design' (p.87). He declared Bach's mastery of technique; at the same time he tried to define where 'Bach followed a course of his own, upon which the text books of his day were silent' (p.74). To identify genius he took, in chapters 5 and 6 ('Bach the Composer'), five aspects of music: harmony, modulation, melody, rhythm and counterpoint. His method was to cite a technical context, state the conventional in terms of contemporary theory or practice, and then consider Bach's handling of such a context. He thus had illuminating things to say about Bach's part-writing, his use of passing notes, of pedal points, of remote modulations, his contrapuntal solo melodic writing, his fugal counterpoint and his use of the voice; for example (p.77):

there is a rule that every note raised by an accidental cannot be doubled in the chord, because the raised note must, from its nature, resolve on the note above. If it is doubled, it must rise doubled in both parts and, consequently, form consecutive octaves. Such is the rule. But Bach frequently doubles not only notes accidentally raised elsewhere in the scale but actually the *semitonium modi* or leading-note itself. Yet he avoids consecutive octaves. His finest works yield examples of this.

For Forkel such transgression on Bach's part always produced a more natural, spontaneous or smooth effect than orthodoxy. The link between genius and nature was axiomatic: 'when [Bach] draws his melody from the living wells of inspiration and cuts himself adrift from convention, all is as fresh and new as if it had been written yesterday' (p.83).

The study of Mozart by Otto Jahn (1813–69) is very different from Forkel's Bach biography. It is closer at once to contemporary theory of composition and to critical writing. Its four volumes describe a single biographical 'progress'. All material, historical, biographical and analytical, is taken in on the way; there is no separate place for stylistic extrapolation or long-distance perspective. There are many analyses of individual works, often very detailed, sometimes occupying whole chapters. Even when he did draw certain groups of works together for consideration as genres – the early instrumental works, the piano music, the symphonies and so on – he generalized only on matters of form before dealing with works individually. But in these chapters there are valuable comparative analyses of two or more works. For Jahn 'the genuine impulses of artistic creation proceed from universal and unalterable laws; the artist does not impress his individual stamp upon the composing elements of the work' (Eng. trans., iii, 41). The more technical analyses tend to approach their subject from three points of view: external form, thematic character and use of instruments or voices. The first of these embodies the 'laws' most strongly, and it is here that Jahn traced the ancestry of individual forms before placing Mozart within the historical continuum. Thus (i, 309):

> The rule that the quartet . . . should consist, like the symphony and the sonata, of four fixed movements, was laid down by Joseph Haydn. It was his inexhaustibly fertile invention and his freedom in the treatment of form which nourished and developed the germ of this chamber-music, until it bore the most beautiful blossoms of German music art. Mozart, destined later to surpass in this direction his freely acknowledged example, displays evident tokens of Haydn's influence even in his youth.

Jahn's analyses are not only historical and analytical, they also contain critical comment: thus, of the C minor Mass 'It cannot be said . . . that the instrumental part of this work is as brilliant and full of colour as others composed at the same period; the tone colouring is on the whole monotonous . . . the inflexibility of form has something in it of pedantry' (ii, 396f).

J. A. P. Spitta (1841–94) organized his *Johann Sebastian Bach* in the same single biographical sweep that one finds in Jahn's *Mozart*, giving the same prominence to examination of individual works and particularly extended treatment to large-scale works. There is, however, rather less formal analysis and much more on musical character. Spitta aimed, by description, 'to call up the spirit which alone can give [music] life and soul' (Eng. trans., i, p.viii). He went further, attempting a symbolic interpretation, notably for the B minor Mass; for example, speaking of the duet 'Et in unum' from the Credo (iii, 51):

33

to represent the essential Unity as clearly as possible, Bach treats the parts in canon on the unison at the beginning of the principal subject each time, not using the canon on the fourth below till the second bar; thus both the Unity and the separate existence of the two Persons are brought out.

There was a second aspect to the growth of historical awareness which in turn contributed to analytical thinking. This was the development of musical text criticism, bringing with it the first of the massive collected editions. Whereas Jahn and Spitta both examined only the finished work in their analyses, Forkel's Bach biography contained the seeds of this new element as well as of stylistic classification. Chapter 10, 'Bach's Manuscripts', though only four pages long, points to the evidence that variant sources of a given piece might yield of Bach's process of composition – his adjustment of a single note, his drastic cutting down, his continual self-correction. Forkel indeed urged the supplementing of a complete edition of Bach's works by the noting of source variants, an initiative that was eventually taken up in the Bachgesellschaft edition. It was another historical scholar involved with textual criticism and the editing of collected editions, Guido Adler, who about this time, in 1885, published a programme for musicology in which historical and analytical research were fully integrated (see Chapter III, §1).

The most influential scholar in this field was Gustav Nottebohm (1817–82), who worked on the collected editions of Beethoven (1862–5) and Mozart (from 1878). In a long series of studies of sketches and other composition materials, published between 1865 and 1887, he tackled the problems of Beethoven's creative processes: how many pieces Beethoven worked on at a time, how he used sketches, drafts and scores, how he worked from single-line draft to full texture, how he conceived and modified formal structure.

Beethoven's sketch materials had been increasingly in circulation from the latter part of the composer's life, and had begun to excite comment. The first significant harnessing of their evidence had appeared in the first volume of Lobe's *Lehrbuch der musikalischen Komposition*. In addition to transcribing some of the sketches, Lobe moulded his whole approach to composition around what he saw as Beethoven's compositional process. The pupil is guided from 'the invention of ideas' (the 'first process', yielding the 'first sketch'), through the expansion of ideas ('second sketch'), then to the 'full sketching-out' (all of which processes use Beethoven's device of the 'continuity line'), and finally to the 'scoring up'. The entire disquisition is sprinkled with analytical examples, all drawn from Beethoven's string quartets op.18 nos.1–2.

What Nottebohm (who, unlike Lobe, was a historian and musicologist by profession) came across in examining Beethoven's painful formulation of thematic material was a living exemplification of the ideas of melodic motif, germ-cell, organic growth, unity – ideas which were rife and had found their way into the theoretical tradition. Here was a way of getting behind the finished text, of showing the composition student how a masterpiece was put together, errors, false starts and all, and at the same time of verifying one's deductive analyses (*Ein Skizzenbuch von Beethoven*, 1865, p.7):

We can observe the progressive development of a plant, learn about its step-by-step growth. Taking shape by continual transformation, following specified rules as it

34

does so, it constantly brings new things to light. But all that is new is always old. Thus it can successfully be explained in genetic terms. It is different with a piece of music; for this in its outward appearance is tied to the expression of a particular individual, and in its very particularity follows not a natural law, as does the plant, but the laws of the spirit [*Geist*]. We can consider a piece of music as an entirety and unity, analyse its structure, enjoy its beauty. Its genesis, however, and how it has come about, is concealed from us. The formal completeness with which it appears to us means that all trace has been eradicated of the development that lies behind it. If we view it as an organic structure we are forced to assume that it came into being by organic means and developed from within itself as a unified whole. Now it is true that in the sketchbooks, where everything that is fixed and unalterable in the finished piece is in a state of flux, is so to speak movable, many a process of birth, of discovery, of shaping, and the like, is laid bare.

One of the first analysts to draw on Nottebohm's findings was George Grove (1820–1900). Each of the analyses in *Beethoven and his Nine Symphonies* (1896) presents a rounded picture of its subject, with a balance of historical and biographical information, text-critical evidence and formal analysis – both plentifully illustrated with music examples – and critical judgment. Each concludes with a survey of the work's critical reception. Grove adopted a narrative approach for his formal analyses which has since become the stock in trade of descriptive writers on music, by animating the orchestra ('This is prolonged by the wind instruments in a humorous passage') or the piece itself ('after a reference back ... a new subject appears ... as harsh and uncompromising as the first subject') or by treating the listeners as visitors ('After this we arrive at a pause'). In another respect, too, Grove differed from the German analysts. He was uninfluenced by the idea of motivic growth. The tangible evidence of how a theme came about was of interest to him, and he was ready to point up similarities between the themes of different composers (e.g. the 'kindred themes' of Brahms, Schubert, Mozart and Beethoven, pp.59f). Similarities were matters of historical influence: 'the links which convey the great Apostolic Succession of Composers from generation to generation'. He recognized resemblance, but refused to construct theories around it: he was down to earth, an empiricist. And in the same spirit he largely eschewed naturalistic descriptions of the music, preferring to cite E. T. A. Hoffmann's imagery, or Schindler's yellow-hammer theory, or Beethoven's alleged 'fate knocking at the door' than to invent his own. For he was at heart a historian: he was interested in the impact of events on Beethoven's creativity, and explored this by drawing together the two strands – music and events – and suggesting the causal connection only with great restraint.

One writer from the early part of the 19th century whose work is properly classified as musical criticism and who was imbued rather with the spirit of Romantic genius than with historical awareness in what he wrote, but who was nonetheless influential, was Robert Schumann (1810–56). His review of Berlioz's *Symphonie fantastique* (1835) is a classic piece of critical writing. Schumann tackled its subject from four distinct points of view: formal construction, style and texture, the poetic 'idea' lying behind the work, and the spirit that governs it. The review ranges itself against critics of the work, examining its structure section by section to show that 'despite its apparent formlessness, there is an inherent correct symmetrical order' (Eng. trans., 1946, p.168); discussing harmonic and modulatory style, melodic and contrapuntal fabric, acknowledging the contravention of many theoretical rules but justifying them by the work's intensity, its 'entirely individual, indestructible energy' (p.172); recounting the work's programme, and arguing that it spurs the listener's imagination to perceive its own further meaning; and finally affirming that the work is 'informed with spirit', though 'not as the masterpiece of a master but as a work outstanding in its originality' (p.182).

In 1887 a writer who rejected both the formal analytical approach and that of naturalistic description, and was at the same time mistrustful of historical information, began publication of a guide to the concert repertory, *Führer durch den Konzertsaal*. This was Hermann Kretzschmar (1848–1924). The guide contains many hundreds of analyses that he had written during earlier years for concerts, classified into 'Symphony and Suite', 'Sacred Works' and 'Oratorios and Secular Choral Works', each category arranged in order by date of composition. It spans nearly 300 years, from Monteverdi to Mahler, including works by French and Russian composers, and was an unprecedented undertaking. Kretzschmar forged his own approach to musical appreciation which saw music as a language, universal in character, with meanings recognizable by those with the necessary aesthetic training (*Satzästhetik*). Such training brought with it an instinctive sense of how a phrase should be performed, a perception of the inner character of the phrase. At the end of this training stood a method of interpretation which Kretzschmar called 'musical hermeneutics', and which he saw as a revitalization of the Baroque doctrine of the Affections (*Affektenlehre*).

In two articles promoting this method (*JbMP 1902, 1905*) Kretzschmar sought to attack the free poetic description of music which many writers of the time indulged in, and to show how his own method was both firmly based on technical criteria and also capable of illuminating whole compositions rather than merely individual passages. At the heart of the method was 'thematic character' as defined by interval and contour. In these terms, the subject of the C major fugue from book 1 of Bach's *Das wohltemperirte Clavier* has an 'energetic disposition' which 'rests on the motif of the 4th as the principal element of the melodic structure'; but 'with the descending final phrase and the cautious approach to the main motif, the flow of the unmistakable energy which forms the middle section is framed on either side with expressions of melancholy' (*JbMP 1905*, p.282).

CHAPTER III

The 20th Century

1. Early 20th Century: Reduction Techniques and Personal Style

It was observed above (Chapter II, §3) that A. B. Marx, while using the word *Gestalt* for a formal 'mould', regarded 'form' as virtually synonymous with 'whole' (*Ganzes*). He felt, too, that formal 'moulds' were not merely conventions: they represented deep-seated principles of organization in the human mind. It was also observed that with Prout and Leichtentritt the subject of musical form (*Formenlehre*) had entered the realm of analysis instead of being a training in composition. It was at the time of Prout and Leichtentritt that a new branch of psychology was emerging, which laid emphasis on perception rather than on motivation: Gestalt psychology. Research gave an experimental scientific basis to some of the new attitudes towards musical experience. In essence it was concerned with form (in keeping with the views of Hanslick, 1854, and of J. F. Herbart, 1811): it laid stress on the power of the perceiver mentally to organize whatever objects or situations he encounters, and to do so in formal terms rather than in terms of individual components and his previous experience of them. Thus, visually, objects which are in close proximity to each other, and objects which are similar in shape or colour, tend to be perceived as a group. Moreover, the perceiving mind seeks the simplest available grouping, looking for basic, complete shapes – for 'continuous wholes'. It looks also for repetition and symmetry, for equal separation in space and time. In short, it tries to place the simplest, most regular, most complete interpretation on the data before it.

Musical sound was used for illustrative purposes by the early Gestalt psychologist Christian von Ehrenfels. He pointed, in 1890, to the fact that a melody does not lose its melodic identity when transposed, despite the change of each note: a melody has a shape which can be heard, recognized and learnt without recognition of its constituent notes, intervals or rhythms. Perception of the shape comes not as a slow process but as a flash of insight; it is like the completion of an electric circuit.

There are three principles which relate to this. 'Closure' is the principle whereby the mind, when presented with a shape that is almost complete but not quite, will complete the shape automatically. 'Phi phenomenon' is the principle whereby the mind, when confronted with two separate occurrences, may link them together and attribute movement from one to the other. 'Prägnanz' is the principle whereby the mind will look for the interpretation of data which yields the most 'pregnant' result – the 'best' interpretation. All these processes can be seen at work in for example perception of a lute transcription of a 16th-century vocal piece, where the original vocal lines are presented only incompletely because of the technical limitations of lute technique; or in a solo violin or cello work by Bach, where several contrapuntal lines are carried, all of them incompletely yet with a general sense of the polyphony.

One final principle is of fundamental importance to music: figure–ground perception. Very often the mind selects from the data before it only certain salient features; these it organizes as a 'pregnant' figure (*Gestalt*), leaving the rest of the data to remain in the field of perception. Ultimately only the figure is passed up from the nervous system (where this organization of sensory experience takes place) to the psychological field where it is 'understood'. The rest of the data remain as the 'ground'. This process is akin to what the musical analyst calls 'reduction', an early example of which is Czerny's stripping away of surface ornament in Chopin, Bach and Clementi to reveal the underlying essential structure (Chapter II, §2 and fig.11). Significantly, but quite conversely to Gestalt terminology, Czerny called the surface ornament 'the moving figure' and the structure 'the ground-melody' or 'the ground-harmony'.

The first full-scale use of Gestalt procedures was probably the examination by Arnold Schering (1877–1941) of the 14th-century Italian madrigal (1911–12), in which he introduced the idea of 'disembellishment' (*Dekolorieren*). This involved removing groups of short note values from melodic lines and substituting fewer notes of proportionately longer value to occupy the same amount of time: 'laying bare from within a melismatic passage the simple melodic progression'. Fig.14 shows an example of this (the reduction – the 'Übertragung' given on the lower staff – shows elements of 'closure' and 'Phi phenomenon', and is a clear example of figure–ground perception). Schering called what he uncovered 'melodic kernels' (*Melodiekerne*) or 'cells' (*Keime*), both terms being familiar from the organic music theorists of the 19th century. But in fact what he set out to reveal were medieval folksongs, since he believed that the elaborate 14th-century madrigals were really keyboard arrangements of folktunes. Such a theory is not inconceivable: there were keyboard arrangements in the 14th century, and Schering was simply reversing the procedure known as 'paraphrase' whereby a melody, usually a passage of plainsong, was embellished in one voice of a polyphonic composition in the late Middle Ages and Renaissance (see the discussion of diminution technique in Chapter II, §1). The difficulty lay in verifying the results as folksongs, and Schering adopted the interesting confirmatory device of reducing two different madrigals by different composers to the same underlying melodic progression. The two madrigals had the same poetic text, and Schering's assertion was that they both present elaborated versions of the original folk melody for these words: see fig.15. Schering's work provided in embryonic form the techniques for both the melodic evolutionists (Réti, Keller and Walker) and also the work of Heinrich Schenker in structural harmony.

In 1906 Schenker (1867–1935) had published his *Harmonielehre*, the first

14. *Johannes de Florentia: 'Nel meço a sei paon'*

15(a). *Lorenzo da Firenze: 'Ita se n'era star'*

15(b). *Vincenzo da Rimini: 'Ita se n'era a star'*

14, 15. From A. Schering: 'Das kolorierte Orgel-madrigal des Trecento', SIMG, xiii (1911–12), 193, 194, 197

volume of his highly influential *Neue musikalische Theorien und Phantasien*. It contained the seeds of two concepts new to harmonic theory, which were to underpin Schenker's later analytical procedures: 'compositional unfolding' or 'composing-out' (*Auskomponierung*) and 'prolongation' (*Prolongation*). He argued several times in the book, citing passages from Fux, Beethoven, Chopin, Liszt and Wagner in support, that arrangements of notes that look on the surface like chords in their own right are not always essential steps (*Stufen*) in a harmonic progression, but are often merely expansions of other essential steps (see especially Eng. trans., pp.141ff, 155, 212). In this way Schenker established a distinction between 'triads' and 'steps' whereby not all of the former in a given tonal context rise to the rank of the latter. Thus he analysed the first 16 bars of Variation 15 of Beethoven's Diabelli Variations op.120 as comprising five 'steps' (his ex.130/164) – see fig.16. He began to represent harmonic progressions graphically on two levels (e.g. his ex.173/234), using in one instance a 'formula' to show short-term triadic movement over longer-term harmonic steps (p.244), in which I – V : I – V is shown as numerator and I as denominator. On the larger scale he saw the key areas to which a composition modulated as either 'established', in which case they functioned as 'steps' at a higher level of form, or 'unestablished', in which case they served only to elaborate other key areas. Schenker's harmonic theory represented a shift away from that of Rameau (*Traité de l'harmonie*, 1722: see Chapter II, §1), introducing the psychological notion of 'valuation'; that is, assessment by the hearer of chords and modulatory key areas in relation to longer-term pulls of tonality,

16. From H. Schenker: 'Harmonielehre' (1906), 206

and interpretation of them as either fundamental steps or elaborations of such steps. This valuation was the starting-point for the new way of hearing music – long-distance listening – for which Schenker has become so famous.

In *Ein Beitrag zur Ornamentik* (1904) Schenker illustrated by reference to form in a sonata of C. P. E. Bach the idea of 'group construction' (*Gruppenbildung*) which was also partly stated in *Harmonielehre* (pp.241ff): the diversifying of a single tonal unit of structure by thematic and motivic variety, by interior harmonic movement, by variety of rhythmic placing and patterning, and by contrast of dynamic levels (pp.11ff). Schenker's scholarly activities – in particular his concern for authenticity in editing and performance, and his respect for the authority of autograph scores and authorized editions – had led him to this study of ornamentation in C. P. E. Bach, Haydn, Mozart, Beethoven and others.

C. P. E. Bach was a seminal figure for Schenker; his *Versuch über die wahre Art das Clavier zu spielen* (1753) not only exerted a powerful fascination over him, but also provided a link back to 16th- and 17th-century theory of embellishment, to which Schenker's concept of diminution closely relates (see Forte and Gilbert, 1982, p.8f). *Ein Beitrag zur Ornamentik* was then a significant study for Schenker's development as an analyst, since he was later to develop a technique of stripping away layers of ornamentation in the process of revealing the ultimate structure of a piece. In his so-called 'Erläuterungsausgabe' of four of Beethoven's last five piano sonatas (1913–21 – that of op.106 did not appear because its autograph could not be found; there is however an unpublished essay on the sonata) he achieved a balance between the analytical and the textual sides of his work. In the last volume of the set, on op.101, he developed the idea of reduction by carrying it through successive stages. Fig.17 (overleaf) shows the stages laid out one above the other. Schenker, however, introduced this example with the words 'Here are shown the lines that Beethoven's imagination followed': he intended it as a tracing of the creative process step by step, not as an analysis. Thus he spoke not of 'reduction' but of the reverse, *Diminution* (i.e. elaboration). The way in which the initial $g\sharp'$–a' in line (a) gives rise in line (d) to $g\sharp'$–a'–$g\sharp'$–a', and in which this is ultimately embellished in the right hand of bars 1–4 of (e) as e'–$g\sharp'$–a'–$b\flat'$–a'–$g\sharp'$–a' shows the technique of his later analyses already formed. Although Schenker's first line (a) does not take the form of his eventual *Ursatz* (or even its melodic component, the *Urlinie*), and he used only the term *Ton-Urreihe* to describe it, the term *Urlinie* is used elsewhere in the study.

It was one of the greatest figures of historical musicology, Guido Adler (1855–1941), who attempted through his book *Der Stil in der Musik* (1911) to change the nature of historical writing about music by introducing the notion of style as the central concern of the historian. As early as 1885 Adler had published a programme for the future of musicology, placing strong emphasis on analysis, arguing for its rightful place in historical inquiry. He set out a series of criteria for the examination of structure in a work, under general headings such as rhythmic features, tonality, polyphonic construction, word-setting, treatment of instruments, and performing practice. In his book Adler criticized his contemporaries for making history out of a string of composers' names.

41

17. From H. Schenker: 'Beethoven: Die letzten fünf Sonaten: Sonate A dur Op.101' (1921), 52–3

What was necessary, he believed, was the formulation of a terminology adequate for the description of music 'without names to prop it up'. If music could be described in this way then it would become possible to compare work with work, and thus to specify what features works have in common – or rather, in the more dynamic terms that Adler used, what features 'link works together'.

Music history was to Adler like a self-weaving textile whose threads, of different colours, thicknesses and strengths, were features of style. Threads might discontinue, change colour, change places or merge. Thus he spoke of 'stylistic direction' (*Stilrichtung*), 'stylistic change' (*Stilwandel*), 'stylistic transfer' (*Stilübertragung*), 'stylistic hybridization' (*Stilkreuzung*), 'stylistic mixing' (*Stilmischung*) (pp.19–48). His view of art was as an organism. Everything in it could be accounted for; nothing occurred by chance (p.13):

> The style of an epoch, of a school, of a composer, of a work, does not arise accidentally, as the casual outcome and manifestation of artistic will. It is, on the contrary, based on laws of becoming, of the rise and fall of organic development. Music is an organism, a plurality of single organisms which in their changing relationships and interdependencies form a totality.

Adler sharply criticized what he called the 'hero-cult' – that is, history written in terms only of leading composers: 'the edifice of style is built out of minor figures just as much as major, and all need investigation if the true picture is to appear'. (It is significant that Adler had been the prime mover in the Austrian national series of editions, Denkmäler der Tonkunst in Österreich, of which he was editor from 1894 to 1938; he must have been particularly conscious of the need to place lesser composers in historical perspective.) The task that he set the historian was to observe and apprehend that edifice of style in an essentially scientific manner; for 'style is the centre of the handling and comprehension of art . . . it is the yardstick by which everything in the work of art is measured and judged' (p.5). He placed emphasis on 'apprehension' as the first stage: that is, a recognition of the facts purely as they are, which avoids value judgments and subjective preconceptions on the part of the historian.

Adler offered two methods of approaching this task, and it is here that his work is important for the analyst. One method is that of taking several pieces and examining them to identify what they have in common and how they differ. This is Adler's 'inductive method', by which the historian can perceive the forces that cause an established group of works to hold together; he can discover which works in a random collection are relatively close in style and which more distant; or he can trace links between works composed in chronological succession. The other, the 'deductive method', is to compare a given work with surrounding works, contemporary and preceding, measuring it against them by set criteria and establishing its position within them. Such criteria are the use of motif and theme, rhythm, melody, harmony, notation and so forth. Other criteria concern the function and medium of music: sacred or secular, vocal or instrumental, lyrical or dramatic, courtly, virtuoso etc. Adler's book is far from a manual of stylistic analysis. It does not offer method in detail. It was a laying of foundations for method. Adler sought to establish a 'framework of laws' (*Rahmengesetz*) by which style operates and within which research could proceed.

Adler made a particular study of the Viennese Classical style. Wilhelm Fischer too, his assistant from 1912 to 1928, completed a dissertation on the genesis of that style in 1915. Two other scholars pursued stylistic studies in scholarly fashion at this time, Ernst Bücken (1884–1949) and Paul Mies (1889–1976), notably in their joint article on the foundations, methods and tasks of stylistic research into music (1922–3). Both also worked on Beethoven; indeed, Beethoven became a centre of attention for studies of personal style, with Hans Gál's examination of individual features in the young Beethoven (1916), Gustav Becking's of Beethoven's personal style (1921), Mies's of the meaning of the sketches for an understanding of Beethoven's style (1925), Ludwig Schiedermair's of the young Beethoven (1925), August Halm's of middle-period works (in *Beethoven*, 1926) and Walter Engelsmann's of Beethoven's levels of composition (1931). Other studies of personal style include Werner Danckert's *Personal Typen des Melodiestils* (1931), later enlarged as *Ursymbole melodischer Gestaltung* (1932). Becking was particularly interested in rhythm as a determinant of individuality (1928) and devised a set of graphic devices, known as 'Becking curves', for representing the rhythmic 'national constants' and 'personal constants': fig.18 shows the curves for the 18th-century Italian–German mixture of styles represented by Handel, and for Wagner's early style.

18. From G. Becking: 'Der musikalische Rhythmus als Erkenntnisquelle' (1928), 58, 110

The most distinguished and influential example of stylistic analysis at this time was however Knud Jeppesen's *The Style of Palestrina and the Dissonance*, first prepared as a doctoral dissertation in Danish in 1923, and subsequently translated into German in 1925 and English in 1927. Jeppesen (1892–1974) provided in this book the detailed analytical procedure that Adler had left wanting. His choice of 'inductive' or 'deductive' method was conditioned by his general purpose: he saw the need for a history of dissonance treatment. He felt that modern manuals of counterpoint, based on Fux (*Gradus ad Parnassum*, 1725), lacked precisely that historical account, that 'genetic' growth of dissonance treatment, which would illuminate the development of musical style in time and place from the Middle Ages to the late Renaissance and from there to the end of the 18th century (pp.3f):

Passing from an absorbing study of Gregorian music to primitive polyphonic forms, from the style of Palestrina to the commencement of dramatic music, or from Bach's polyphony to the classical art of Vienna, would be the best manner of proceeding for recognizing immediately the essential peculiarities of the new style.

In taking Palestrina as his special study Jeppesen was starting with a 'central' point, and a stable one, from which he could look backwards (since Palestrina's work was a 'vast summary of the musical development of the preceding centuries') and forwards. At the same time he was starting with the best-known phenomenon in the field, and investigating it against a background which was in his terms virtually uncharted. He was therefore driven to the 'inductive' method, with no established criteria and only the possibility of comparing case with case until such criteria began to appear.

Jeppesen himself called this method 'empiric-descriptive', and identified it expressly with Adler's method. He stated it clearly (p.8):

> through comparison of variants of homogeneous forms of [the] language [of music] – whether taken from contemporary or from historically separated periods – to indicate and fix common qualities, which with certainty can be supposed to possess the essential accentuations of these forms. The material thus obtained may then serve as a basis upon which to build up the laws of the language, the laws of musical evolution. These, psychologically translated, finally develop into certain regulations and directions of will – the hidden force behind these laws.

Jeppesen in this way extended Adler's inquiry from the surface of music, considered empirically, to the subconscious controls of style, considered psychologically. In so doing he enunciated the motivation for most present-day feature analysis, including computer-assisted analysis (see §5 below), and for formulations of musical grammars (§6). His method of working is indeed particularly well suited to computer operation.

Jeppesen presented first an account of Palestrina's melodic style (pp.48–84) with regard to pitch contour, rhythmic flow and the width and direction of intervals. The preliminary work for this analysis must clearly have been an exhaustive search through every vocal part of Palestrina's entire output (in the Leipzig collected edition of 1862–1903) in order to count and note every interval in relation to its metrical placing. Thus he located and listed for the reader (p.55, note 3) the occurrence of major 6ths and descending minor 6ths as 'dead' intervals (i.e. between two phrases rather than during a phrase: 32 cases in all). The investigation of upward leaps in rhythmic context led to the uncovering of a subconscious law: 'on considering the style with regard to crotchets . . . we meet with the astonishing fact, not previously observed, that a rule (almost without an exception) forbids the leap upward from an accentuated crotchet' (p.61). By contrast, Jeppesen listed no fewer than 35 melodic patterns in which a downward leap occurs from an accented crotchet, and charted all the places in which these patterns occur. It is in the much larger second discussion, that of dissonance treatment (pp.84–287), where he defined each dissonance in turn and discussed its degree and manner of use by Palestrina, that Jeppesen entered into historical comparison. Thus for example he considered the use of the 'portamento dissonance' (the anticipation of a note on a weak beat), stating: 'by Palestrina it was most frequently employed immediately before a syncope [i.e. syncopation] and in descending movement . . . though the syncope is not an invariable condition' (pp.184f). He then contrasted this limitation with the use by other composers, citing cases in Josquin, Obrecht, Carpentras, Cara and La Rue.

The aspect of Jeppesen's work that makes it scientific is the fact that the analyst is not selecting and summarizing: he is presenting the entire data for each case and adducing laws from them objectively.

2. 1920–45: Tension Theory and Structural Layers

One of Adler's pupils was Ernst Kurth (1886–1946). Kurth's ideas were closely allied to those of the Gestalt psychologists, but also used Schopenhauer's concept of the 'Will' and Freud's of the subconscious mind. The Gestalt theorists saw three levels of aural perception: physical perception by the ear, sensory organization in the nervous system, and understanding at the psychological level. Kurth saw three levels of activity in musical creation, which he expounded as part of his theory of melody in the first part of *Die Grundlagen des linearen Kontrapunkts* (1917). The first of these levels is the operation of the 'Will' (which in art is unselfish and disinterested) in the form of kinetic energy (*Bewegungsenergie*); this, a continuous flow, is the living power of music; 'the origin of music . . . is the will to move'. The second level is the psychological: the submerged stirrings of the unconscious mind draw on this energy to produce a 'play of tensions' (*Spiel von Spannungen*), each tug of tension describing an arc of growth and formation (*Ur-Formung* or *Erformung*). This play of tensions does not become conscious until the moment that it takes form in musical sound – the third level, the acoustic manifestation (*Erscheinungsform*). Because these three levels are activated one after the other to produce melody, the resultant line has unity and wholeness. Its shape is conceived before either notes or harmonic implications are brought into play; it is thus a 'closed progression'. This is the essence of Kurth's concept of the 'linear'. He saw it particularly at work in the music of Bach – a texture made up of lines, each of which is powered by kinetic energy and internally unified, and which make harmonic sense together only as a secondary phenomenon. This is what Kurth called 'linear counterpoint'. He evolved a concept of 'linear phase', a unit of growth and decay, quite separate from the conventional idea of 'phrase' in that it did not depend on rhythmic patterning, only on proportion and contour. The motif was such a phase: unified, distinctive, not losing its identity when its pitches, intervals and durations are modified (pp.21ff, 68ff).

Notes forming a melody contain kinetic energy; notes forming a chord contain 'potential energy'. Tonal harmony is a system of internal coherence, carrying the possibility of change, brought about by potential energy. The most powerful tension in this system is that of the leading note. In his next book, on Romantic harmony (1920), Kurth first expounded chromatic alteration as a process of placing the leading note where it would not normally occur. He distinguished between two forces at work in Romantic harmony, creating a polarization: 'constructive' and 'destructive' forces (pp.272ff). It is the cohesive forces of tonality that are constructive, and the dissolving forces of chromaticism that are destructive: alteration, the use of chords of the 7th, 9th etc in place of triads, and the use of chords for coloristic effects. Kurth took Wagner's *Tristan*, and in particular the many statements of the famous 'Tristan chord', as the central material for this book; it contains little actual analysis, yet it offered a new perspective for handling the large-scale tonal structure of Wagner's operas, giving insight into long-term tonal relationships despite pervading chromaticism and movement to remote key areas for long periods.

The scholar who grasped the problem of form and tonality in Wagner and exposed its 'secret' analytically was Alfred Lorenz (1868–1939). After a doctoral dissertation on form in the *Ring* (1922) and a study of the *Tristan* prelude (1922–3) he published the first of his four volumes of *Das Geheimnis der Form bei Richard Wagner* which were to analyse form in the *Ring* (1924), *Tristan* (1926), *Meistersinger* (1930) and *Parsifal* (1933). Lorenz's work was a landmark in the history of analysis: a large-scale piece of sustainedly analytical writing, matched only by Schenker's 375-page analysis of Beethoven's Ninth Symphony (1912). It uses graphic and tabular techniques of presentation in a thorough-going way: the 'sine curve' for harmonic movement, the 'projectile curve' for extended formal contour, the graph for modulatory scheme (see fig.19 (overleaf) for the graph representing the whole *Ring* cycle as a vast unified structure in D♭ major, with lateral spacing marking 40 pages of score and each horizontal line a major and each space a minor key area) and type-set diagrams for more detailed tonal movement (see fig.20 for the diagram of *Das Rheingold*, which is complementary to fig.19 and shows the opera as an introduction (748 bars) in the dominant of the dominant followed by a massive symmetrical section (3128 bars) in D♭ pivoting round the relative minor, B♭).

Lorenz's work is the confluence of all the main earlier developments in analysis. It contains ideas from the Gestalt writers; his notion of periodization and symmetry derives from Riemann; his defining of structure draws on traditional *Formenlehre*; his perception of harmonic movement comes from Kurth (to whom he dedicated his *Tristan* volume). It is also built from a large body of existing writings on Wagner's musical and dramatic structures (especially those by Hostinský, 1877; Grunsky, 1906, 1907; von Ehrenfels, 1896, 1913; and Mayrberger, 1881 (see fig.13, p.27)) and on his leitmotifs (e.g. Mayrberger, 1881; von Wolzogen, 1876, 1880, 1882), and above all from Wagner's own prose writings.

Lorenz saw formal construction (*Formbildung*) as created out of three primary things: harmony, rhythm and melody. He segmented the entire *Ring* cycle into periods according to key area (pp.23ff). He also analysed the distribution of leitmotifs into formal groupings: repetition forms, arch forms, refrain forms and bar forms. It is in this last area that his main contribution to music theory lies. Lorenz perceived a hierarchical structure in music, the two extremes of which are his *kleine Rhythmik* and *grosse Rhythmik*. The second of these arises out of the first by forms being 'raised to a higher power' (*potenzierte Formen*). By this process, three consecutive passages of music may each be constructed in arch form (*ABA*); the third of them may be a restatement of the first and so create

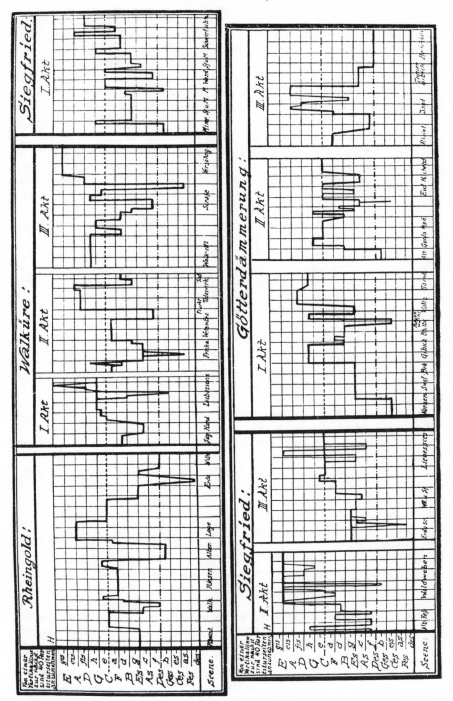

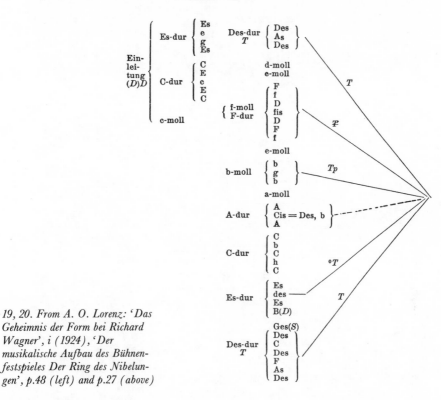

19, 20. From A. O. Lorenz: 'Das Geheimnis der Form bei Richard Wagner', i (1924), 'Der musikalische Aufbau des Bühnenfestspieles Der Ring des Nibelungen', p.48 (left) and p.27 (above)

an arch form at a higher level. The process may be traced at more than two levels. He also described the embedding of small-scale units within forms, extending them and changing the balance, and very large-scale forms which contain small-scale forms of different sorts. By analysing formal units in this way, Lorenz sought to uncover the architectonics (*grosse Architektonik*) of very large musical structures.

A year after Lorenz had issued the first volume of his *Geheimnis der Form*, Schenker produced the first issue of a yearbook, *Das Meisterwerk in der Musik*, which was to run to only three issues (1925, 1926, 1930). It contains ten analytical studies, of works by J. S. Bach, Domenico Scarlatti, Mozart, Beethoven and Chopin, accompanied by Schenker's new type of graphic analyses, together with a long essay on 'Die Kunst der Improvisation' (itself containing important analyses of keyboard works by C. P. E. Bach and Handel), a polemic 'Weg mit dem Phrasierungsbogen' ('Away with phrase-marks') and a study-in-progress of the concept of 'fundamental line' (*Urlinie*). This was not the first journal that Schenker had produced: he had published ten issues of *Der Tonwille* between 1921 and 1924, the first two of which contain preliminary studies of the *Urlinie* idea together with analyses using the so-called *Urlinie-Tafeln* – graphic analyses showing the fundamental line. The most important analytical product of *Der Tonwille* was the study of Beethoven's Symphony no.5, produced in instalments

49

and later issued separately (1925). (The two journals contain material exclusively by Schenker.)

The *Urlinie-Tafel* as developed at this stage was usually a presentation of a piece in full or partly reduced, with normal use of note values and complete with time signature and the original barring (numbered for reference). This was overlaid with auxiliary analytical symbols: horizontal and sloping square brackets over the staff to show the movement of the fundamental line; note heads printed large to indicate structural importance; curved lines like phrasing or bowing marks to indicate important progressions (often also labelled *Quintzug, Quartzug* etc); dotted curves to indicate the longer-term structural retention of a particular pitch (or transfer to another octave) despite intervening pitches; and the fundamental harmonic steps (*Stufen*), symbolized below the staff by roman numerals, with conventional bass figuring to show the overlying harmonies. In some cases Schenker added a parallel staff above the *Urlinie-Tafel*: this carried his reduction of the piece to bare harmonic essentials – already termed *Ursatz* – and partly abandoned the durational significance of note symbols in favour of a valuation whereby greater duration denoted greater structural importance. Fig.21 (*Das Meisterwerk*, i, *Urlinie-Tafeln*, pl.2) illustrates all these features and many others (the *Urlinie-Tafel* showing the Largo from Bach's Violin Sonata no.3 BWV1005 bar-for-bar but in skeletal form): bar 7, and bar 17 a 5th lower, show how the fundamental line ($f''–e''–d''$) moves from the top line of the texture to the bottom and back, and how the last of its notes is not actually sounded but only implied (hence the parentheses). For this particular piece, Schenker chose also to give a three-layer graph (see fig.22) of which the bottom layer is a partly reduced form of the piece, the middle one an intermediate stage of reduction, and the top one a complete reduction corres-

21, 22. From H. Schenker: 'Das Meisterwerk in der Musik', i (1925), 'Urlinie-Tafeln', pl.2 (top left) and graph between pp.61 and 62 (below)

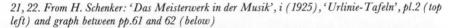

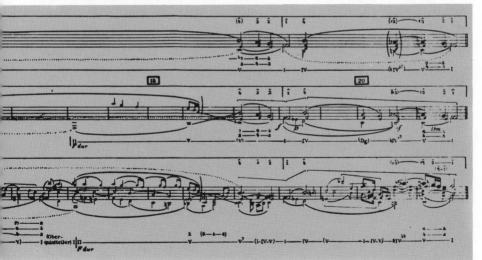

ponding to the upper parallel staff of the *Urlinie-Tafel*. These two graphs are accompanied by 11 pages of closely reasoned text with further music examples.

The main achievements of the yearbook were a long and lucid essay on Mozart's Symphony no.40 in G minor (vol.ii) and the massive analysis of Beethoven's 'Eroica' Symphony (vol.iii). The layers (*Schichten*) are identified as 'foreground', 'middleground' and 'background'; horizontal brackets are abandoned in preference to the beaming together of structural notes, and many other graphic devices are adopted. Such was the sophistication of Schenker's graphs during the last five years of his life that he felt able to discard verbal commentary altogether. His *Fünf Urlinie Tafeln* (1932) are self-sufficient graphings of works by Bach, Haydn and Chopin. The full range of his terminology is to be found in these graphs. Moreover, the *Ursatz* had by then taken its final form in Schenker's mind as a melodic progression of 3–2–1 extensible to 5–4–3–2–1 or rarely 8–7–6–5–4–3–2–1, over a 'bass arpeggiation' (*Bassbrechung*) of 1–5–1: the ultimate projection of the major triad into the dimension of time which Schenker saw as lying at the heart of his theory. This meant that the basic structure of any tonal piece of music was diatonic, and all modulations were considered as 'prolongations' of diatonic harmonic steps. The fullest statement of Schenker's approach is his posthumously published *Der freie Satz* (1935), which was itself 20 years in writing. Here, Schenker's linear conception of music – music as organically based 'voice-leading' – is systematically expounded, proceeding from background to foreground. The work concludes with valuable chapters on metre, rhythm and form. While Schenker never arrived at a free-standing theory of metre and rhythm, it is often argued that their function was implicitly recognized within Schenker's view of tonal organization.

Further formulation of the rhythmic component of Schenker's analytical method had to wait 40 years. Maury Yeston's *The Stratification of Musical Rhythm* (1976) explores the way in which rhythmic elements interact with pitch elements in musical structure. Carl Schachter's studies of 1976 and 1980 investigate durational reduction, exploiting the long-term metrical effects produced by whole bars and even regular multiples of bars, or 'hypermeasures', and devising durational graphs on the Schenkerian model. Fundamental work on rhythm and metre has also been done by Wallace Berry (1976) and Allen Forte (1983).

Schenker's analytical work was directed towards the performer as well as the scholar, and his final graphic method led the reader stage by stage from the familiar text of a work through to an understanding of it in its complex totality. His analyses were thus always pedagogical in function. (For Schenker's method see also Chapter IV, §2.)

In his *Unterweisung im Tonsatz* of 1937 the composer Paul Hindemith (1895–1963) believed himself to have laid down the basis of a *lingua franca* for modern composition, 'proceeding from the firm foundation of the laws of nature'. He was by 1926 thoroughly familiar with Schenker's writings and declared that 'in them the foundations of musical creativity are laid bare' (Schubert, 1980). There was a personal link between the two men in Herman Roth, whom Hindemith consulted closely on the *Unterweisung*. The work of

Schenker and Hindemith in a sense had a common origin in the crisis that music was undergoing before World War I. Whereas the former looked backward, confirming the 'immutable laws' of German music from the Classical period and calling for a return to these from the errors of the 19th century, the latter affirmed the forward movement of 20th-century music, seeking rational principles for it – hence Schenker's antagonism towards Hindemith (Schenker, 1925, p.219). Hindemith, like Schenker, believed in the force of tonality and the primacy of the triad; but his theory is far more systematically acoustical. To Hindemith, if any one of the notes of the chromatic octave scale be taken, then the other 11 notes can be ranged in descending order of relationship to it. This order he called 'Series 1'. Adopting the principle of inversion (by which, for example, minor 7th = major 2nd), he determined an order for intervals based on combination-tone curves in increasing complexity. This produced 'Series 2', of intervals in descending order of value with respect to a given note. This series acknowledges no point at which consonance ends and dissonance begins. From this Hindemith developed a system of chordal analysis, which first allocates to any chord a root – always present in the chord, unlike the roots of Rameau's harmonic system – and then measures the intensity of that chord. Hindemith classified chords containing three to six notes into separate groups and sub-groups in terms of their harmonic intensity. Using these groups, a composer might put together a succession of chords in any desired 'harmonic crescendo and decrescendo'. Such an increase and decrease of intensity he called a 'harmonic fluctuation' (a concept closely related to Kurth's idea of *Spannung*); and he devised a graphic means of demonstrating this beneath the staff (see fig.23, which shows the group and subgroup of each chord as well as the graphic fluctuation). Hindemith proceeded from there to determine harmonic relationships on a larger scale by measuring the progression of prevailing roots, the 'degree-progression', against Series 1.

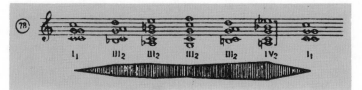

23. From P. Hindemith: 'Unterweisung im Tonsatz' (1937; Eng. trans., 1942), i, 120

Although *Unterweisung im Tonsatz* was intended as a constructional tool for composers, and stressed the realms of harmony that Hindemith felt were not adequately covered by conventional harmonic theory, its theories were meant to apply equally to the harmony of the past and thus to function as a means of interpreting and analysing the music of any period. Hindemith himself supplied, at the end of the first volume, a set of analyses of music ranging from plainchant to Schoenberg and his own music. As an analytical method his system is like Schenker's in being based on a theory of melody and harmony with no separate theory of rhythm. It is unlike it in that there are no structural levels: all notes at the surface can be related to the tonal centre, and modulation is an accepted tonal procedure which is not reduced out of existence.

In 1932 Arnold Schoenberg (1874–1951) wrote: 'For nearly 20 years I have been collecting material, ideas and sketches, for an all-inclusive textbook of composition'. The project was never completed, though it survives in skeletal form as an inquiry into musical ideas, the 'Gedanke Manuscript', now in the Arnold Schoenberg Institute in Los Angeles. Only *Harmonielehre* (1911) and *Models for Beginners in Composition* (1942) were published in his lifetime, and *Structural Functions of Harmony* (1954) shortly after his death. Since then, two sets of notes designed for teaching purposes, both dating from the 1930s, have been assembled and issued: *Preliminary Exercises in Counterpoint* (dating from *c*1936; 1963) and *Fundamentals of Musical Composition* (dating between 1937 and 1948; 1967). The last is a small manual of form. Not at all radical in conception, it sets out definitions of terms in thematic construction before proceeding to small forms, the subsidiary parts of larger forms, rondo forms and the sonata-allegro. The material was intended for composers, but it rests on analytical exemplification and is to some extent a manual of analysis, drawing particularly on examples from Beethoven's piano sonatas.

Schoenberg saw form as implying comprehensibility in two dimensions: as subdivision, which enables the mind to grasp the whole through units; and as logic and coherence, without which such units remain disconnected. It was on questions of coherence that Schoenberg was at his most original. He adhered to the 19th-century view of music as organic. Construction thus begins with the motif, the motif must by its nature be repeated, repetition requires variation. He thus explored rhythmic, intervallic, harmonic and melodic means of variation, subdividing each systematically, then considered variation by addition of ancillary notes and the connecting of different motif forms. All this is demonstrated with analytical examples. In the course of his exposition he supplied the analyst with a valuable set of working definitions for terms such as 'motif', 'phrase', 'antecedent' and 'consequent', 'period', 'sentence' and 'section'. Among the melodic concepts that he introduced was that of 'liquidation', whereby a unit gradually loses its characteristic features until only a residue remains.

The most influential aspect of the book, as it was disseminated through his teaching, is his atomic splitting of the motif into 'element' or 'feature'. The 'element' is often a single interval underlying a pattern of notes, and itself undergoes repetition, transposition, inversion, internal multiplication, enlarge-

24. From A. Schoenberg: 'Fundamentals of Musical Composition' (1967), 11

ment, contraction and all the other processes to which the motif is subject. His reduction of the first theme of Brahms's Symphony no.4 to a succession of 3rds is perhaps the most famous example in the book (see fig.24).

Several subsequent writers have pursued Schoenberg's insights for analytical purposes. Of these, Rudolph Réti and Hans Keller have raised the notion of the single underlying motif to the status of background unity (see §4 and Chapter IV, §3). Erwin Ratz (1951) took up Schoenberg's exhortation, given in 1950 (1975, pp.396f), to solve the 'hidden mystery' of J. S. Bach's non-fugal keyboard works. He engaged in a comparative analysis of the two- and three-part inventions of Bach – on which he lighted as the source of the Viennese Classical style – with Beethoven's middle- and late-period sonatas. Ratz used Schoenberg's concepts of the 'model' and its treatment (*Modell* is a term traceable back to Lobe in 1850), and of liquidation. He distinguished two constructional types which articulate structures powerfully: 'fixed' (as in main themes and codas) and 'loose' (as in second themes, transitions, bridges and development sections).

In seeking a synthesis of Schoenbergian and Schenkerian ideas, David Epstein (1979) harnessed Schoenberg's term *Grundgestalt* ('basic shape' – a term in fact rarely used, and then not very deliberately, by Schoenberg himself) in the analysis of Classical and Romantic music. He showed an acute awareness of the many dimensions of music, paying particular attention to tempo relationships and rhythmic structure, and to ambiguity as a force in structure.

Walter Frisch (1984) took up Schoenberg's concept of 'developing variation' and applied it to the music of Brahms – whose innovations in musical language had been a lifelong preoccupation of Schoenberg. Developing variation was the principle whereby the structural ingredients of themes (motifs, phrases, ideas) were reiterated only in varied forms, some with their internal elements (intervals, rhythms, harmony, contour) undergoing modifications at each restatement. Such modifications yielded 'variants' and 'motif forms', some of which might take on identities of their own in a sort of motivic bifurcation.

3. *Empiricist Dissent*

The most significant British contribution to analysis in the first half of the 20th century was that of a man who rejected abstract thinking and systematic theory in music: Donald Francis Tovey (1875–1940). He took issue with most of the dogmas of his time. He castigated the theorists of harmony and tonality as being 'in a tangle of abstruse confusion', stating that 'what is hopelessly beyond' their range is 'precisely . . . the relation of harmonic resources to the time-scale of the whole music' (*Essays and Lectures on Music*, ed. H. J. Foss, 1949, pp.166, 198). He was no less sceptical of the notion of Schoenbergian 'thematic logic'. Characteristically trenchant is his observation: 'themes have no closer connexion with larger musical proportions than the colours of animals have with their skeletons'; and moreover 'if themes cannot determine the logic of music, neither can a single figure really form the "idea" of a whole movement or section' (ibid, pp.275, 278). He did not deny the existence of thematic organization; but unless a derivation is presented to the listener as a continuous process of development it will not be perceived; a long-range thematic link may indeed exist, but it will be perceived as a contrast. However, even if a sonata were to swarm with thematic relationships, 'the "logic" of the music would still depend on principles deeper and radically different' (ibid, p.281).

Tovey rejected equally derisively the teachings of late 19th-century *Formen-lehre*. He spoke of 'the idiotic terminology of sonata form' and 'the mechanical triviality of the accepted doctrines of sonata form' (ibid, pp.120, 123); he ridiculed the notion that the 'classicists . . . reduced all instrumental art-forms to pre-established jelly-moulds' (ibid, p.224). He discarded the terms 'first subject' and 'second subject' as having 'worked such havoc in our notions of sonata form and sonata themes' (1935–9, i, 2), preferring the neutrality of 'theme' (often qualified as 'major theme', 'horn-theme' and so on), 'sentence', 'phrase' and the more down-to-earth 'melody' and 'tune'. He declared: 'there are no rules whatever as to the number or distribution of themes in any sonata movement'. In his view, 'the art forms of Haydn, Mozart, and Beethoven were not moulds in which music could be cast, but inner principles by which the music grew' (1949, pp.274, 289). He accused theorists of confusing the 'normal' with the 'usual'. The normal may be extremely rare, and freedom is a function of normality, not an opposing principle (ibid, pp.183f).

The principles of sonata form were stated by him in 1927 as: 'key system and phrase system, both of which can be reduced to technical analysis; and dramat-ic fitness, which can be discussed only descriptively and analogically' (ibid, p.275). This admixture of technical analysis and metaphor, illustrated by frequent music examples, their figures and themes marked by letter symbols, correctly characterizes his analytical style; for whereas he rejected emotive writing about music, he accepted that metaphor was the means by which artistic expression is to be related to life. Only in his study of the Beethoven piano sonatas is his analysis substantially technical. He also rejected the separa-tion of form from content: 'form and matter are different aspects of the same thing', 'every genuine work of art grows . . . from within' (ibid, pp.178f).

What Tovey produced as six volumes of analyses, published together for the first time in 1935–9, is not outwardly unlike what Kretzschmar produced in 1887 (see Chapter II, §4). They began life as programme notes for the Edin-burgh Reid Concert Series in the mid-1910s (though some go back to 1902). Like Kretzschmar's, his material was arranged by genre, and within that in chronological order, the final volume in his case containing supplementary essays and a glossary. As a whole, the volumes make a substantial analysis book of the 18th- and 19th-century orchestral and choral repertory, to which he added in 1944 a further volume on chamber music (some of whose essays go back to 1900). The two works thus have broadly the same scope. Both writers had rejected most of the received wisdom of musical theory, both sought firm technical criteria, both rejected flowery prose yet ended up using it, both used exemplified prose as their means of communication. The results, however, are totally different, Kretzschmar describing a secret interior world of the spirit, Tovey narrating a purely musical process.

Tovey had earlier produced two sets of analyses: *A Companion to Beethoven's Pianoforte Sonatas (Bar-to-Bar Analysis)*, and *A Companion to the 'Art of Fugue'* (both in 1931). These books, and his articles for the *Encyclopaedia Britannica* written between 1906 and 1910, have exerted the strongest influence on British analytical and critical writing.

That Tovey dissented from the abstract theory of his age is not to be taken as signifying radically forward-looking thought. He was out of sympathy with most of the modern music of his day, for he was a true Victorian man-of-letters, brought up on classical Austro-German repertory from Bach to Brahms (precisely that to which Schoenberg and Schenker devoted their analytical energies). One aspect of his analytical approach which might at first appear novel is his 'naive listener'. This was the image of the reader to whom he addressed himself: one with no technical training in music, but open to experience. Tovey was concerned always with audibility – perceptibility without recourse to orthodoxy. If a feature was not observable by the innocent ear of the non-expert hearer, then it was not worth observing. The 'naive listener already possesses the right musical sensations. These are as direct as the colours of a sunset or the tastes of a dinner. Connoisseurship comes from experience, not from verbal explanations' (1949, p.271). However, his idealized reader is not so very far from the amateur music lover who was the addressee of much mid-19th-century analysis; nor so far from the well-educated Victorian gentleman or lady. What is clear is that the naive listener and Tovey's dislike of theorizing are counterparts within a single system.

Tovey's analyses have influenced British writing about music at all levels and in every context. Since 1950, they have had one vigorous repudiator: Hans Keller, for whom mere description is no substitute for real analysis, and who attached the memorable tag 'eminently professional tautologies' to Tovey's mode of expression. Tovey had little impact on continental Europe or the USA, but since 1970 has undergone a revaluation among certain American scholars, notably Charles Rosen (1971, 1980) and Joseph Kerman (1975–6, 1985). For the latter, in his championing since the 1960s of a species of musicology which fuses the objectivity of the historian with the personal experience of the critic, Tovey has in some measure become prototypical.

4. 1945–60: Linguistics, Cybernetics and Thematic Unity

In the years after World War II, two highly influential lines of intellectual thought came to impinge on musical theory. To some extent both were approaches to phenomena – methodologies – rather than fields of study in their own right. The first was linguistics, founded as a modern science by Ferdinand de Saussure about the turn of the 20th century; this began to influence musical theory in the 1930s and 1940s before making a great impact in the 1950s and 1960s in conjunction with the closely related approaches of structuralism and semiotics (or semiology: the two terms are virtually synonymous with slight overtones of different intellectual traditions within the field). The second was

57

cybernetics and information theory, which as mechanistic views of the world originated at the end of the 1940s with the work of Norbert Wiener (*Cybernetics*, 1948), and Claude Shannon and Warren Weaver (*The Mathematical Theory of Communication*, 1949).

Linguistics examines social communication through natural language, seeking to uncover the rules by which a given language operates, the deeper rules by which language as a general phenomenon operates, and the processes by which individuals intuitively learn the complex rules of their own language. It took important strides forward with the work of three circles of linguistics scholars: that in Prague, including Roman Jakobson and N. S. Trubetzkoy; that in Copenhagen, including Hjelmslev; and the American scholars including Zellig Harris and Noam Chomsky. The kindred approaches of semiotics and structuralism both tend to reduce all kinds of non-linguistic social communication to the state of natural language, semiotics by treating all the ways in which human beings signal to each other (by the clothes they wear, the gestures they make, the food they eat, and so on) as 'codes' containing 'messages' which can be encoded and decoded by those familiar with that code, structuralism by seeing all social phenomena as 'wholes' (or 'structures') whose elements are governed by well-defined laws. Semiotics has derived much from the mechanistic view of cybernetics, while structuralism (which developed in the 1950s and 1960s with the work of the Belgian anthropologist Claude Lévi-Strauss, the Swiss psychologist Jean Piaget and the French literary critic Roland Barthes) has been constructed on a special field of mathematics known as group theory.

Cybernetics sees all activities, human, animal and machine, in terms of control systems. Thus the nervous system of a human and the electronic system of a computer and the servo system of a complex machine plant are seen as analogous processes, with inputs and outputs, with information feeding back to modify the operation of the system, and so forth. Information theory measures the capacity of systems to receive, process, store and transmit information. Information is thought of as a choice of one message from a set of possible messages; some messages come more frequently than others, thus setting up different probabilities for the arrival of any one message. Information theory reduces any existing range of choices to a network of two-way or 'binary' choices. When a highly probable choice is presented within a message, that choice is said to contain 'low information'; and conversely when an unlikely choice is presented then that choice contains 'high information'. In other words, information is generated by non-confirmation of expectation. Information theory spread rapidly in the early 1950s to fields of application as widely differing as genetics, neuro-physiology, sociology and philosophy, and soon to aesthetics, where it came upon certain difficulties. For in the arts what information theory calls 'redundancy' (namely, confirmation of expectation, non-information) plays a special role in creating form and structure.

The first 15 postwar years also saw a considerable extension of the notion of motivic growth in music, and its reshaping into an analytical theory. In the course of this reshaping, the theory took over elements of Freudian psychology. The Jungian concept of the collective subconscious also figured briefly in analysis in the 1960s.

The first musical contribution in either of the new fields of thought was probably an address to the first International Congress of Phonetic Sciences in Amsterdam as early as 1932 by the musicologist, style analyst and ethnomusicologist Gustav Becking (see §1 above). It was phonology (the science of distinguishing between elements in a stream of vocal linguistic sound and the apprehension of the rules by which these sounds are linked together), as developed by Trubetzkoy, that seemed relevant to music. And in particular it was the scholars of non-Western music, with their rapidly developing scientific approach to their material, by whom the relevance was first seen. Becking, in discussing Serbo-Croat popular epic, pointed to a certain parallel between basic problems in phonology and those in musicology, illustrating this by the different constructions that people of different world cultures place on a given single musical sound. Such people operate within different musical systems, and Becking tried to set up a typology of systems, 'unidimensional', 'bidimensional', 'tridimensional' and 'quadridimensional'. The great linguistics scholar Roman Jakobson took up Becking's point in the same year, stressing that the particular property of music, as of poetry, is that its conventions are wholly phonological in operation, and do not concern etymology or vocabulary. He urged musical analysts to study the model of phonology.

13 years later Milos Weingart explored the analogies between musical and language phrase structure, with reference to Czech, and in 1949 Antonín Sychra examined folksong by means of linguistic method. In 1956, in a volume of essays to Jakobson, George P. Springer provided a comparison of language and music which surveyed the progress of linguistic analysis in music. He discussed the distinction between repetition (i.e. identity) and difference as a binary opposition, and the modification which the idea of variation brings to this, concluding that music (1956, p.510):

> is subject to conventional rules of combination and distribution, and *ipso facto*, of probability. . . . Moreover, music turns out to be not only a stochastic process (producing a 'sequence of symbols . . . according to certain probabilities') but the special kind of stochastic process known as the Markov chain (where 'probabilities depend on previous events').

In his first important book (1956) the aesthetician Leonard B. Meyer came close to information theory in his view of styles as culturally conditioned systems of expectations, and of musical meaning as deriving from the arousing, frustrating and fulfilling of such expectations. Meyer was still working within the Gestalt concepts of *Prägnanz* and closure. In the following year, however, he introduced the fundamentals of information theory into his argument and revised his definition of 'meaning' in music. As early as 1956 R. C. Pinkerton and Abraham Moles had produced articles relating information theory, as presented by Shannon and Weaver, to music, and in 1958 and 1959 a spate of material was issued on the subject: two basic presentations by David Kraehenbuehl and Edgar Coons, an article by Joseph Youngblood, a monograph by W. Fucks, and an extended book on the broader application of the theory to aesthetic perception by Moles that devotes a chapter to perception of 'sonic material'. But Meyer, in his redefinition, fashioned three stages of what he called 'embodied meaning': the 'hypothetical meaning' before a sound-pattern has been heard, the 'evident meaning' when the sound-pattern has become a concrete event, which initiates a stage of 'revaluation' comparable with 'feedback' in control systems, and the 'determinate meaning' that arises later in the total experience. Meyer dealt, as Moles had previously done, with the concept of 'noise' whereby information is distorted. The maturity of Meyer's thought is shown in his subsequent essay (1961), which subjects the view of music as information to the actual situation of music frequently reheard. Two of the articles from 1958 appeared in the second issue of a new journal published at the Yale School of Music, the *Journal of Music Theory*, begun in 1957 as a forum for musical theory in a creative spirit rather than as dry academicism; it has regularly found space for detailed analyses, studies in the nature and problems of analysis, and analytical symposia.

During the 15 years just described, new approaches to organic motivic analysis already mentioned in passing were being forged, which have influenced analytical writing in Britain but have found little sympathy elsewhere in Europe or in the USA. They were first expounded by Rudolph Réti in two books (1951, 1958), of which the earlier, *The Thematic Process in Music*, is his classic exposition. But before that, Réti, who had lived in Vienna most of his life until emigrating to the USA in 1938, had worked intensively on analyses of sonatas by Beethoven between 1944 and 1948 in an attempt to grasp Beethoven's compositional process. These analyses were published, ten years after his death, in 1967. Réti started from the two-dimensional view of formal construction that was implied in Schoenberg's *Fundamentals* (see §2 above): motivic expansion, and division and demarcation. Réti reconciled these two dimensions. His method in itself produces, by reduction of thematic material, a series of 'cells'. Each cell is the extracted contour of a motif, and it comprises usually one, two or three intervals presented without rhythmic values in Réti's music examples. Each cell can undergo transposition and inversion. But Réti saw specific sequences of such cells recurring in each of the movements of a large-scale work and forming what he called a 'thematic pattern'. Such a pattern supplies its own natural thematic grouping which, in Beethoven's work, often takes the place of strict textbook form, and creates a symmetry or unity between movements, which Réti considered a conscious act of composition.

Réti's first book, *The Thematic Process in Music*, extends these ideas, dealing more fully with his architectural concept of thematic evolution and resolution, and also with key relationships, presenting a greater diversity of examples and attempting a historical survey of the thematic process. His second book expounded what he saw as a new kind of tonality 'which does not appear on the surface but is created by the ear singling out hidden relationships between various points of a melodic or contrapuntal web' (p.65). At the heart of his idea was the 'moving tonic'. Réti supplied a wide range of contemporary analytical examples in support of his thesis. (For Réti's method see also Chapter IV, §3.)

Two years before this last book of Réti, Hans Keller presented the first of a succession of short, pithy articles in which he put forward the principles of 'functional analysis'. 'Functional analysis postulates that contrasts are but different aspects of a single basic idea, a background unity' (1956–7, p.15). Criticizing conventional Toveyan analysis as 'anatomical', and thus concerned with 'dissection', Keller proposed a method that would attempt 'to elucidate the unifying *functions* of the living organism that is a musical work of art' (*MR*, xviii, 1957, p.203). He saw his analytical work as the purely objective isolating of background unities, and strongly refuted charges of subjectivity. Unlike Réti's treatment of a single movement, Keller saw the whole musical structure proceeding from a single idea. He added to this view the idea of the 'suppressed background', too obvious to be stated by the composer yet vitally important for the analyst to reconstruct in order that the unity of what followed might be demonstrated. For him, the contrasts on the surface of a piece of music were 'manifest', and the unity that lay behind it was 'latent'. It was precisely the analyst's job to demonstrate that what appeared new was not new at all. This concept of background and foreground was comparable with Schenker's structural layers in that the structure lies at the back, but is totally different in that Schenker's background comprised the *Ursatz* projected, stretched, 'composed out', whereas Keller's background comprised an everpresent idea, a model that contains the common elements of all the work's themes. Keller in 1957 took a bolder step even than Schenker when the latter abandoned the word for the graph: Keller abandoned word and graph for sound, by preparing an analytical score which demonstrated what he saw as the background unities of Mozart's String Quartet in D minor κ421/417*b* entirely in musical sound. Several such analyses were prepared and broadcast in Britain and on the Continent. (For Keller's method see also Chapter IV, §3.)

The traditional idea of motif was later to be developed by Forte in studies of the first movement of Brahms's String Quartet in C minor (1983) and of the Adagietto of Mahler's Fifth Symphony (1984–5). In these, the motif is seen to operate not only on the surface but also – as Schenker had recognized – at middleground level. These studies bring Schenkerian graphing techniques into the service of motivic analysis.

In the later 1950s there were significant developments in the linguistic analysis of music: a brief proposal by Bruno Nettl (1958), and the first contribution by the most influential figure in this field, Nicolas Ruwet, in which he sought to define the aural problems of listening to integral serial music by reference to phonology and the need for a 'margin of error' between the phonemes in a phonemic system (1959).

The trains of thought discussed above had their impact not only on analytical work but also on the work of composers. There is a striking similarity, for example, between the work that phonologists did with phonemes to test the point at which modification converts one phoneme into another and the work that Pierre Schaeffer did with recorded natural sound in the late 1940s and early 1950s in *musique concrète*. Similarly, probability theory came to be used as a means of generating compositions mechanically, for example in the work of Lejaren Hiller (who in 1958 completed a master's dissertation which included the famous *Illiac Suite* for string quartet by Hiller and Isaacson).

Finally, the postwar years were a period of revival for the ideas and teaching of Schenker, with important books by Adele Katz (1945) and Felix Salzer (1952), and with a resurgence of practical analyses along Schenkerian lines (e.g. Forte, 1955). There was a revival, too, of hermeneutic theory in *The*

Language of Music by Deryck Cooke (1959), who argued for the materials of music as a quite specific vocabulary of intervallic contours with the connotations of emotional states. These connotations arise not by convention but from the inherent forces of the intervals that make up the contours: forces of tension and direction. The analysis is thus apparently based on natural phenomena, translating a musical expression of psychological states and events (presumably those of the composer) into a verbal expression.

5. 1960–75: Set Theory, Computers and Concurrent Developments

The output of analytical writing since 1960 has been prodigious, and yet only two significant new factors have been introduced in that time. The first is mathematical set theory, which has its origin in the work of Georg Cantor between 1874 and 1897, and which had already entered the theory of musical composition with the work of Webern before becoming of paramount importance to the serialists of the early 1960s. The second is the use of the digital computer, a device for the rapid processing of information, which was developed during the latter years of World War II and whose use for purposes other than number calculation developed enormously during the 1950s.

The fundamental concept of set theory is that of membership. A 'set' is made up of the 'elements' that are members of that set. The set may contain 'subsets' all of whose elements are members of the set itself. Where several sets exist, certain relationships can apply among them: relationships of equivalence (in which one set can be reduced to another by some simple procedure), intersection (in which sets have certain elements in common), union (in which sets are joined together), complementation (in which sets have no elements in common and together make up all the elements of some larger order, often called the 'universal set') and so forth. In the realm of atonal music, set theory seemed to offer both a way of increasing the sophistication of the 12-note system and a way of relating pitches systematically that was as highly organized as the tonal system without depending on traditional tonality in any acoustical sense.

The importance of the computer for research in the fine arts, especially for literature and music, is twofold: it can count, and therefore can produce statistics concerning features of style which may lead it to suggest or question authenticity or simply to define a style as an aggregate of 'features'; and it can compare, and thus detect identity and difference (the binary opposition spoken of earlier), and can use such comparison to define the way in which elements are distributed, which of them occur in combination and under what conditions, and which never occur in combination – in short, it can deduce a 'syntax' for the behaviour of the material in a given work or style. There is no essential difference between a human doing these operations by hand and a computer carrying them out electronically, but a computer has the advantages of speed, accuracy and exact memory. It is here that the largest quantity of analytical work has been done in music since 1960, and the very large amount of published material is the more astonishing when one realizes that it is only the tip of an iceberg whose main bulk exists in the form of computer printout, punched cards, punched or magnetic tape, floppy disk and hard disk.

One further external factor entered into discourse on music at about this time: the philosophical view of the world known as 'phenomenology'. Phenomenology is a 'science of experience'. It is concerned not with the world as natural object or with mind as a store of knowledge. It deals with the contact between object and mind; it studies consciousness directed towards objects ('intentionality'), and aims to describe the structure of consciousness. The principal work of this type in music is the massive two-volume study by the Swiss conductor and mathematician Ernest Ansermet (1961). Ranging across mathematical, acoustical and philosophical issues, it reaches a study of musical structures that centres on the idea of the 'melodic path' (*chemin mélodique*). Classifying intervals as 'active extrovert', 'active introvert', 'passive extrovert' and 'passive introvert', it tries to give a value to the degree of tension in a melody. The method reckons tension between phrase-units and calculates the total tension for a melody (pp.237ff). Other phenomenological work has been carried out by Batstone (1969) and Pike (1970), but no working method of analysis has yet emerged.

Alongside these new developments there was a crescendo of activity in linguistic analysis, a slightly diminishing flow of work in information theory, a steady stream of functional analysis, and a continued resurgence of Schenkerian work. A number of independent approaches resulted, including a study by Albert B. Lord (1960) of Yugoslav epic which proceeds from the concept of oral composition and examines the mechanism by which a singer spontaneously creates or re-creates a song. This mechanism operates through the 'theme' and the 'formula'. The crux of the theory (which originated with the classical scholar Milman Parry: see *The Making of Homeric Verse*, 1971) is the capacity of formulae to group into 'systems' which provide the singer with alternatives to match different metrical situations in the poetry that he is creating. This idea, though scarcely applied by Lord to music, was taken up by Treitler (1974) for the analysis of plainchant.

Aspects of mathematical set theory already existed in the compositional technique of Webern in the 1930s, not to mention Josef Hauer's theory of 'tropes' 20 years earlier still. They also emerge in the writings of Leibowitz (*Introduction à la musique de douze tons*, 1949), Rufer and Perle. More important is the theory of hexachords presented by Rochberg (1955, 1959), and the statements concerning musical technique made by Boulez (1964, chap.2; 1966, part ii). But the proper formulation of a set theory of music has been the work of Milton Babbitt (1955, 1960, 1961, 1972), Donald Martino, David Lewin and John Rothgeb (*JMT*, iii–v, x, xi). Although Babbitt, using particularly the mathematical concept of the group, has dealt with harmony and with the functions of melodic and rhythmic configurations in 12-note music, and also with the interaction of components over longer spans of time, his work belongs to the realm of compositional theory rather than analysis. Set theory in serial composition is concerned with the 'ordered' set – the set whose elements exist in an inherently prescribed order. More generally applicable to analysis, notably to analysis of non-serial atonal music, is the notion of the 'unordered' set

– the set which is simply a 'collection' of elements. The most significant analytical contribution has been made by Allen Forte (1964, 1965, 1972, 1973). Forte has extended the notion of pitch-class set (i.e. a set of pitches irrespective of their octave register) and its relationships to include the association of sets in 'set-complexes' and 'subcomplexes' – a 'complex' being an array of all the sets that are related by inclusion to any one given central set. This additional concept establishes a type of organization which has analogies with tonality. It makes possible the elucidation of tonal coherence in large-scale musical structures and the links between sections of such structures. With this theory Forte has provided analyses of atonal works by Berg, Schoenberg, Stravinsky and Webern. Two works have been analysed as full-length studies by this method: Stravinsky's *The Rite of Spring* (Forte, 1978) and Berg's opera *Wozzeck* (Schmalfeldt, 1983).

For Forte, the use of the computer has facilitated the compilation of a roster of such complexes. It has also made possible the analysis of compositions into sets and set-complexes and the formulation of a 'syntax' for these compositions; and this has opened up the possibility too of formulating a syntax for individual styles (*JMT*, 1966). Forte's method of set-theory analysis has been implemented variously on microcomputers and has been marketed for home computers by at least one independent programmer. The use of the computer in music goes back to 1949, when Bernard Bronson, editor of the melodies of the Childe ballads, analysed range, metre, modality, phrase structure, refrain pattern, melodic outline, anacrusis, cadence and final of folksongs, using data on punched cards. The measuring of such quantities and the production of sets of statistics was the facility most readily available from the computer. 'Languages' for encoding music into a form that a computer could 'read' were rapidly developed, and special compilers (internal programmes that translate the user's simplified way of giving the machine instructions into the computer's own terms) with biases towards the demands of musical material were created in the early 1960s. An important article by Selleck and Bakeman (1965) explains two strategies for analysing melodic structures: one through probabilities, which derives from information theory, the other through comparing and sorting melodic units, which derives from linguistics.

Two important publishing events occurred at this time. The first was the inception of the journal *Computers and the Humanities* in 1966, which, apart from including material on computers and music, for a while maintained a directory of projects in progress, enabling scholars to be aware of other work in their field and encouraging collaboration. (The journal abandoned this bibliographical function in the 1970s to concentrate on articles and reviews.) The second was the publication in 1967 of a collection of essays on electronic data processing in music, under the editorship of Harald Heckmann; this presents a cross-section of work, including 'languages' for representing music, strategies of computational analysis, sample analyses and articles raising more general issues. Discussions of the application of information theory include the writings of Bean (1961), Hiller (1964), Meyer-Eppler (1962), Winckel (1964) and Brincker (1970), but the most significant study of mathematics and music has been Xenakis's treatise *Musiques formelles* (1963). Although his exposition of

64

probabilities, stochastics, Markov chains and the theory of games is intentional, is focused on the means of production, and resorts to analysis mostly in order to trace the compositional means in works of his own, the framework that he set out places the art of music on a more universal plane, opening it up to investigation according to precise laws. His book (which inherits the theoretical tradition of Messiaen, 1944, and which pours scorn on existing cybernetic and linguistic analyses of music as tending towards 'absurdities and desiccations', as elementary and pseudo-objective) proposes 'a world of sound-masses, vast groups of sound-events, clouds, and galaxies governed by new characteristics such as density, degree of order, and rate of change' in place of traditional 'linear' musical thought; it puts forward a 'distinction in musical architectures of categories between "outside-time", "in-time" and "temporal"' (see pp.180ff), whereby the elements of a composition outside time are 'mapped' into time. Apart from his discussion of ancient Greek and Byzantine music Xenakis offered only one example of analysis by his methods: a bar and a half of Beethoven's 'Appassionata' Sonata subjected to 'vectorial algebra' – 'a working language which may permit both analyses of the works of the past and new constructions by setting up interacting functions of the components' (pp.163f).

A work that has much in common externally with Xenakis's treatise is Pierre Schaeffer's *Traité des objets musicaux* (1966). This is not a work on musical analysis in any conventional sense, but a dissertation on the sonorous material from which music is made: an attempt to present a full typology of that material, and to discover its general laws. Like Ansermet's phenomenological book referred to earlier, Schaeffer's treatise is underpinned with acoustics and with philosophy (Schaeffer, like Ansermet, brought special technical training to bear on his subject), and is centred on 'l'expérience musicale'; but it is much more tangible in its formulation of a 'solfège des objets musicaux'. This 'solfège' is in practice a system of classification by seven criteria: mass (one of the central notions in Schaeffer's thought), dynamic, harmonic timbre, melodic profile, mass profile, grain and inflection (*allure*).

Xenakis's and Schaeffer's treatises both represent the work of teams of experts: Xenakis's group of mathematicians, electronics engineers, psychologists and philosophers at his Equipe de Mathématique et d'Automatique Musicales (EMAMu) and Schaeffer's comparable team of technicians at the French radio. Both groups work in Paris, as does the even larger team of specialists which was built up by Boulez at the Pompidou Centre: the Institut de Recherche et de Coordination Acoustique/Musique (IRCAM). IRCAM was initially divided into four departments: instrumental and vocal, headed by Vinko Globokar; electronic and electro-acoustical, headed by Luciano Berio; synthetic and analytical, headed by Jean-Claude Risset (in close collaboration with EMAMu); and of 'mobile unity', headed by Diego Masson. With these organizations the history of analysis perhaps reaches its most esoteric realms. To them should be added the work of analysts and composers at Princeton University: Benjamin Boretz's 'Meta-Variations' articles in the journal *Perspectives of New Music* (which he founded with Arthur Berger at Princeton in 1962 as a forum for musical theory and of which he remained co-editor until 1982), which survey the existing 'models' for music, examine the bases of these models, conceptual, perceptual and theoretical, and move towards analyses of single works; that of Babbitt, Westergaard and others; and the computer work of Robison, Regener, Howe and others – all these activities represent the most highly sophisticated level of thought.

One other institutional group deserves mention within the esoteric realms of analysis: the Groupe de Recherches en Sémiologie Musicale at the University of Montreal, founded in 1974 and headed by Jean-Jacques Nattiez. The formation of this group, with its series of monographs in musical analysis, came after 15 years of development in the field of musical semiotics, of which the backbone was a series of brilliant articles by the professor of linguistics at the University of Paris at Vincennes, Nicolas Ruwet. The most important of these was 'Méthodes d'analyse en musicologie' (1966), in which he took a simple melody (a 14th-century flagellant song), proceeded to segment it crudely and then to pass the segmentation through a sequence of transformational rules which in effect recognized similarities and equivalences. This yields a phrase-structure analysis that is a syntax of the melody. The success of this exercise was not so much the quality of the finished analysis as the fact that it had been produced by an exact and verifiable procedure. The article triggered off a dispute among semioticians as to whether in such a mechanized procedure the analysis should begin with musical units of large proportions and work towards a microscopic finished analysis, or begin with a microscopic segmentation and gradually construct the larger formal units by the recognition of equivalents (i.e. phrases with differences of detail which a machine would treat as 'different' but which have the same function in the musical syntax). Ruwet had taken an intermediate course by starting with middle-size units, 'niveau (level) I', refining these by subdividing them ('niveau II'), and then reconstituting 'niveau I' before associating its units to reach a large-scale 'niveau 0'. (For Ruwet's method see also Chapter IV, §7 and fig.39, p.96.) The immediate dispute was won by the second school of thought, and Nattiez produced intensive analyses which proceed from small-scale segmentation (e.g. 'Densité 21.5', 1975; see Chapter IV, §7 and figs.40–42, pp.98–9). Other writers on this subject have been Eco (1968: an important general treatise, expanded and translated as *A Theory of Semiotics*, 1976), Arom (1969), Mâche (1971), Lidov (1975) and Morin (1979: an essay in comparative semiotic analysis); and semiotics has been given generous space in the journal *Musique en jeu* (1970–78). Perhaps the major subsequent products of this tradition are the full-scale analytical study of Berio's *Sinfonia* by Osmond-Smith (1985) and Nattiez's study of the 1976 Bayreuth performance and production of the *Ring* cycle (1983; see also 1985). One isolated attempt was made to implement a wholly aural method of analysis by structuralist principles (Chiarucci, 1973). Aural analysis remains a seriously neglected field and a systematic theory will become an imperative when input of musical sound to computers for analysis becomes truly practicable.

Two further collections of essays on computer applications, published in 1970 (Brook, Lincoln), between them present a useful picture of the range of activity and the then current state of development. In the second half of the 1960s important research was in progress, including that by Lindblom and Sundberg which continues the earliest computer applications but at a much higher level

(1969). Their work combines concepts of linguistic syntax with probabilities, first analysing simple nursery tunes, producing 'tree-diagrams' (see, for example, fig.40, p.98) of their structures, and then verifying by synthesizing such melodies according to the syntax deduced (see §6 below for further development in this field).

Techniques of great sophistication were demonstrated by Norbert Böker-Heil at the International Musicological Society conferences in 1972 and 1977, analysing features, defining and differentiating styles. A project at Princeton University between 1963 and the late 1970s under the direction of Arthur Mendel and Lewis Lockwood aimed to define the style of Josquin's music. The programme for example made studies of all the simultaneities (i.e. all the harmonic effects, no matter how incidental) and of suspension formations; it could also compare the variants of a single piece in several sources, and determine the filiation between the sources and their comparative authority. During the 1960s a computer-implemented project of similar proportions, handling the 16th-century chanson repertory, was in operation at the University of Chicago under the direction of Lawrence Bernstein.

Parallel with this was a resurgence of interest in style analysis. Richard Crocker produced *A History of Musical Style* (1966), and in 1970 Jan LaRue published his *Guidelines for Style Analysis*. In the latter, LaRue established a 'style-analytical routine' which examines each of the elements of a piece or style in turn at various 'magnifications' (large, middle and small dimensions), and then tries to understand the functions and relationships of those elements. For LaRue the four contributing elements of music are sound, harmony, melody and rhythm, and a fifth 'combining and resultant' element is 'growth'. Growth is subdivided into 'movement' and 'shape'. For the coordination between these elements LaRue introduced the concept of 'concinnity' (for which he quoted Webster's dictionary: 'the skillful arrangement and mutual adjustment of parts'). LaRue's approach is commonsense and empirical: its use of acronym and simple symmetrical classification, its measurement by direct alternatives ('coloristic–tensional', 'active–stable' etc) and its single-level treatment of music (its three 'dimensions' owe virtually nothing to Schenker's structural layers) all lend it to direct practical analytical work. It controls and channels the analyst's personal judgment rather than by-passing it. It also makes a useful contribution to the graphic representation of musical style: a system of letter- and number-symbols with brackets (deriving from the parsing of language) maps what LaRue called 'shape' in a neat shorthand, and a device termed a 'timeline' enables the analyst to diagram the rhythmic and formal structure of a piece with indications of the fabric. (For LaRue's method see also Chapter IV, §6.)

A number of scholars have been working on questions of proportion in musical structure, in particular on the division of works into 'golden sections'. Tovey once observed, in passing, that the first movement of Haydn's String Quartet in F op.50 no.5 'falls into golden sections in every way' (1935–9, i, p.19), though he was sceptical about their general significance in the Classical repertory. However, the first scholar to undertake a systematic investigation of proportion in the work of a major composer was Ernő Lendvai (1955). From careful measurements of the passage of time (achieved by counting the number of quavers in the score), he demonstrated the presence of the golden section at various levels in several of Bartók's compositions. In making his calculations, Lendvai took advantage of the special property of the so-called Fibonacci series (0, 1, 1, 2, 3, 5, 8, 13, 21, 34, 55, . . .), whereby the ratio between successive numbers in the series (e.g. 8:13, 34:55) closely approximates to the golden section. Similar studies in what is now being called 'proportional analysis' have been carried out on other repertories, notably by Marianne Henze on Ockeghem (1964), Ernest Sanders on Philippe de Vitry (1975), Brian Trowell on Dunstable (1978–9) and Roy Howat on Debussy (1983). In a more occult vein, golden sections in the music of Obrecht (M. van Crevel, 1959, 1964) and Bach (Siegele, 1978) have been related to special 'cabbalistic' numbers (whereby, for instance, 888 is associated with the Greek name for 'Jesus') or to numbers derived from simpler alphabetical summations (e.g. B–A–C–H $= 2 + 1 + 3 + 8 = 14$), whose presence in a piece may similarly be determined by counting metric pulses. The credibility of these types of analysis is based on either or both of two factors: the frequency and consistency with which a composer appears to apply golden sections and other numerological devices over a wide range of his work; and any external circumstances (sketches and autograph corrections with a numerical basis, the composer's knowledge of and interest in mathematics, and his awareness of other art forms based on numerical principles) that enable us to infer a composer's interest in such matters.

The work of Réti and Keller was furthered in the 1960s by two books of Alan Walker. In the first of these (1962) he argued for the validity of mirror forms, and introduced the Freudian elements of repression and preconscious association into the theory of motivic unity. Walker's second book, on musical criticism (1966), offers much analytical material, demonstrating above all the 'all-pervading background forces' that operate in musical creation, and furthering the Freudian theory. The book contains a useful exposition of 'historical background', a concept fundamental to Keller's work.

Schenkerian analytical work continued in great strength, and an occasional publication under the title *Music Forum* was founded by Felix Salzer and William J. Mitchell in 1967 to present extended analyses of which some in each issue would use Schenkerian techniques. The series has particular value because of the attempts made in it to extend Schenker's techniques to music outside the domain for which it was created: to medieval and Renaissance music (Salzer, 1967, Bergquist, 1967, Schachter, 1970), to late Romantic music (Mitchell, 1967, Bergquist, 1980), to contemporary music (Travis, 1970) and to non-Western music (Loeb, 1976). Among the non-Schenkerian material in *Music Forum* is Lockwood's masterly study of the autograph of Beethoven's Cello Sonata op.69, a rare blend of rigorous historical musicology and analytical method (1970).

L. B. Meyer, in his third book (1973), advocated a mode of discourse which he termed 'critical analysis'. Unlike music theory, which seeks to discover the principles which govern styles and structures (and which is seen as close to pure analysis), critical analysis seeks to elucidate that which is singular about a work. In this he showed kinship with Joseph Kerman, whose search for a higher form of musical criticism to replace 'positivistic' musicology has already been mentioned. Meyer's book shows a shift away from the Gestalt-based concept of expectation and towards the notion of 'implication'. The critic whose goal is to explain a work seeks 'what kind of patterning underlies it, and hence . . . what sorts of implications are suggested by its melodic, rhythmic, and harmonic organization, and whether and how these are actualized' (p.17). Eugene Narmour (1977), a pupil of Meyer, took this up and outlined a new model: 'implication–realization'. Musical formations carry certain implications as to how they will continue. Those implications are manifold; they relate to the way things have gone in the work so far ('idiostructure'), but also to the stylistic context of the work ('style structure'). As Meyer's statement suggests, each parameter of a musical event carries its own separate implications. The implications in play at any one moment are bound to be to some extent mutually contradictory, hence no more than part-realization is possible. That which is unrealized remains potential. Realization yields 'closure', non-realization 'non-closure'. Narmour's book has perceptive insights into historical evolution of style as viewed from this model. This outline model was presented within a fierce onslaught on Schenkerian theory; a fully formed and free-standing statement of the model is promised.

Among the many independently minded analytical publications, those that stand out include Donington's Jungian interpretation of Wagner's *Ring* (1963) and Rosen's perceptive books on the *The Classical Style* (1971) and on *Sonata Forms* (1980); the latter question in Toveyan spirit the orthodoxies of their time, providing penetrating analyses in pungent prose. Lomax's study of 'cantometrics' (1968) offers a classificatory 'grid' not totally dissimilar from LaRue's, but adapted to the analysis of non-European song. (For Lomax's method see also Chapter IV, §6.)

Useful surveys of analysis also began to appear during this period. Above all, Hermann Beck's *Methoden der Werkanalyse* (1974) is a remarkable systematic account of analytical method from early times to the early 1970s, though with some German-language bias. Diether de la Motte's *Musikalische Analyse* (1968) is a skilful demonstration of different approaches to analysis, each monitored with comments by Carl Dahlhaus. There was a spate of important studies of the history of music theory from Dahlhaus and his circle, of which two notable products were Dahlhaus's own *Die Musiktheorie im 18. und 19. Jahrhundert* (1984–) and Renathe Groth's *Die französische Kompositionslehre des 19. Jahrhunderts* (1983). Hellmut Federhofer (1981) produced a major revaluation of the systems of Riemann, Kurth and Schenker, and of analytical writing since 1940.

6. Since 1975: Grammars of Music

An upsurge of interest during the late 1970s in the broad field of music theory has been reflected in a spate of new journals, some of them edited by graduate students in America, and in the formation of new societies of music theory. *Theory and Practice*, the organ of two student societies in New York State, began in 1975; so too did *In Theory Only*, journal of the Michigan Music Theory Society; and *Indiana Theory Review* followed them in 1978. All three contain analytical articles, with emphasis on the traditions of Forte and Schenker. Most important among the new organizations is the Society for Music Theory, founded in 1977, and its journal, *Music Theory Spectrum*, launched in 1979. *Music Analysis*, originating at King's College, London, in 1982, is the first periodical (at least since the days of Schenker) to be devoted specifically to analytical matters, representing a wide range of theories and approaches; and *Contemporary Music Review*, launched from Nottingham in 1984, features largely analysis of contemporary music. A series of monographs, Studies in Musical Genesis and Structure, connecting source- and sketch-studies with analysis, was launched in 1985 with Lewis Lockwood as editor. In Germany the periodical *Musiktheorie* was inaugurated in 1986.

The University of Michigan was the provenance of a powerful, broadly based theory of musical structure formulated by Wallace Berry: *Structural Functions in Music* (1976). While plainly receptive to the Schenkerian concepts of hierarchy, level and linearity, the book maintains a clear independence from the implementation of Schenkerian method in procedure and terminology. Central to this theory is the tetrad of 'progression', 'recession', 'succession' and 'stasis'. The first three denote subtly distinguished varieties in sense of direction, the last the absence of such a sense. 'Fluctuation' is the term used for such sense of direction. 'Progressive fluctuation' is movement away from a given starting-point, hence intensification; 'recessive fluctuation' a return to that point, hence resolution. Such fluctuation creates a sense of distance and gives rise to feelings of stability and instability. This notion applies not only to tonality but also to texture and to rhythm and metre. Thus, for texture, progressive fluctuation might be, for example, an increase in the independence of the parts which make up a given texture (a given degree of independence being the starting-point from which the fluctuation occurs); or an increase in density; or an expansion of the placing of sounds within a given pitch-range. These aspects of texture may work 'complementarily' (i.e. progress or recess in tandem), 'compensatorily' (offsetting each other), 'in parallel' or 'counteractively'. Berry has provided a detailed taxonomy of texture, allowing the concept of hierarchical levels to be applied to textural structure just as to tonal structure. By this means, a particular peak of structural complexity may be seen as a long-term goal, while other peaks are seen as subservient or preparatory to it. Hence there can be a 'deep structure' of texture as of tonality.

Berry has attributed to every aspect of musical substance (every 'element') the possibility that the changes which such an element undergoes in the course of a piece may constitute an 'element-structure'. As such element-structures unfold simultaneously, the interactions between them will be of great significance to the piece functionally and expressively (and Berry is always attentive to expressive effect) – they will 'underlie morphology and meaning' in the music. Every element-structure (it might be melodic contouring, harmonic rate, instrumental colour, changes in tempo) has its own pacing and patterning, and therefore constitutes an 'element-rhythm'. Berry's discussion of rhythm stresses the need to separate out the levels of metric units and to identify the operating of four functions: 'initiative' (i.e. accent-bearing at some level), 'reactive' ('absorbing the force' of an accent), 'anticipative' and 'conclusive' impulses. Durational reduction is used in association with a repertory of graphic symbols to express these functions and succeeds in representing long-term rhythmic functions, thus uncovering a hierarchy of rhythm.

Berry's treatment of tonality recognizes the ambivalence of harmonic events: a single harmony may perform different functions at different levels of structure. Tonality's capacity to project multiple levels gives to music its sense of depth of significance. While using the notions of tonicization and modulation, Berry's handling of tonal and linear events is not predicated on the structures of 18th- and 19th-century music. Consequently, his theories apply with an ease that Schenker's theories lack to music outside this era. Indeed, some of his most successful analyses are of music from the Renaissance and the 20th century.

The analysis of music as sonorous material had remained comparatively undeveloped, apart from the work of Pierre Schaeffer, who followed his *Traité* of 1966 (see §5 above) with his *Guide des objets sonores* (1983), and from that of two Norwegians, Lasse Thoresen and Ulav Anton Thommessen, who in the early 1980s were formulating a verbal and symbolic language for formal description of sound qualities. Robert Cogan and Pozzi Escot took phonological analysis, as performed in the field of linguistics, as a model for investigating what they called 'sonic design' – the way in which sound-spectra are shaped in musical space. Their contention is that compositions are just as much formations of basic sonic stuff as formations of tonal or rhythmic materials; and that composers and eras of music often bear sonic 'fingerprints' which can be recognized if the right technology is available. Their first book (1976) makes brilliantly resourceful use of graphs to carry out tone-colour analysis of single instrumental sounds and ensembles; this material is then subsumed, along with the study of other dimensions of sound, within a method of describing formal musical structures. Technology came to their assistance in the form of sound-spectrum analysis. This was a technique being developed at IBM's Watson Research Center, and made available at the Sonic Analysis Laboratory of the New England Conservatory: a technique whose output was the spectrum photograph (see fig.25 overleaf: a section of computer tape from Jean-Claude Risset's *Little Boy*, 1968). It was capable of photographing the sonic 'content' of a whole composition. Cogan and Pozzi Escot have evolved an analytical theory which deploys the evidence of these photographs: a theory strongly influenced by the writings of Roman Jakobson in linguistics, and based around opposition pairs. Cogan first provided an analysis of Stravinsky's *The Rite of Spring* in his new and exploratory journal *Sonus* (1982), and then presented a series of analyses with an account of the theory (1984).

The work of Chomsky in the late 1950s had caught the imagination of theorists and practitioners in the arts. His first major book, *Syntactic Structures* (The Hague, 1957), is a seminal work. It presents several models of systems for generating 'utterances' in natural language. Of these, the 'transformational model', developed and modified in *Aspects of the Theory of Syntax* (Cambridge, Mass., 1965), is the most comprehensive. Chomsky became convinced that all humans possess an inborn grasp of the formal principles of syntax, and that this

71

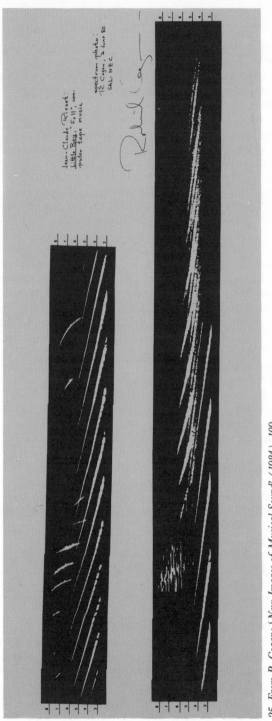

25. From R. Cogan: 'New Images of Musical Sound' (1984), 109

grasp is 'universal' in that it underlies all languages.

In its first form, Chomsky's model comprises a set of rules ordered in three groups or 'components': the 'phrase-structure component', which derives an initial sentence-structure, called the 'terminal string', from the primary categories 'noun-phrase' and 'verb-phrase' (NP + VP); the 'transformational component', which converts this sentence structure from active to passive etc; and the 'morphophonemic component', in which the individual sounds of words are modified under the requirements of language (e.g. 'ride + en' becomes 'ridden').

Such a system is modelled on what in mathematics is known as a 'formal system'. A formal system comprises four things: a set of symbols, the rules for combining these symbols into expressions, certain combinations of such symbols which form axioms, and rules by which statements may be made by inference from these axioms. In a formal system, the number of symbols and rules is finite, the number of inferences infinite. What Chomsky produced was a 'generative grammar', that is, a formal system whereby a finite set of symbols and rules is capable of generating an infinite number of grammatically well-formed sentences of a natural language. His generative grammar is of the transformational type, which posits the existence of a 'deep structure' by which utterances that are different in their 'surface structure' may be similar.

Under Chomsky's influence, questions such as 'Does music have a deep structure?' and 'Do universals exist in music?' fascinated musicians. The series of lectures given by the conductor Leonard Bernstein in 1973, later televised and published in 1976, raised these in a challenging fashion. In a series of articles beginning in 1977 and culminating in *A Generative Theory of Tonal Music* (1983), Fred Lerdahl and Ray Jackendoff, composer and linguist respectively, evolved a theory whose central purpose was to elucidate the organization which the listener imposes mentally on the physical signals of tonal music. Using principally music by Bach, Haydn, Mozart and Beethoven as their 'idiom', they compiled a grammar which 'models the listener's connection between the presented musical surface of a piece and the structure he attributes to that piece. Such a grammar comprises a system of rules that assigns analyses to pieces'. The system is thus like Chomsky's grammar in that it is 'mentalistic', i.e. concerned with mental processes rather than with end-products, and in that it is at heart an analytic procedure in which the generative function of the theory is a system for deriving or testing analyses.

The theory of Lerdahl and Jackendoff has an outward resemblance to Chomsky's in that it is a set of rules operating on four components. These four are 'dimensions' of musical structure, and all are hierarchical: 'grouping structure'; 'metrical structure'; 'time-span reduction' (reduction in the Schenkerian sense, but based equally on pitch and rhythmic criteria); and 'prolongational reduction', which takes account of the intuitive sense of tension and relaxation in music. Two types of rule govern each category: 'well-formedness rules', which control the making of possible structural descriptions of pieces; and 'preference rules', which determine which of a number of possible descriptions corresponds to a listener's preferences.

Three graphic conventions are adopted for demonstrating the operation of

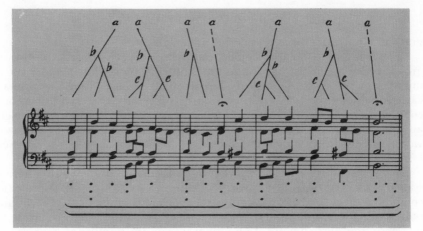

26. From F. Lerdahl and R. Jackendoff: 'A Generative Theory of Tonal Music' (1983), 132

these rules. Grouping structure is shown as horizontal braces, and metrical structure as lines of dots, both below the staff and reiterated vertically to express hierarchy; reduction is shown as branching trees above the staff. Fig.26 gives a small-scale example, which is a local time-span reduction.

For prolongational reduction, the three diagrams acquire solid and void circles at the nodes to indicate the type of prolongation which the branching represents; reductive levels are displayed on separate staves below, adopting Schenkerian conventions for solid and void note-heads and solid and dotted phrase-marks. Fig.27 shows the *St Anthony Chorale* analysed in this way (the original is already slightly reduced).

Lerdahl and Jackendoff claim that much of their grammar is 'idiom-independent' (i.e. holds good whatever the musical style), and thus that certain of their rules constitute 'universals' of musical perception and can be taken to represent innate aspects of musical cognition.

Their grammar was developed without the aid of a computer. With the advance of 'artificial intelligence' throughout the 1960s and 1970s, it was to be expected that mechanistic models of musical systems would be implemented on computers. The rules of such systems could be expressed as logically sequenced steps in the form of computer programs; when such a program was 'run', causing it to generate music according to the rules of the system, the well-formedness of the rules could be tested intuitively as the quality of the musical output. Between 1962 and 1967 Michael Kassler had constructed a formal system embodying the rules of Schenker's prolongational techniques (see §§1–2 above) (1967, p.97):

> the primitive symbols . . . are the constituents of current musical notation; the formation rules select from all possible sequences of primitive symbols those sequences which . . . are 'well-formed' with respect to this system of notation; each axiom . . . is an *Ursatz*; each rule of inference . . . specifies a prolongation technique; each proof . . . is an S-derivational sequence [i.e. a sequence of compositional layers which starts with an *Ursatz* and finishes with a foreground]; and each theorem . . . is an S-derivational composition.

74

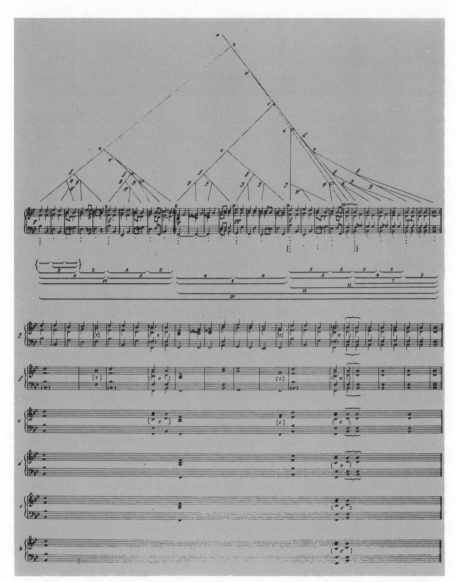

27. From F. Lerdahl and R. Jackendoff: 'A Generative Theory of Tonal Music' (1983), 205

Kassler's system limits itself to major keys and to music in two voices (the latter making those of Schenker's procedures that generate inner voices impossible to implement). It provides three axioms (the *Ursätze* 3–1, 5–1, 8–1), and 13 rules of inference (i.e. prolongational techniques of bass arpeggiation, neighbour note (i.e. auxiliary note) and so forth).

Stephen Smoliar has also attempted to construct a system for generating compositions according to the Schenkerian theories. In an article published in *Computers and the Humanities* (1976–7) he used a type of data-structure known as the 'linked list', which enabled him very easily to mirror transformational processes by inserting material into or deleting it from the coded musical data, or copying part of it to some other point (such material constituting a 'sublist' within the main 'list'). List-processing offers a potentially good way of thinking about deep structure in music.

James Snell designed a system whose Schenkerian theoretical basis took account of recent work on rhythm by Yeston, Schachter and others. Like Kassler's, his system (as described in 1979) handles only the major key, and generates music in only two voices; however, it does proceed from the *Ursatz* right through to the foreground. At every level a new pitch-structure is generated; and at certain levels a new set of durations is assigned (with stress-patterns so as to preserve metre). Snell subsumed the great variety of transformational procedures under a small number of pitch-derivational rules and a single duration–distribution rule. The whole process is seen as a tree-structure in which elements closer to the foreground are 'branching' from others closer to the background. This allows the system to foster musical parallelisms, by making certain branches dependent on others either in the early stages and not the later (to effect sectional parallelisms) or in the later stages only (to effect motivic parallelisms). As to the overall working of the system, the results of the operating of rules at any one structural level are passed down as the parameters for the operating of rules at the next level.

Formal modellings of Schenkerian analysis have the property that 'routines' which give effect to such devices as repetition or linear progression (*Zug*) can be called again and again as the generation of the composition proceeds; that is, as the composing-out (*Auskomponierung*) moves from level to level. A formal system based on the concepts of musical semiotics would work quite differently. It would need to provide the reverse of the segmentational process of semiotic analysis: in order to generate a melody, it would have first to establish a series of melodic 'functions' along the axis of time, and then to set up a 'lexicon' of segments and supply the rules for selecting these and assigning them to such functions. A formal system of this type was first aired by Mario Baroni and Carlo Jacoboni in 1973. Whereas Schenkerian theory was already symmetrical around the finished score (composing-out leading to the score, analytical reduction leading away from it), musical semiotics was single-mindedly analytical. Baroni and Jacoboni therefore had to develop a generative theory, and did so by drawing on Chomsky. Working on the melodies used by J. S. Bach for his four-part chorales, they divided each phrase into three functions: initial crotchet, central body, cadence. The possibilities within each were expressed as a set of 30 rules determining how notes might occur in succession. They used

76

techniques similar to those of Lejaren Hiller in the 1950s (see §4 above): random numbers are generated first to establish the lengths of the constituent phrases, and then to represent notes, which are in turn rejected if they do not conform to the rules or accepted into the melody if they do. Their acceptance, however, is only provisional. A pair of phrases as a whole, once generated, is subjected to a set of 26 global rules: if it fails these in more than an acceptable number of respects, it is rejected wholesale.

By 1978 their system was a functioning set of computer programs, and the authors were bold enough to print out some of their melodies so generated alongside the corpus of melodies (all in a major key, non-modulatory and in 4/4) which formed the analytical sample. The authors subsequently recognized certain limitations in their system, and moved away from a procedure in which notes are generated immediately at the surface to one which is transformational. In their revised system, a 'kernel' is established first, comprising the first and last notes of the phrase. 'Rules of insertion' are then supplied to furnish the intervening notes, first as a scale (the 'kernel scale'). Each note of that scale is then taken as the starting-point for a possible 'deviation'. Deviations are specific figures whose character will depend on the prevailing style (for Bach chorales they are repetition, appoggiatura, neighbour note and skip). From this emerges the 'primitive phrase', a sequence of intervals in a metrical scheme. This will eventually be subjected to a succession of transformations which will pass it through 'modified' and 'adapted' levels to produce a 'surface phrase'. Before this can happen, a program must provide an abstract description of the whole melody. More than one primitive phrase can be derived from a kernel, and similarly also at every level of structure. Thus, the abstract description must determine the number of phrases in the melody, the degree of the scale on which each will cadence, the total number of kernels required, and the route by which each surface phrase is to be derived. The melody can then be generated in its entirety, and will have form, tonal organization and thematic unity.

A conference of musical grammars and computer analysis, held in Modena in October 1982, reviewed progress in the constructing of grammars of musical style and repertory (in Schubert's lieder, in Inuit songs, in 18th-century French chansons, for example) and of performance; it also examined issues of musical perception and cognition. The issue which promises to be of longest-term significance is perhaps that of constructing 'expert systems' in musical analysis. An expert system is a computer program which can pursue a line of reasoning on the basis of what information it has, build up a repertory of rules of thumb ('heuristics') and make decisions, constantly adjusting its rules and amplifying its stock of knowledge. It must always be able to explain its path of reasoning, and thus be transparent in all that it does. Otto Laske, long active in the application of artificial intelligence research to music (1973, 1977, 1981), reported on a knowledge-based system that he designed (with Debussy's *Syrinx* in mind) which receives sound-input and segments it into 'sound-objects', reads and parses scores, adopts rules of thumb to establish 'concepts' about the piece, looks for 'instances' of such concepts and stores the information in 'frames' of knowledge which can be supplemented, corrected and updated. Its rules, too, are stored in frames, and so can be developed in the light of experience.

With the celebrated Japanese project for a fifth generation of computers for the 1990s (ICOT) under way, the 'knowledge base' and 'knowledge engineering' are likely to become familiar ideas, and computer languages such as PROLOG which perform such engineering will furnish the basic tools. Herein lies a prospect, exciting or terrifying, but in any case inevitable: machines which evolve methods of analysis tailor-made to the music under scrutiny, and which store large bases of knowledge about all the music that they analyse.

CHAPTER IV

Analytical Method

1. Introduction

A variety of classifications have been formulated for musical analysis as a whole. There is the widely accepted division into 'stylistic analysis' and 'analysis of the individual work' which is described at the beginning of this book as pragmatic but theoretically unnecessary. There is the threefold classification into 'constructional analysis', 'psychological analysis' and 'analysis of expression' put forward by Erpf in *MGG* (1949–51). This classification does not correspond exactly with, but is roughly equivalent to, Meyer's distinction (1967, pp.42f) between 'formal', 'kinetic-syntactic' and 'referential' views of musical signification. Meyer characterized the 'formal' view as placing central importance upon the 'relationships existing among the structural units that constitute a musical event', as looking for such things as 'symmetry, balance, ... proportion', and as essentially 'somewhat static'; the 'kinetic-syntactic' as concerned with music as a 'dynamic process', with 'tension and repose, instability and stability, and ambiguity and clarity'; the 'referential' as depicting the 'concepts, actions, and passions of "real", extra-musical experience'. The first tends to centre on the musical structure itself (hence Erpf's 'constructional'), the second on the listener's response (hence 'psychological'), the third on the interaction of the two, on communication.

Roughly equivalent, but again not exactly homologous, is the classification into 'autonomous' and 'heteronomous' values of music, where the former designates music as to be 'understood and enjoyed for whatever it is', the latter as either 'a partial manifestation of some cosmic force or principle' or 'a means of communication among men'. Dahlhaus (*RiemannL 12*, 1967) made a fourfold distinction: 'formal analysis', which explains the structure of a work 'in terms of functions and relationships between sections and elements'; ' "energetic" interpretation', which deals in phases of movement or tension spans; and Gestalt analysis, which treats works as wholes; these three make up between them the field of analysis proper, which he distinguished from his fourth category, 'hermeneutics', the interpretation of music in terms of emotional states or external meanings. The first, second and fourth of these correspond broadly with the three categories of Erpf and Meyer, while the third deals with analyses based on the idea of organism.

The difficulty with these classifications is that their categories are not mutually exclusive. Thus, for example, Riemann is cited always as the prime example of a formal and constructional analyst, and yet Riemann's work rests on a fundamental idea of 'life force' (*Lebenskraft, lebendige Kraft, energisches Anstreben*) which flows through music in phases and is actualized in phrase contours, dynamic gradings, fluctuations of tempo and agogic stress. This idea is closer to the kinetic view of music; it suggests that Riemann's work belongs to two of Meyer's three categories.

A thorough-going typology of musical analysis would probably have to encompass several axes of classification. The analyst's view of the nature and function of music would certainly be one of these. But his approach to the actual substance of music would be a second; his method of operating on the music would be a third; and the medium for presentation of his findings would be a fourth. Then there might be subsidiary axes of, for example, the purpose for which the analysis was carried out, the context in which it was presented, the type of recipient for whom it was designed.

Under approaches to the substance of music would be categories such as that a piece of music is (*a*) a 'structure', a closed network of relationships, more than the sum of its parts; (*b*) a concatenation of structural units; (*c*) a field of data in which patterns may be sought; (*d*) a linear process; and (*e*) a string of symbols or emotional values. These five categories embrace the approaches of formal analysts such as Leichtentritt and Tovey, structuralists and semioticians, Schenker, Kurth and Westphal, and Riemann, hermeneutics, stylistic analysis and computational analysis, information-theory analysis, proportion theory, Réti and functional analysis, set-theory analysis and much else. The categories are still not exclusive. For example, (*a*) and (*c*) are not wholly incompatible in that approach (*c*) may lead to approach (*a*). Then again, two approaches may co-exist at two different levels of construction: perhaps (*a*) or (*b*) for large-scale form and (*d*) for small-scale thematic development.

Under methods of operating would be categories such as (*a*) reduction technique; (*b*) comparison, and recognition of identity, similarity, or common property; (*c*) segmentation into structural units; (*d*) search for rules of syntax; (*e*) counting of features; and (*f*) reading-off and interpretation of expressive elements, imagery, symbolism.

Under media of presentation would be categories such as (*a*) annotated score or reduction or continuity line (see figs.36–7); (*b*) 'exploded' score, bringing related elements together (fig.39); (*c*) list, or 'lexicon' of musical units, probably accompanied by some kind of 'syntax' describing their deployment (see figs.41–2); (*d*) reduction graph, showing up hidden structural relationships (figs.29–30); (*e*) verbal description, using strict formal terminology, imaginative poetic metaphor, suggested programme or symbolic interpretation; (*f*) formulaic restatement of structure in terms of letter- and number-symbols (see §7 below); (*g*) graphic display: contour shapes (fig.23), diagrams (figs.20, 40, 43), graphs (fig.19), visual symbols for specific musical elements (fig.18); (*h*) statistical tables or graphs; and (*i*) sounding score, on tape or disc, or for live performance (see §3 below). Such media can be used together within an analysis, and elements of two or more can be combined.

The types of analysis described below are arranged according to method of operation, beginning with reduction techniques and proceeding through comparative method to different types of segmentation, category measurement and feature counting, syntax formulation, probability measurement and set-theory analysis. For each type, some description of the underlying aesthetic approach is supplied, and also of the medium of presentation.

2. *Fundamental Structure (Schenker)*

Schenker's unique view of a musical composition is that works that are tonal and exhibit mastery are 'projections' in time of a single element: the tonic triad. The projection of this triad comprises two processes, its transformation into a two-part 'fundamental structure' called the *Ursatz*, and the 'composing-out' (*Auskomponierung*), i.e. the elaboration of the structure by one technique or more of prolongation. The *Ursatz* is made up of a linear descent to the root of the triad – the 'fundamental line' (*Urlinie*) – accompanied by an 'arpeggiation' in the bass (*Bassbrechung*), from the tonic to the dominant and back to the tonic. In the simplest form of the *Ursatz* the linear descent begins with the 3rd of the tonic triad, and each note in it is accompanied by one chord in the bass (see fig.28).

28. From H. Schenker: 'Der freie Satz' (1935), 1

But this is a highly abstract notion, and in practice the elaboration begins with the structure in an already articulated form, representing the 'background' (*Hintergrund*) of the work. The number of possible forms of the background is theoretically infinite.

The elaboration of a basic contrapuntal design, as a way of viewing composition, emerged early in Schenker's development as a theorist (see Chapter III, §§1–2), and the method of analysis logically entailed by it was reduction. The concept of projection from a universal starting-point, which came to him only gradually during the last decade of his life, added a new factor to his analytical method: the tracing and highlighting of a structural 'norm', a kind of phasic process. The crucial idea in Schenker's theory is 'the perception of a musical work as a dynamic totality, not as a succession of moments or a juxtaposition of "formal" areas related or contrasted merely by the fact of thematic or harmonic similarity or dissimilarity' (Babbitt, *JAMS*, v, 1952, p.262 [review of Salzer, 1952]). Its reduction down to a small structural core which embraces the entire composition – the reverse of projection – is thus the crucial analytical operation.

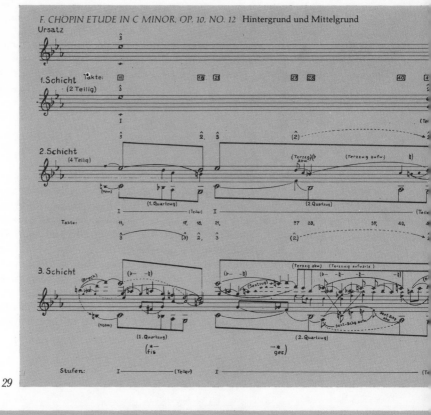

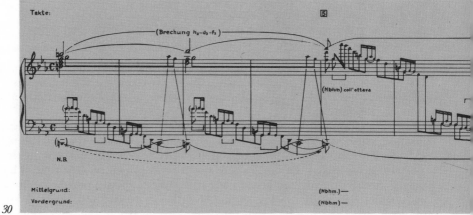

29–30. H. Schenker: 'Fünf Urlinie-Tafeln' (1932; from Eng. trans., 1969), 54–5, 56–7 (fig.29 shows t[...] fundamental structure; fig.30 shows the foreground 'graph')

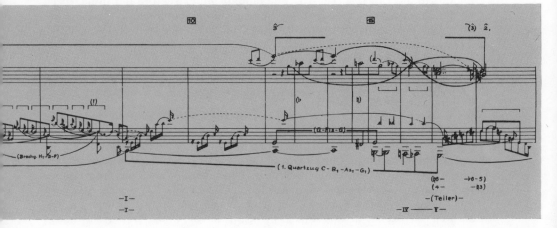

Schenker controlled this reduction by the establishment of three structural layers (*Schichten*). Of these, the 'foreground' contains the elements of the contrapuntal design that are immediately perceptible, eliminating only ornamentation and note repetition from the surface of the work. The 'middleground', which might consist of more than one layer, presents the work without any of its surface detail, and so brings together structural elements that might be widely separated in the foreground. The 'background' presents the basic core, with as little as one melody note and harmonic function representing a theme or section of the work.

In order to present this Schenker devised a graphic notation whereby all the layers except the foreground are set out one above the other. Each of these layers is laid out on a single staff and makes use of notational symbols (though with unconventional meaning), slurs, brackets and parentheses. Roman numerals are used for harmonic steps (from I to VII), capped arabic numerals for melodic degrees of the scale ($\hat{1}$, $\hat{2}$, $\hat{3}$ etc), ordinary arabic numerals for bar numbers and bass figuring; words and auxiliary symbols are also used. The layers are aligned vertically, so that any element of the composition can be traced upwards to its place in the structural core.

Figs.29–30 (pp.82–3) show Schenker's analysis of Chopin's Etude in C minor op.10 no.12, as published in *Fünf Urlinie-Tafeln* (1932). The analysis is laid out on no fewer than six staves. The foreground is in this case presented separately, occupying far more lateral space than the other layers and thus not aligned with them (fig.30, showing only bars 1–18). Then three layers of middleground are presented in vertical alignment. Above these the background layer, represented by the fundamental structure (*Ursatz*) is set out, so that its transformation into middleground can be observed. The fundamental structure has in fact been broken into two parts: the first two elements of the fundamental structure are presented before the statement is broken off, recommenced and concluded. This transformation is known as 'interruption' (*Unterbrechung*), and the point of breaking off is marked by the word '(Teiler)' ('divider' – often indicated by two short vertical lines just above the staff, especially later, when *Teiler* tended to signify small-scale anticipatory interruption). At level 2 this interruption is multiplied to three occurrences.

In layers 2 and 3 of fig.29, void note-heads are used to indicate notes of relatively greater structural importance, black note-heads notes of relatively less. The void note-heads are linked together by large beams, pointing up the fundamental two-part movement of the composition. Black note-heads are linked together by slur marks, which pick out detailed melodic progressions, and these progressions are often labelled verbally (e.g. *Terzzug abwärts*, 'conjunct progression down a 3rd', *Sext-Brechung-aufwärts*, 'upwards arpeggiation across a 6th'). They are also linked by beams to void notes. Dotted slur marks indicate not progression but recurrence of a structural note after the intervention of other notes (thus the recurrence of d'' in the first half of layer 2). Black notes with tails (quaver symbols) are used to point up small-scale events of special interest (such as the neighbour-note patterns g'–$f\sharp'$–g' and $b\natural''$–c''' in layer 3).

Spatially the treatment of bars 1–10 is most striking. The fundamental structure first emerges in bar 11, and the preceding three melody notes are considered functionally as an 'ascent' (*Anstieg*) to the first melody note of this structure: they 'open the space' between the tonic note C and the first melodic structural note E♭. Moreover, in layer 3 the first ten bars are compressed into a melodic arpeggio of three notes (*b♮″–d‴–f‴*), the B♮ being interpreted also as a bass note and the harmony being labelled as neighbour-note (*Nebennotenharmonie*). This is further compressed into two notes in layer 2, and disappears altogether at layer 1.

The harmonic indications at the bottom of fig.30 show that what is considered as I–IV–V at foreground level becomes entirely I at the middleground. Moreover, Schenker's analytical method completely rejects the conventional idea of modulation: key changes are viewed as harmonic elaborations of diatonic harmonies. Thus the moves to B♭ minor, D♯ minor, C♯ minor and F minor around bar 30 are seen ultimately as prolongations of C minor harmony.

Although Schenker's analytical method was designed, and can be used in its full form, only for tonal music, some of its principles and most of its techniques can be applied to non-tonal music. Salzer (1935, 1952) analysed medieval and Renaissance compositions and 20th-century works, and other applications can be found in *Music Forum*. The concepts of prolongation and directed motion are relevant, as are the graphic devices and the structural layers; but Schenker's norm, the *Ursatz*, has to be discarded.

3. Thematic Process (Réti) and Functional Analysis (Keller)

Réti's view, overtly expressed in his writings, is of music as a linear compositional process: the composer starts not with a theoretical scheme but with a motif that has arisen in his mind, which he allows to grow by constant transformation – by transposition, inversion, reiteration, paraphrase, variation. Its growth is evolutionary. In time, he makes a significant modification to the motif or picks up a detail from his elaborative material, and this becomes the centre of focus. A work is thus seen as 'a musical improvisation, a true thematic song around a few motifs'. The succession of motifs itself forms a grouping at a higher level, a 'thematic pattern', and this pattern recurs from movement to movement, becoming 'the skeleton of all themes in all movements; it determines the modulations, the figurations and the bridges, and above all, it provides an outline for the overall architecture' (1967, p.94).

Underlying the motivic material of a work are several 'prime cells'. These are small-scale melodic contours comprising two or three intervals and in origin non-rhythmic. Thus the two prime cells of the 'Pathétique' Sonata of Beethoven are as shown in fig.31 (overleaf). Réti arrived at these cells by reduction of all the thematic material of the work to its abiding common elements. He gave them separate functions by designating them 'prime cell' and 'concluding motif' respectively. Fig.32 shows where the cells are located in the opening bars of the first movement. The motifs (still without rhythm) which can be derived from these cells may be set out in a table: fig.33. An entire

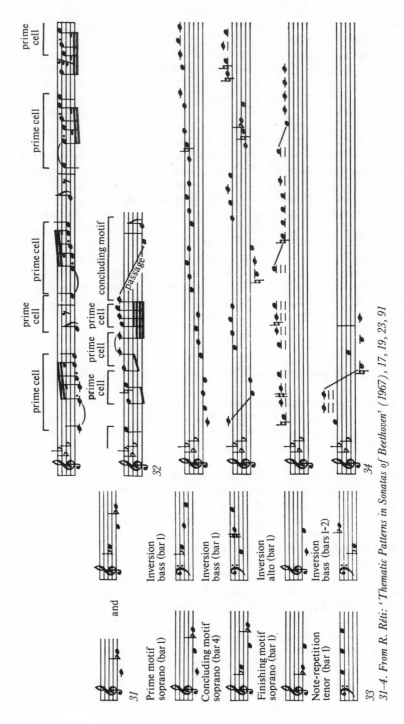

31–4. From R. Réti: 'Thematic Patterns in Sonatas of Beethoven' (1967), 17, 19, 23, 91

86

movement can then be set out, in non-rhythmic form with its melodic shapes grouped to reveal the motif forms, as a 'thematic song' (see fig.34, the slow introduction).

Réti's view of music is considerably simpler than Keller's. It is a single process passing from beginning to end, almost like a chain except that some of the links overlap or occur side by side, and except also that certain large patterns recur. Keller's view is of music as a double process: a linear development – argument would be a better word, for Keller's view is that music communicates and that the listener 'understands' it – but one controlled by a single cell-like 'basic idea'. The singularity of the basic idea introduces an element of projection into the compositional process. Keller spoke of musical thought as two-dimensional: that is, as having 'background' and 'foreground'. The background proceeds by the law of identity, the foreground by the law of contradiction. Thus music has the quality, not open to logical thought, that something may both be and not be something. In context, Keller's view of a piece of music (a piece, as with Schenker, that exhibits mastery) is of unity within diversity: of constant 'latent' presence of a single basic idea, articulated in time as a succession of 'manifest' contradictions.

The diversity of the foreground is meaningless unless it occurs against a background of unity. It is thus the job of analysis to discover the basic idea from which all the foreground material springs. However, this 'idea' has nothing apart from its singularity in common with Schenker's 'fundamental structure'; it is not a structural norm but a small-scale idea, a germ-cell, whose internal elements are reproduced at the surface in close proximity, and which recurs again and again. All the principal thematic material must be brought together, and by reduction the highest common factor within that material must be isolated. To identify the pervasive, all-embracing idea is the first task of the analyst, but to account for the continuity of the foreground is the second. This involves not only explaining how each manifestation of the basic idea is derived from the original but also why that particular derivation occurs at that point. Analysis elucidates the functions of a piece as if it were a living organism.

As with Réti, the basic idea is usually a melodic outline, a succession of intervals out of time. Its manifestation is thus a rhythmicization. The foreground derivation may involve transposition, inversion, retrogression or 'interversion' (the reordering of the elements of the idea). Keller, however, was less open than Réti to the criticism of neglecting rhythmic aspects of a structure, for his method recognizes fundamental rhythmic patterns, and thus augmentation and diminution are further types of derivation. Also very important in foreground continuity are the separation of two phrases latently in antecedent–consequent relationship – called 'postponed complementation' by Keller – and the reversing of the order of two such phrases.

Early presentation of functional analysis was by verbal text with music examples. Such examples showed thematic material with labelled motifs and derhythmicized reductions. Soon, however, Keller stated the principle that 'music about music is immeasurably more objective than words about music, because music is absolutely concrete' (*MR*, xix, 1958, p.200). He devised a method that involved composing a score, for the same forces as the work under analysis, in which passages of the original are interspersed with aural demonstrations of the links between themes. He claimed for this method the advantages that it avoids the transition between musical and verbal thought, that the through-composition of the analytical score leads along purely musical lines, and that the subjectiveness of verbal description is eliminated. (Unfortunately it has the disadvantage that after the controversial broadcasts in the late 1950s Keller's analytical scores were completely unavailable – but see Keller, 1985.) As to the last of these, a further distinction between the work of Réti and that of Keller is that Réti regarded what he produced not (in the words of his widow) as 'graven in stone, but ... as creative insights, ... by which the listener ... might be stimulated to new discoveries' (1967, p.8), whereas Keller regarded his best analytical work as incapable of being improved. For him, where two functional analyses ('FAs', as he abbreviated them) differ, 'one will be objectively better' (1958, p.199). (For the history of functional analysis see also Chapter III, §§4–5.)

4. Formal Analysis

In Chapter I, §2 the three basic form-building processes were proposed as 'recurrence', 'contrast' and 'variation', expressible as AA, AB and AA'. Formal analysis is concerned with the recognition of these three processes and the description of works in terms of them.

During the late 18th century and the 19th, music theorists defined certain structural patterns – not genres or species such as concerto or minuet, but more widely applicable processes of formal construction common to many genres and species, and now often called formal models (see Chapter II, §§2–3). These are in turn reducible to two fundamental patterns: AB and ABA, subsumed in German terminology under the single term *Liedform* (first proposed by A. B. Marx, 1837–47) in its 'two-part' (*zweiteiliges*) and 'three-part' (*dreiteiliges*) form, and distinguished in English terminology as binary form and ternary form. Broadly speaking, these terms refer to small-scale forms; they apply most directly to instrumental dance movements of the 17th and 18th centuries, and rely on the concept of regular phrase structure with the eight-bar period as the principal unit of construction. Larger-scale formal models are regarded as extensions of one or other of the two fundamental patterns: thus sonata form is the extension of the binary pattern, and rondo of the ternary.

There is however an additional distinction to be made between two basic processes of extension: that of a succession of formal units, and that of development. The former (in German, *Reihungsform* or *plastische Form*) relies on proportion and symmetry, and is architectural in nature; the latter (*Entwicklungsform* or *logische Form*) on continuity and growth. The rondo, $ABACADA$, extends ternary form by succession; sonata form extends binary form by development. And the two processes are both brought into operation in the so-called sonata rondo: $ABACAB'A$.

There is a further process by which larger forms may be created out of one of the two basic patterns: by the operating of one or both patterns at more than one level of structure (*Potenzierung*, 'exponentiating'). By this means, such structures as *A* (*aba*)–*B* (*cdc*)–*A* (*aba*) are produced. Related to this is the concept of 'cyclic form', whereby movements in recognizable forms are grouped together to form larger units such as the suite and the sonata. (For Lorenz's use of *Potenzierung* see Chapter III, §2.)

Manuals of formal analysis vary in the extent to which they see the totality of musical formations, from the Middle Ages onwards and for all vocal and instrumental media, as governed by these fundamental patterns. Many manuals now have separate descriptions of 'the contrapuntal forms' and allow a category of 'free forms'. Nonetheless, the underlying idea of formal analysis is that of the 'model', against which all compositions are set and compared and measured in terms of their conformity to or 'deviation' from the norm. It was against this *a priori* concept that Tovey rebelled so vociferously (1931, 1935–9).

Quite apart from the universality of the basic models, there are many difficulties in determining criteria for their recognition. For some analysts, identity or non-identity is determined by thematic character; for others, by key scheme; for others, by length of units. Thus, for Dahlhaus (*RiemannL 12*, 1967), the prime conditions of the two-part *Liedform* |:*A*:|:*B*:| are, first, that the first part ends on a half-close in the tonic or a full-close in a related key, and, second, that the parts are melodically different (or related |:*AX*:|:*AY*:| or |:*AX*:|:*BX*:|). For Scholes ('Form', *Oxford Companion to Music*, 1938, 10/1970), binary form rests on the key scheme |:tonic–dominant (or relative major) :|:dominant (or relative major)–tonic:| and on the absence of 'strong contrast' in thematic material. For Prout, key scheme is not really a determinant at all for binary form, for he allowed |:tonic–tonic:|: remote key–tonic:|; nor is thematic relationship, for he allowed *AA'BA''* as well as *ABCB*. The basic determinant for Prout is that the form shall constitute 'two complete sentences'. Thus the form |:*A*:|:*BA*:|, which for Dahlhaus is three-part *Liedform*, is for Prout binary form unless the first part is itself a complete binary form, self-contained and rounded.

Tovey (see Chapter III, §3) felt a basic antagonism towards the formal analytical approach, and yet his method, which represents the tradition of analysis and descriptive criticism in Britain as a whole, accepted the standard forms and framed its analyses in terms of them. Terms such as 'transition', 'development', 'return', 'recapitulation', 'episode', 'coda' and 'codetta' are part of his normal vocabulary. He disliked 'first subject' and 'second subject' because 'there is no prescribed number of subjects to a movement in sonata form', and substituted 'group' for 'subject', 'which has the merit of not necessarily implying themes at all' (1935, p.2). Thus his analyses of sonata form movements (in 1931) are laid out under subheadings 'First Group', 'Transition', 'Second Group', 'Development' and 'Recapitulation'. Under each subheading there appear bar numbers at the left-hand side of the page, with verbal commentary and music examples (the themes and 'figures' being labelled with letter-symbols). Hence Tovey called his method 'bar-by-bar' or 'bar-to-bar', and it was the successive aspect of his description that was most important to him, since he saw analysis as tracing the same process in time that the 'naïve listener' experienced.

89

Tovey's verbal commentary contains technical information on phrase structure ('Eight-bar theme (A); 2 + 2 in sequence, followed by 1 + 1 in sequence'), thematic identity ('New theme (B) rhythmically allied to (a) + (b) [figures of (A)]'), key structure and formal process ('interlocking thrice in self-repetition, and the third time augmenting its last notes to two full bars'). But it also contains metaphor. Thus the scherzo of Beethoven's Fifth Symphony seems 'finished, exhausted, played out' – because the main section that is 'dark, mysterious, and, in part, fierce' has 'suddenly collapsed', after which a trio 'dies away' and the return of the scherzo is 'one of the ghostliest things ever written' (*Beethoven*, 1944, pp.16f). What he did was to 'describe the technical means and the aesthetic effect and invite the reader to contemplate, if not their logical or necessary connection, at all events their simultaneity and likely association' (Kerman, 1975–6, p.798). His method is thus partly hermeneutic, and he achieved it by animation of the orchestra ('A piccolo, a contra-fagotto and a triangle contribute with grotesque poetic aptness') or animation of the work itself ('When this has died wistfully away on an inconclusive chord, the original theme sternly reappears in the windband'), or by treating the commentary as a guided tour ('We are now in the full swing of a perfectly regular recapitulation'). The style is almost that of Schumann at times, and it achieves a humanity, an accessibility and yet a formality which makes it an excellent tool for introducing a listener to a work he is about to hear or a performer to his subject of study.

5. *Phrase-structure Analysis (Riemann)*

Riemann's theory of phrase structure rests on the postulate that the pattern weak–strong is the 'sole basis for all musical construction' (1895–1901, i, 132). This fundamental unit is termed the *Motiv*. It is fundamental because it represents a single unit of energy passing from growth to decay by way of a central stress point. It is thus a dynamic trace, a flux, and is far removed from the traditional notion of 'beats' in a 'bar', each beat being separate and having its own 'weight'.

Where two such *Motiv* units occur in succession they form the two elements of a *Motiv* at the next level of structure: the first forming the growth phase, the second the stress point and decay phase. And in turn, two such larger *Motiv* units form a still higher-level *Motiv*, and so on in a hierarchy. The result is a kind of grid, made up of equal units of energy: a grid that is conceptual in the sense that very few pieces of music are made up of equal-length phrases and unvarying tempos, and yet is not as imaginary as, say, the grid of a map because the lines of this grid bear an intrinsic relationship to the topography of the music they concern (but only to the topography: *Motiv* has no connotation of thematic identity in Riemann's theory).

Given this theory, the process of analysis is one of locating the lines of the grid behind the articulated surface of a piece or passage of music. A piece that is totally slavishly aligned to its grid would be made of regular modules, each

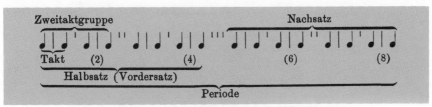

35. *From H. Riemann: 'Präludien und Studien' (1895–1901), i, 163*

module comprising eight bars of 2/4 or 3/4 and pairing off into units of 16 bars, 32 bars, 64 bars and so forth at higher levels. The eight-bar module is shown for 2/4 in fig.35 (*Zweitaktgruppe* is Riemann's term for a pair of *Motiv* units in weak–strong relationship; *Halbsatz* for a four-bar unit – either antecedent or consequent; *Periode* for an eight-bar module: 1895–1901, i, 163). But in practice music adopts certain 'symmetry-disturbing processes', some of which stretch or compress the grid, others of which temporarily upset the internal relationships without affecting the regularity of the grid itself. Chief among these processes are:

(*a*) Elision (*Auslassung*): the suppression of the growth phase of a unit (the first element of a *Motiv*, the first *Motiv* of a two-bar group, the first two-bar group of a four-bar half-phrase etc), thus yielding a strong–weak–strong pattern. An example is the minuet of Mozart's G minor String Quintet κ516: fig.36 (1900, 8/1912, p.84).

(*b*) Cadential repetition: restatement of the stress point and decay phase of a unit at any level of structure. A classic example is the introduction to Schubert's Symphony no.9: fig.37 (ibid, p.80). This example contains double repetition, and the doubling of values on the second restatement.

(*c*) Dovetailing: a transfer of function whereby a final stressed unit is converted into an initial unstressed one (i.e. decay is converted into growth phase), for example when the eighth bar of a period becomes the first of a new period.

(*d*) General upbeat (*Generalauftakt*): a large-scale upbeat, often occupying only

36. *From H. Riemann: 'Handbuch der Phrasierung' (1912), 84–5*

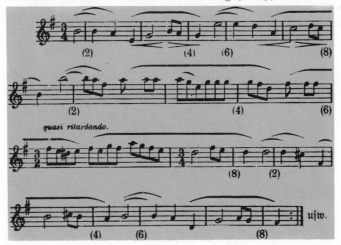

91

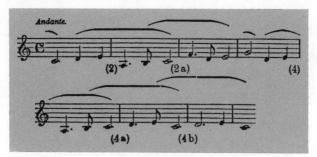

37. From H. Riemann: 'Handbuch der Phrasierung' (1912), 80

the space of the upbeat to a *Motiv* but functioning as the upbeat to a larger formal unit (see ex.6, p.116).

(*e*) Annexed motif (*Anschlussmotiv*): a subsidiary phrase unit placed immediately after the strong beat of a main phrase unit. It serves to generate a second strong beat where a weak beat would normally occur (see ex.1, p.110).

The first three of these processes alter the temporal distance between points on the grid, the last two may alter the impression of such distance but do not necessarily alter the number of intervening beats.

Riemann's own analyses take one of two forms: books of analyses (those of Bach's *Das wohltemperirte Clavier*, 1890, and Beethoven's string quartets, 1903, and piano sonatas, 1918–19), or 'phrase-structure editions' (of sonatas of Mozart, Beethoven and Haydn). The latter are editions which use special phrase-marks and signs, as shown in Table 1, and number the bar-functions beneath the staff. The former adopt as their method of presentation the 'continuity line': a single staff which shows all the main thematic material, accompanied by the special signs and numbering used in the editions, and employing also Riemann's system of harmonic symbols (fully explained in his *Anleitung zum Generalbass-Spielen*, 4/1917, pp.12ff). These books also use conven-

TABLE 1

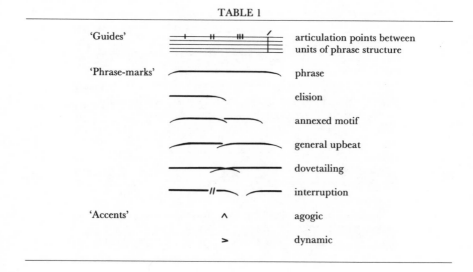

92

tional terminology when dealing with thematic material and aim at fully rounded 'technical and aesthetic analyses of pieces of music'. Yet it is in his theory
of phrase structure, much disputed and now somewhat neglected, that
Riemann had most to offer: in the field of metre and rhythm, where analysis has
been most deficient, offering a set of criteria for segmentation and at the same
time a means of defining the functions of large time spans.

6. *Category and Feature Analysis*

These two types of analysis both take a wider view of musical material than any
of the types so far described. In both, structure is only one of the aspects brought
under examination. Consequently they are both particularly useful as methods
for stylistic analysis, where construction and cohesion are but two of the terms
of reference, along with techniques of instrumentation and vocal writing,
usages of consonance and dissonance, of metre and rhythm, of texture and such
like, which characterize a style or repertory. Usable though both types are for
analysis of the single work, they tend to analyse that work synchronically (i.e.
out of the continuum of time), treating it as a style rather than as a piece, usually
with reference to other pieces in the same style or comparable styles, and
present their findings in non-temporal form as tables, statistics, graphs or summarized descriptions.

Category analysis starts with the recognition that music is too complex a
phenomenon to be comprehended without some way of breaking down its
material into elements – not so much its temporal elements (phrase, motif etc),
though these may be part of the 'breaking-down' process, as those facets that
are constantly present: the 'parameters'. What the analyst requires is, in
LaRue's words, 'a set of categories that are satisfactorily distinct, yet without
undue branching and proliferation' (1970, p.10). Each category is then given
a scale of measurement, and it is this measuring that is the critical operation in
the analysis.

Two fully worked-out systems will serve to illustrate the type: that by LaRue
(1970) for style in Western Classical music (designed with the 18th-century
instrumental repertory in mind) and that by Lomax (1968) for singing style
(hence its name, 'cantometrics') in the folk music of world cultures.

In abstract, category analysis establishes a two-dimensional grid, a 'matrix',
one dimension comprising categories, the other the scale of measurement.
Lomax's 'behavioral grid' is made up of 37 categories and 13 degrees. It
operates on a single level. It ultimately locates any singing style somewhere
along a spectrum of style whose extremes are 'highly individualized and group-
dominating performance' and 'highly cohesive, group-involving performance'
(p.16). It can easily be coded for comparative analysis by computer, and the
computer will present its results in a graph (pp.75ff).

LaRue's system has only five categories (its 'four Contributing Elements' and
'fifth Combining Element') and three degrees (the Aristotelian 'Rule of Three':
two extremes and a mean). In practice, however, the system contains hierarch-

ies and is consequently much more complex to operate. The five categories are: Sound, Harmony, Melody, Rhythm, Growth (acronymically known as 'SHMRG'). But sound is subdivided into 'Timbre', 'Dynamics', 'Texture and Fabric'; harmony into 'Color' and 'Tension'; melody into 'Range', 'Motion', 'Patterns' and so on. Each subcategory has its own set of degrees of measurement: thus melodic patterns are measured as Rising, Falling, Level, Waveform, Sawtooth or Undulating (abbreviated R, F, L, W, S and U); and the number of degrees varies from subcategory to subcategory (which is true also of Lomax's degrees, but the variation is there built into the system). Moreover, each category is considered at each of three levels of structure (LaRue's 'Dimensions'): Large, Middle, Small. The resultant analytical grid is really three-dimensional, with categories and subcategories as one dimension, the three levels of structure as the second, and the variable degrees of measurement as the third. However, a finished analysis is displayed as a table, with categories as rows and dimensions as columns: each box in the table contains (if anything, i.e. if relevant) a verbal description that does not limit itself to quantification but also supplies information about context and function.

LaRue appended to his analytical system a method of extracting the essential and relevant information from analyses of individual works so that comparative analysis may be performed without drowning in data. It comprises three headings: 'Sources of Shape' (subdivided into articulation, recurrence/development/response/contrast, connection/correlation/concinnity, and conventional forms), 'Sources of Movement' (subdivided into states of change, stability/local activity/directional motion, and types of change, structural/ornamental), and 'Conventional and Innovative Features' (which isolates distinctive features from the stylistic background: LaRue stressed the need for large sampling of any given repertory as a frame of reference for judging distinctiveness).

Feature analysis involves taking not variables (categories) into which values (measurements) are placed, but invariables (features, such as a particular interval or chord or rhythmic unit or dynamic level) to which frequencies of occurrence within a given passage or piece or repertory are assigned after a counting operation. Such invariable features will tend to be small and indivisible, but can be larger units or 'patterns'. This method is of particular application in stylistic analysis, where counts for individual pieces are being compared and correlated for 'affinity'. It is one that views music as a universe of features, and any one style as a clustering of certain of those features in differing frequencies; style is seen as statistical in nature.

Crane and Fiehler, for example (in Lincoln, 1970, chap.15), expounded a method (derived from R. Sokal and P. H. A. Sneath: *Principles of Numerical Taxonomy*, 1963) by which affinity can be calculated so as to produce three classes: coefficients of association, coefficients of correlation and coefficients of distance. The last conceives a work's style as a unique point in multi-dimensional Euclidean space. As Crane and Fiehler said, the result of any of these affinity calculations will be a 'matrix like a mileage-between-cities table, whose columns and rows are headed by the identifications of each work. At the intersection of row i and column j will be entered the affinity between works i and j'. Their essay goes on to describe ways in which the clustering of works, the

94

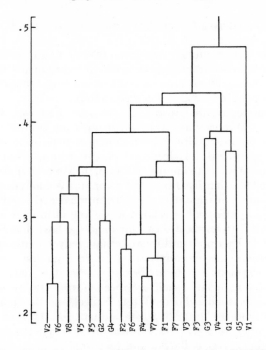

38. From H. B. Lincoln, ed.: 'The Computer and Music' (1970), 217

'mutual relations among a set of works' may be determined and graphically expressed. Fig.38 shows a 'dendrogram' displaying the clustering of 20 chansons from the 15th century: each horizontal line shows the coefficient of distance at which the two works or clusters below it join; the lower the coefficient the greater the affinity.

Mention has already been made of the notion of 'context', in connection with LaRue's category analysis. 'Context-sensitivity' has direct relevance to feature analysis. The statement, about a piece of music, that 'The rising 4th followed by falling minor 3rd occurs 247 times' takes on greater significance when completed by 'with conjunct motion preceding it in all but 30 cases and following it in all cases'; and even more if information about the points in the metrical structure at which the pattern begins and about the three note values involved can be included.

Context-sensitivity (a term used in linguistics) may lead to another concept with wide application outside music: the 'equivalence-class'. Where two (objectively distinct) features have an identical context or set of possible contexts for a given piece or repertory, they may be described as 'functionally equivalent'. The set of all such features that have their contexts exactly in common constitutes an equivalence-class. Context-sensitivity and equivalence are, however, concepts not of feature analysis as such but of syntactical analysis, which deals with the ways in which elements combine and the rules by which they may or may not do so. This type of analysis is considered in the next section.

95

7. Musical Semiotics (Ruwet and Nattiez)

Musical semiotics views music as a stream of sounding elements governed by rules of 'distribution': that is, of ways in which the elements associate with or complement or mutually exclude each other. Its aim is to state these rules as 'adequately' as possible for any given passage of music, or work or group of works; to formulate, in other words, a syntax for the music. Its method is to break the stream of music into component units (or 'unities' – i.e. units that either cannot be further subdivided or do not need to be because their sub-units never occur independently). It does this by comparing all possible units with all other possible units; when an identity is found, the contexts of the two occurrences are examined for identity. From this comparative analysis emerges a list of all 'distinctive units', an account of the distribution of each, and a grouping into units distributed in identical or related ways; and ultimately a restatement of the stream of music in terms of these units and the laws that govern them.

This method differs from traditional formal analysis in recognizing no standard formal templates. Every analysis thus starts from first principles, striving to avoid preconceptions and to achieve scientific objectivity. The method is used by musical semioticians (such as Ruwet, Nattiez, Lidov and Mâche) and syntactical analysts (such as Forte, Boretz, Selleck and Bakeman). It is carried further by those who, under the linguistic influence of Chomsky, attempt to test their syntax by using it to generate musical utterances in the same style (Lindblom and Sundberg, Laske, Baroni and Jacobini).

The restatement of the stream of music in terms of units and laws usually employs simple labels made of letters and numbers. A typical example is the labelling system of Ruwet (1966). Units at the middle level of structure that Ruwet called 'niveau I', which repeat and are thus defined, are allocated capital letters from the beginning of the alphabet; non-repeating material is then allocated capital letters from the end of the alphabet. These produce a string of symbols such as $A + B + A + X + B + Y$. Units at the smallest level of structure, Ruwet's 'niveau II', are assigned lower-case italic letters, the late letters of the alphabet again being allocated to non-repeating units. The segmentation of middle-level units may reveal relationships between such units.

39. From N. Ruwet: 'Méthodes d'analyse en musicologie', RBM, xx (1966), 81

Thus, if $A = a + b$ and $X = a + c$, then it may be possible to rewrite $A + X$ as $A + A'$. Middle-level units may also be aggregated into high-level units, Ruwet's 'niveau 0', and these latter are assigned arabic numerals in parentheses. Thus $A + X + A + Y$ may become (1).

Using this system of labelling and of rewriting, Ruwet (1972) analysed a troubadour song, *Molt me mervoil* by Guiot de Provins (see fig.39). His initial segmentation at level I produces X (bars 5–8) $+B$ (bars 1–4) $+Y$ (bars 9–28) $+B$ (bars 29–32). On grounds of phrase length, X is then rewritten as A, and Y as $C + D + E + F + G$. But at level II, $C = z + a$ and $G = z' + a'$, so that G is rewritten as C'. The result so far is: $A + B + C + D + E + F + C' + B$. Level II now comes into operation:

$$
\begin{array}{ll}
A = x + a & B = y + b \\
C = z + a & D = w + b \\
E = v + a'' & F = ? \\
C' = z' + a' & B = y + b
\end{array}
$$

Level 0 now also comes into operation, since by the laws of 'equivalence' the pairs of segments $(A + B)$, $(C + D)$ and $(C' + B)$ are seen as 'manifestations of the same abstract structure', which can be set out as:

$$
\left\{ \begin{array}{c} x \\ z \end{array} \right\} \quad a \qquad \left\{ \begin{array}{c} y \\ w \end{array} \right\} \quad b
$$

This formula indicates that x and z are distributionally interchangeable and that the same applies to y and w. Each pair forms an 'equivalence-class', as discussed in §6 above. The pair $(E + F)$ is more problematic, but Ruwet suggested that $E(v + a'')$ is equivalent to the first part of the formula, and F externally (but not internally) equivalent to the latter part. Ruwet did not rewrite the string of symbols, but it would presumably appear as $(1) + (1) + (1) + (1)$, or $(1) + (1) + (1)' + (1)$, or $(1) + (1) + (2) + (1)$, depending upon how one viewed the pair $(E + F)$.

This kind of comparative analysis can be carried out very efficiently by computer, especially when using a computer language designed for 'pattern matching' (a process whereby a string of characters is scanned to see whether a second string of characters is contained within it) such as SNOBOL or SPITBOL. The highly sophisticated work of Forte (especially his article in *JMT*, 1966) shows the computer used in this way to parse and rewrite the structure of music by Webern.

Nattiez has developed other modes of presentation, including the tree-structure diagram (borrowed from linguistics; see fig.40, overleaf: Nattiez, 1975, p.311, of Brahms's Intermezzo op.119 no.3), the lexicon of items (see fig.41: ibid, p.346, of rhythmic elements in Debussy's *Syrinx*) and the table of distributions (see fig.42: ibid, p.296, of Varèse's *Intégrales*).

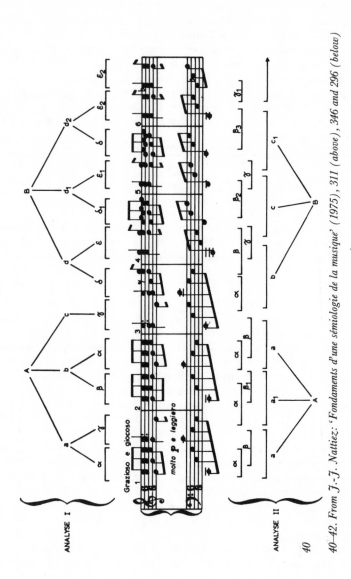

40–42. From J.-J. Nattiez: 'Fondaments d'une sémiologie de la musique' (1975), 311 (above), 346 and 296 (below)

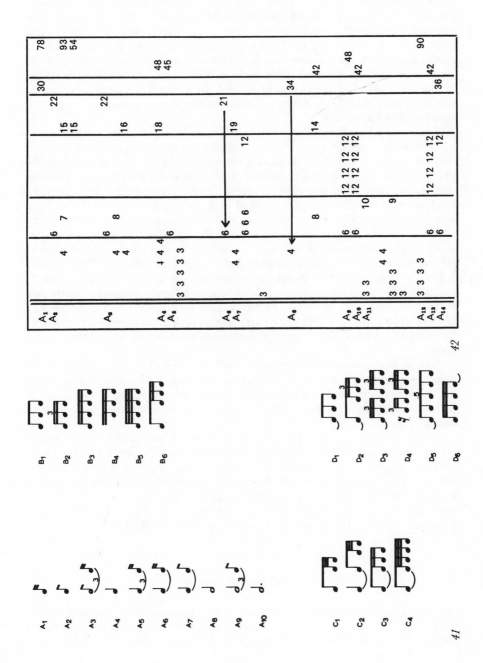

8. Information Theory

Information-theory analysis views music as a linear process. The process is governed by a syntax, but the syntax is stated in terms of the probability that any one element will occur next in the line rather than in terms of grammatical laws. Music is treated by analogy with the transmission of a message from sender to receiver, but neither that nor the word 'information' should give the impression that the method deals with meaning and communication in the hermeneutic sense. It deals exclusively with the arousal, satisfaction or frustration of expectation in the receiver. The history of its application to music is sketched in Chapter III, §4.

A message is a chain of discrete sense-units. In music these units are taken to be 'events' in a composition: usually isolated notes, chords or simultaneities. Any one event in the chain arouses a prediction of its following event. If the prediction is confirmed then no information is imparted; if it is 'non-confirmed' then information is imparted. But events in music form into patterns, and the total amount of information contained in a pattern can be calculated by a formula and expressed as an 'index'. Coons and Kraehenbuehl (1958) offered two indices, one of articulateness which they described as measuring 'how neatly the conditions of "unity" and "variety" have been arranged so that the force of neither is dulled', and one of hierarchy, which measures 'how successfully a "variety" of events has been arranged to leave an impression of "unity"' (p.150). Their method, in other words, measures the phenomena of unity and variety, which are so important in analysis, in an objective and tangible way rather than a subjective and vague way. It can do this for a single structure, or it can do it for a work with respect to the known terms of reference of that work's style.

Artistic 'communication' is, however, different in nature from other forms of communication in that it is not primarily concerned with transmitting maximum information: it is concerned rather with transmitting structure. It therefore requires a certain degree of what information theory calls 'redundancy'.

Information theory analysis generally presents its findings in statistical tables, which can be converted into graphs for easier understanding. Computers lend themselves naturally to the complex calculations which are involved in any but the simplest analysis of this type; and they in turn can produce graphic representations directly by means of a plotter, such as the three-dimensional representations of style in madrigals by Palestrina, Rore and Marenzio produced by Böker-Heil (1972, pp.117ff; see fig.43).

9. Set-theory Analysis

Set-theory analysis has been formulated with a rigour and comprehensiveness unusual among theories of musical analysis (e.g. Forte, 1973; Rahn, 1980). This formulation has necessarily been modelled upon formal theory in mathematics

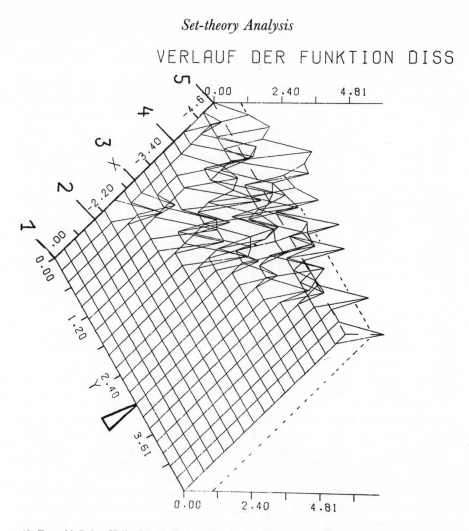

43. From N. Böker-Heil: 'Musikalische Stilanalyse und Computer: einige grundsätzliche Erwägungen', IMSCR, xi Copenhagen 1972, i, 120

(see Chapter III, §5); and even when softened by 'informal discussion' (Babbitt, 1960), its specialist language has tended to deter many musicians – even to offend musical sensibilities because of its apparently automaton-like nature. This is unfortunate, since the method offers a powerful and penetrating tool, especially for musical analysis. It is as capable of being employed by the sensitive and musicianly analyst, and its results of being interpreted, as any other method. It has proved itself in extended analyses of large-scale works (e.g. Forte, 1978; Schmalfeldt, 1979; Baker, 1986) as well as in countless shorter analyses.

What follows is not a summary of published formulations – these are already expressed with as great an economy as is possible, and the glossary at the end

101

of this volume explicates the principal terms and concepts; rather it is an attempt to characterize the nature of the method.

Let us take tonality as the starting-point. A theory of harmonic tonality needs to embody a mechanism for, first, the recognition of the basic building-blocks of the harmony (the underlying chord formations), and second, for demonstrating the ways in which these building-blocks may be combined (the laws of structure). In harmonic tonality the number of basic building-blocks is relatively small (and all are familiar to Western musicians), while the laws of structure are complex. When we turn to the world of 'free' atonal music – the non-tonal, non-serial works of Schoenberg, Berg and Webern, certain works of Stravinsky and Bartók, and a host of more recent music, American and European – we at first find a bewildering variety of chord formations, many of them unfamiliar, and their structural sense may not be immediately apparent. Could there be, for a given piece, or a given repertory of pieces, a 'vocabulary' of building-blocks? Could there be an underlying 'logic'? Could there be properties which parallel in a general way the tonal system? It was to address these questions that musical set-theory analysis was initially developed. Before the 1960s, attempts to analyse free atonal music tended to refer back to tonal categories and to explain progressions as if they were tonal structures with elaborate chromatic alterations. Set theory deliberately broke away from this line of inquiry and sought to interpret atonal harmony as a set of free-standing structures with their own logic independent of tonal laws.

Consider for a moment how, in tonal music, we perceive in the elaborate sound-surface of music a small vocabulary of building-blocks. Our minds intuitively perform certain transformations. For example: (1) when we hear two notes separated by a whole octave or number of octaves, we attribute to them broadly the same tonal significance (indeed, they even have the same letter-name); (2) when we hear a chord whose notes are widely spaced, we recognize it as an expanded form of a chord in 'close position'; (3) when the lowest note of a triad (or chord of the 7th, 9th etc) is shifted by octave transposition above the other notes, we recognize the same chord changed from 'root position' to 'first inversion' and so on. With all three we see in operation the notion of 'octave equivalence'; and with (3) we see that rotation of the elements of a chord does not eradicate its identity. Moreover, (4) when a pattern of notes (whether chordal or melodic) is shifted as a whole to any different pitch level, it retains its identity. With this we see in operation the notion of 'transpositional equivalence'.

All four are familiar parts of our listening experience. Set theory posits that they are not exclusive to listening in the tonal domain: that they apply also when we listen to non-tonal music (it does not go so far as to claim them as universals). It therefore builds them into its procedures. Thus it often speaks not of a 'pitch', but of a 'pitch class'. 'C' is a pitch class when it is thought of irrespective of the octave register in which it is sounded.

But here the difficulties begin. In tonal analysis we can speak of a 'minor triad', a 'diminished 7th' and so forth; the categories of atonal analysis have yet to be defined, and we should aim to define them without reference to tonal ones. Neutral descriptions are to be preferred. The alphabet (which we use in

102

describing pitch) is one neutral ordered system; numbers are another. In set theory whole numbers are assigned, normally treating C as the starting-point, 0, proceeding chromatically to D♭ = 1, D = 2 and so on to B = 11: 12 pitch classes in all, represented by the whole numbers 0–11. (The numbers can be extended beyond 11 to show pitches beyond the octave, as they are in the example below, but will usually eventually have a multiple of 12 subtracted from them to reduce them to pitch classes.) Following 12-note theory, set theory makes no distinction between A♯ and B♭, or between any other pair of enharmonically equivalent pitches. The chord (or melodic pattern) E♭–D–A–B♭, for example, can then be designated simply as [3,2,9,10] (note the square brackets and the separation of numbers by commas).

With this simple notation, the process of reducing surface phenomena to basic categories can begin. Again, consider a tonal chord: it may be contracted into the space of one octave and then rotated until its root position, in which the notes are piled up in 3rds, is reached (see fig.44*a* stages *1–5*). In the case of our atonal chord, contraction into the space of one octave is achieved simply by writing the whole numbers in ascending order: [3,2,9,10] → [2,3,9,10]; and rotating them until packed as tightly as possible: [9,10,14,15] (i.e. stage *4* in fig.44*b*). This establishes the 'normal form'. Transposition so as to start with

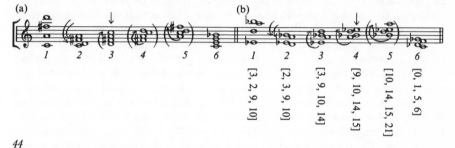

(a) stages *1 2 3 4 5 6*   (b) stages *1 2 3 4 5 6*

[3, 2, 9, 10]   [2, 3, 9, 10]   [3, 9, 10, 14]   [9, 10, 14, 15]   [10, 14, 15, 21]   [0, 1, 5, 6]

44

zero, [0,1,5,6], yields finally the 'prime form' (fig.44*b* stage *6*). The prime form provides a reference point for all transpositions and distributions of this underlying chord formation; hence '[0,1,5,6]' is a description comparable to that of 'dominant 7th' in tonal harmony (whereas in fig.44*a* stage *6* is redundant).

It is important to grasp that these methods of representation are adopted not in order to 'mathematicize' music, but in order to arrive at an objective way, uncoloured by tonal concepts, of reducing the great multitude of surface phenomena to a much smaller number of basic categories. The prime forms are ultimately reducible to 208, and have been placed in an order and tabular arrangement which is now widely accepted, each with its own label. Thus our [0,1,5,6] is, in the table of prime forms with four notes, the eighth prime form: accordingly it is labelled '4–8'. (This table is given in Forte, 1973, pp.179ff.) Of course, the basic categories of tonal harmony can be expressed in these terms as well. Thus the minor triad is 3–11 [0,3,7], the diminished 7th is 4–28 [0,3,6,9], the diatonic major scale (the prime form of which gives the scale starting on its leading note) is 7–35 [0,1,3,5,6,8,10] and so on.

However, not all tonal categories are represented straightforwardly. This is because in addition to transposition and rotation, inversion is widely accepted as a further basis for equivalence. Thus, for example, the dominant 7th chord C–E–G–B♭, when its rising succession of intervals (major 3rd, minor 3rd, minor 3rd) is arranged downwards from C, yields the 'half-diminished-7th chord' D–F–A♭–C. These two chords are thus 'inversionally related'. And since the prime form of the latter is reducible to an arrangement that is more tightly-packed to the left (C–D–F–A♭), it is the latter which provides the prime form for both: 4–27 [0,2,5,8]. Similarly, the major triad 'inverts' to the minor triad; as the latter, [0,3,7], is more tightly-packed to the left than the former, [0,4,7], it is the minor triad which provides the prime form for both.

To clarify terminology at this stage, when an analyst isolates a number of pitches at the surface of the music for examination, then these are called a 'pitch collection' or 'pitch combination'. When they are reduced to pitch classes with repetitions eliminated, they are called a 'pitch-class set'. All pitch-class sets which reduce to the same prime form are described as 'equivalent'.

As was said earlier, a harmonic theory needs to embody a mechanism by which basic building-blocks can be recognized and, further, to determine the laws for combining such blocks. The primary internal structural property of a pitch-class set is the network of intervals which exists between the constituent elements. Just as the inversion of a pitch-class set is considered when determining its prime form, so too the inversion of an interval is considered in arriving at the 'interval class' to which it belongs. Hence the interval between F and C, counted in semitones, is 5 rather than 7 (i.e. the perfect 4th rather than perfect 5th). From this, the most powerful tool can be forged for determining the relationships between sets. The 'interval vector' is a tally of the number of occurrences, within the network, of each possible interval class. The chord in fig.44*b*, C–D♭–F–G♭ in its prime form, contains two minor 2nds (C–D♭, F–G♭), one major 3rd (D♭–F), two perfect 4ths (C–F, D♭–G♭), one diminished 5th (C–G♭); but no major 2nds or minor 3rds. If we arrange a series of numbers which shows the number of minor 2nds followed by the number of major 2nds and so forth, we arrive at an 'interval vector' of [200121]. This may seem artificial, but it carries, as it were, the genetic code of that set: it essentializes the character of the set.

We can see immediately how the interval vector reveals relationships. There are certain pairs of sets which, while not reducible to the same prime form (i.e. not transpositionally or inversionally equivalent), have one and the same interval vector. Thus, for example, in the table of prime forms with five notes, the 12th and 36th prime forms have an identical interval vector: [222121]. Such pairs of sets are called 'Z-related' (a purely arbitrary designation), and to reflect their membership of such a pair their labels include 'Z'. The two sets in question are: 5 –Z12 [0,1,3,5,6] (C,D♭,E♭,F,G♭) and 5–Z36 [0,1,2,4,7] (C,D♭,D,E,G). To have identical genetic code and yet be outwardly different is a fascinating property; and analysis confirms that these pairs have a special role to play in atonal structures. That is, where one of a pair of Z-related sets occurs, the 'Z-correspondent' of that set is often used in the same composition, perhaps in close conjunction with it, or perhaps to create a link with a remoter part of the structure. The Z-related pairs of six-note sets have special properties and are frequently encountered in association.

So far, the relationships discussed – equivalence, Z-relation – are definitive in nature. But what of the greyer area of similarity, which is so important in musical structure? In set theory there are two means of measuring similarity between sets containing the same number of pitch classes (that is, 'of the same cardinality'): we can look for pitch classes common to them or we can compare their respective interval vectors to see how many (if any) of the corresponding numbers match each other. Any two sets which have certain pitch classes in common might be said to have some degree of similarity; such shared pitch classes are described as a 'common subset'. If two sets of the same cardinality have all but one of their pitch classes in common, then they are said to have 'maximal similarity with respect to pitch class', a relationship designated by the symbol R_p.

The remaining, and in some respects more important, levels of similarity are determined by comparing the interval vectors of two sets of the same cardinality. If these vectors are identical, the sets are, as we have seen, Z-related. If four of the six numbers in each of a pair of interval vectors match in size and position, the sets are said to have 'maximal similarity with respect to interval class'. (Two degrees of this relation are distinguished, the stronger designated R_1, the weaker R_2.) If none of the numbers matches, they are said to have 'minimal similarity with respect to interval class' (designated R_0).

The measuring of similarity achieves considerable sophistication when the compound relationship of R_p, R_0, R_1 and R_2 is recognized. A relationship might, for example, combine the weaker of the two degrees of maximal interval-class similarity (R_2) with maximal pitch-class similarity (R_p); this is represented as '$\cdot(R_p, R_2)$'. Or it might be maximal as regards interval class, but not maximal as regards pitch class; this is written as '$\cdot(+R_1, R_2), -R_p)$'. In this way, properties that are not especially significant when considered in isolation become more useful in delimiting the number of 'similar' sets.

But can set theory provide a construct which is in any way comparable to the harmonic tonality of European music? Harmonic tonality is a system comprising chords, each deriving its identity and function directly or indirectly from a central, referential chord (the 'tonic'). Among all the chords in that system there exists a network of interrelationships. When harmonic tonality is defined in this rather partial, functional way, set theory does indeed provide a construct which, while by no means a direct analogue, operates on a similar scale and exists by virtue of a network of interrelationships by reference to a central entity. The construct is the 'set complex', and the central entity is the 'nexus set'.

In fig.44*b* we saw a four-note set [0,1,5,6]. By sounding those four pitch classes, the set does not sound the remaining eight pitch classes which go to make up the chromatic scale, i.e. [2,3,4,7,8,9,10,11]. These pitch classes form a set in their own right and have a special relationship to [0,1,5,6]: they form its 'complement'. Indeed, each of these two sets is the 'complement' of the other. The complement relationship is of pivotal importance to the 'set complex'. So too is the notion of 'subset' alluded to earlier, though we need to broaden the

notion. If set (1) is a subset of set (2), then (2) is equally well a 'superset' of (1).
The relationship between (1) and (2) in this sense is known as 'inclusion'. Taken
together, 'complementation' and 'inclusion' lay the basis for the set complex.

The complement just mentioned, [2,3,4,7,8,9,10,11], is not, of course, in its
prime form. That prime form is in fact [0,1,2,3,4,7,8,9], and in this form it no
longer appears to be the complement of [0,1,5,6], as now has two elements in
common with it. Nonetheless, the two are considered complements of each
other, and this is reflected in the labels which are assigned to them in Forte's
table of prime forms: [0,1,5,6], as shown above, is 4–8; [0,1,2,3,4,7,8,9] is 8–8.
The table is so arranged that complementary sets have the same second number: thus 3–1 and 9–1 are complements, as are 4–19 and 8–19, 5–32 and 7–32
and so on. (The only exceptions to this are the 6-note sets, which are, if we leave
aside the Z-related sets, their own complements.)

Similarly, a set in its prime form may not at first sight appear to be a subset
of another, also in prime form, and yet it may turn out to be so as a result of
transposition and/or inversion. For example, the set 3–7 [0,2,5] does not appear
to be a subset of either 4–8 or 8–8. Yet if 3–7 is transposed upwards by a whole
tone it becomes [2,4,7], at which pitch level it is a subset of 8–8: [0,1,2,3,4,
7,8,9]. This process is called 'mapping' 3–7 'into' 8–8. And if 4–8 were our
'nexus set', then 3–7 would belong to the set complex around that nexus set by
virtue of the fact that it can be transpositionally mapped into its complement,
8–8. The set complex, therefore, broadly defined, comprises all those sets which
are related by inclusion to either the nexus set itself or its complement.

Set complexes tend to be rather large and unwieldy for practical analytical
purposes; a more useful construct emerges if the 'either'/'or' of the previous
sentence is changed to 'and'. The construct which results is known as the
'subcomplex'. 'Complex' is often abbreviated to 'K', and 'subcomplex' to 'Kh'.
Thus the subcomplex Kh, broadly defined, can be said to comprise all those sets
which are related by inclusion to the nexus set itself and its complement. Set 3–7

*45 (below and opposite). From A. Forte: 'The Magical Kaleidoscope: Schoenberg's First
Atonal Masterwork, Opus 11, No. 1', JASI, v/2 (1981), 139–40*

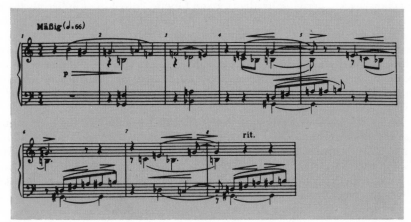

does not meet this requirement because it maps only into 8–8 and not into 4–8. If, on the other hand, we take the set 3–5 [0,1,6], it can be seen immediately to map in its prime form into 4–8 [*0,1,5,6*]; and if it is transposed up by a semitone, [1,2,7], it can be seen to map also into the complement of 4–8: 8–8 [0,*1*,2,3,4,7,8,9] (in fact it maps into it at several transpositions). Our subcomplex around 4–8 in all comprises 16 sets: 3–4, 3–5, 5–6, 5–7, 5–20, 5–22, 6–5, 6–Z6/Z38, 6–7, 6–16, 6–Z17/Z43, 6–18 and 6–Z19/Z44. Subcomplexes vary in size between four and 32 sets around the nexus set and its complement. Here

(a) **Principal Sets:**
    6–Z10/39, 6–16, 6–Z44
    6–21, 5–Z37, 5–Z38

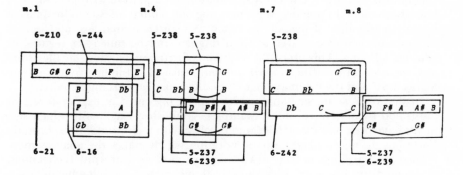

(b) **Other Features:**
    4–7, 4–19, 6–Z10/39,
    6–16, 6–21

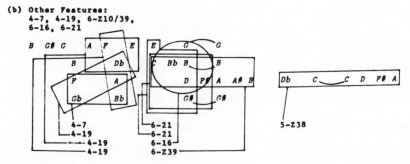

(c) **Trichords:** 3–3, 3–4, 3–5, 3–8
    Pentachords: 5–13, 5–21; **Tetrachord** 4–19

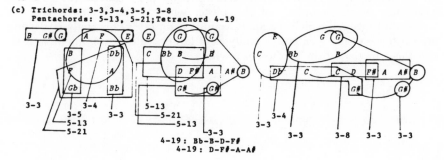

107

then is a construct which can be used to demonstrate structure. When the constituents of one subcomplex are found extensively in two sections of a piece which are widely separated, then a long-term linkage might be posited between the two sections concerned; conversely, when the constituents of two different complexes are found at close quarters to each other, then a short-term opposition might be posited.

A number of important aspects of the theory have been passed over in the above account: the property of 'invariance', for example, and the device of the 'basic interval pattern' (or 'bip'). Nor has there been the opportunity to introduce some of the independent ideas of writers other than Forte. However, two matters must be demonstrated in conclusion: segmentation; and the presentation of set-theory analysis in readable form. This discussion has been exemplified by reference to chords, as if atonal music were written entirely in block harmonies. In practice, the separating out of pitch collections for analysis involves extraction of melodic as much as chordal formations, and indeed mixtures of these two as well as what might better be called 'aggregates' or 'clusters' of notes. This process is itself one of extreme delicacy, for the entire analysis rests on its being carried out with musical sensibility. While phrase marks, rests and the like may offer clues, the task demands much more.

In the main, set-theory analyses have been presented as explanatory text illustrated by annotated music examples – published excerpts in which segments have been boxed or circled and labelled with their prime forms. Latterly Forte has devised a diagrammatic notation which makes the analysis more immediate. Used in parallel with a passage in score, it extracts pitch collections, retaining distribution but discarding rhythmic, metric and dynamic information. These it then encloses in rectangles, circles and ovals, the result leaving space for set labels, bar numbers and other items. It also allows for separate levels of organization to be unpacked and set out in a coordinated way.

Fig.45 (pp.106–7) comes from Forte's analysis (1981) of the first of Schoenberg's Three Piano Pieces op.11. It shows bars 1–8, during which, as can be seen in (a), eight of the six-note sets (or 'hexachords') which are to be of great importance for the structure of the piece are presented, 6–Z10/Z39, 6–Z13/Z42, 6–16, 6–Z19/Z44 and 6–21, along with several of the five-note sets ('pentachords') which together with their seven-note complements are destined to be significant. Level (b) shows new ways of segmenting the musical fabric; level (c) shows in particular some of the three-note sets ('trichords') which play on the surface of the music. The recurrent hexachords and pentachords are seen as the basic harmonic vocabulary of the piece, whereas the trichords are the foreground through which the analysis must penetrate. This analysis, despite the existence of more extensive analyses of larger-scale works, might well be taken as a model for the method as a whole.

A Glossary of Analytical Terms

by William Drabkin

This glossary explicates terms used in the generally current methods of musical analysis examined in Chapter IV. The basic descriptive vocabulary of tonal and formal analysis (e.g. 'passing note', 'German 6th chord', 'cadence', 'relative major', 'ternary', 'rondo'), common to many analytical approaches, is not included; adequate definitions of such terms will normally be found in standard musical reference works. Nor are there explications of general words encountered in analytical writings (e.g. 'growth', 'sound'), in particular those whose meanings change slightly from one writer to another but should be clear from their context (e.g. 'articulation', 'transformation'). Terms of historical importance, which are no longer part of current analytical vocabularies (e.g. 'Abschnitt', 'Dessin'), are explained in Chapters I–III.

Some emphasis has been placed upon Schenkerian analysis, which depends upon a large number of concepts and techniques underpinned by a precise vocabulary, and which current writings on music suggest to be among the leading methods of tonal analysis. Basic terms employed in atonal and 12-note set theory, semiotics and proportional analysis are also defined and discussed, as are terms used by Réti, Riemann, Schoenberg, Tovey and their disciples.

Terms first used in foreign-language theoretical writings are mostly entered under the word in that language, with cross-references from their current English equivalent (e.g. 'Grundgestalt', with a cross-reference from 'Basic shape', and 'Niveau', with a cross-reference from 'Level'; such English terms appear frequently in translations of the original writings as well as in discussions orientated towards the theories they cover). Where an English equivalent has gained universal acceptance, however, the main entry is under the English word, with cross-references from the original term (e.g. 'Arpeggiation', with cross-references from 'Bassbrechung' and 'Brechung').

Anschlussmotiv (Ger.: 'annexed motif'). A term used by Riemann (see Chapter IV, §5) to denote a subsidiary phrase unit, usually two or three beats in length, placed immediately after the last strong beat of a main phrase unit. It occupies the relatively weaker beats that follow that strong beat, and serves to generate a second strong beat, equal in stress to the first, on one of those weaker beats. Thus it falls within the natural metrical structure of the main phrase; that is, it cannot itself give rise to an extension of the phrase's natural metrical pattern although it can occur within such an extension. In practice the *Anschlussmotiv* is either a reiteration of the strong beat itself or an elaborate form of feminine ending.

The former is illustrated by the theme from the Andante of Beethoven's Piano Sonata in G op.14 no.2 (ex.1; after Riemann, 1918–19, i, 86), where each of the first three two-bar groups has a two-note figure which is 'annexed' to the first beat of the second

Ex.1

bar and fills out the last part of the bar; the resultant secondary stress on the third beat is shown by the dotted bar-lines. Riemann indicated *Anschlussmotiv* here with a slur that is either open-ended at the left or appears to grow out of the slur marking the previous phrase. For an illustration of an *Anschlussmotiv* in the form of a feminine ending, see ex.26, p.140.

Anstieg (Ger.: 'ascent'). In Schenkerian analysis, a method of PROLONGATION consisting of a preliminary stepwise ascent from a note in the tonic triad to the first note of the fundamental line (URLINIE), as shown in ex.2. The term is usually translated as 'ascent'

Ex.2

or 'initial ascent', sometimes as 'space-opening motion'. As the *Anstieg* is only preparatory to the fundamental line, not part of it, it need not be diatonic (Schenker, 1935, fig.38*a* and *c*). It can even have a raised 4th, which may give the effect of a TONICIZATION of the dominant; this is illustrated by Schenker's analysis of the 'Emperor Hymn' from Haydn's String Quartet op.76 no.3 (ibid, fig.39/3; see ex.17, p.133).

Antecedent. *See* PERIOD.

Arpeggiation (Ger. *Brechung*). In Schenkerian analysis, the progression of the bass from the tonic to the dominant and back again as it spans an entire piece; the lower voice of the fundamental structure (URSATZ). Also, a method of PROLONGATION by which any voice is elaborated in the form of a broken chord: in either case a vertical configuration (i.e. an interval or chord) is made linear or (as it is sometimes said) 'horizontalized' (Ger. *horizontalisiert*).

In tonal music, harmonic interest is maintained over an entire piece by establishing the tonic key, moving away from it (usually to another key, or other keys), and returning to it by way of a dominant preparation. The arpeggiation of the bass I–V–I, which Schenker specifically referred to as *Bassbrechung* ('bass arpeggiation'), represents the establishment of the tonic, the dominant preparation and the return of the tonic. Without it, harmony would be essentially 'fixed' to the tonic and true modulation impossible (Schenker, 1935, §15).

Ausfaltung

As a method of prolongation, arpeggiation can be used in an upper line in the service of a structurally important note; in the minuet from Mozart's String Quartet in D minor K421/417*b* the first violin part rises from *d″* through *f″* to *a″* (as indicated by the set of slurs in ex.3), which is the first note of the fundamental line (URLINIE) of the movement.

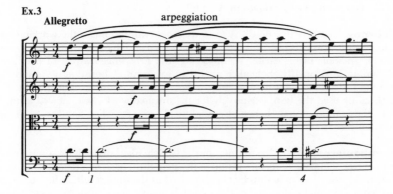

It may similarly be used to serve a harmony of structural importance (STUFE), as is illustrated by the arpeggiation *e′–c–A′* which leads to the first tonic harmony of Chopin's Study in A minor op.25 no.11 (ex.4; after Schenker, 1935, fig.100/3*c*); this example is of particular interest because of the wide spacing between the notes in the arpeggiation, and also because the arpeggiations connect notes in different voices. Sometimes an

arpeggiation appears in conjunction with another method of prolongation (especially ÜBERGREIFEN), and often it effects a transfer of register up or down an octave (*see* HÖHERLEGUNG and TIEFERLEGUNG).

It is not necessary for the arpeggiated chord to be a triad (diminished chords and 7th chords are frequently arpeggiated), nor does an arpeggiation have to be modally 'pure': in Schenker's analysis of *Auf dem Flusse* from Schubert's *Winterreise* (ibid, fig.40/2), the first note of the fundamental line is approached by the arpeggiation *e′–g♯′–b′–e″– g♮″*.

Ascending register transfer. *See* HÖHERLEGUNG.

Ascent. *See* ANSTIEG.

Ausfaltung (Ger.: 'unfolding'). In Schenkerian analysis, a method of PROLONGATION whereby the separate voices of a contrapuntal idea are amalgamated as a single line.

Ex.5

Allegro vivace

pp

Ex.5 shows the derivation by *Ausfaltung* of the opening bars of the first theme from the finale of Beethoven's Cello Sonata in A op.69.

Ausführung (Ger.: 'realization'). A term used generally to mean the working-out of the plan of a musical passage, be it the composer's own sketch or an analyst's conceptual reduction. In some of his earlier writings (e.g. the *Erläuterungsausgabe* of Beethoven's Piano Sonata in A op.101) Schenker used it to mean an elaboration of a more basic contrapuntal design – what he was later to describe as a middleground LAYER. From about 1926 he used the term exclusively for the finished work itself, viewed as the last stage in the compositional (hence also analytical) process. (For another meaning of 'realization', *see* IMPLICATION–REALIZATION.)

Auskomponierung (Ger.: 'composing-out'). In Schenkerian analysis, a term used to describe the articulation and elaboration of the structural basis of a tonal piece, namely its tonic triad; the piece may thus be characterized as the final result of the 'composing-out' or 'compositional unfolding' of this chord. The first stage in this process results in the 'fundamental structure' (URSATZ), whose upper voice or 'fundamental line' (UR-LINIE) is supported by an ARPEGGIATION of the bass. The fundamental line consists of a diatonic descent linking one of the notes of the tonic triad to its root; the bass arpeggiation, a move from the tonic to the dominant and back to the tonic, similarly outlines this triad. *Auskomponierung* is achieved at subsequent 'structural levels' (*see* LAYER) by the application of the various methods of PROLONGATION.

'Composing-out' is sometimes used more generally by Schenkerians, as well as by non-Schenkerians, to mean the working out of the implications of some special feature of the musical fabric, for example the play on C♯/D♭ in the first movement of the 'Eroica' Symphony (see J. Kerman and A. Tyson: *Beethoven*, The New Grove Composer Biography Series, ed. S. Sadie, London and New York, 1983, pp.105ff).

Auslassung (Ger.). *See* ELISION.

Background. *See* LAYER.

Basic shape. *See* GRUNDGESTALT.

Bassbrechung (Ger.). *See* ARPEGGIATION.

Brechung (Ger.). *See* ARPEGGIATION.

Cell. A term conventionally used in thematic analysis to denote a small melodic shape; a part of a musical figure or MOTIF (see ex.9, p.123). Because of their size, cells lack the identity, or recognizability, normally associated with motifs.

The distinction between motif and cell was developed in a different way by Réti in the second of his books on thematic process (1967). A cell represents the essence of a motif, a melodic contour, a neighbour-note figure or note repetition. A motif might be no more than a fleshing out of a cell, for instance the scalic filling-in of an interval. Thus the distinction between cell and motif is not one of size, but of particularity: a motif is a form of a cell as it appears in a specific piece. The analyst must then identify the few shapes

112

in the piece which govern its motivic vocabulary and, by their recurrence in a particular sequence throughout the piece, its 'thematic pattern': these are the 'prime cells' of the work. (For an illustration of Réti's method, see Chapter IV, §3 and figs.31–4, p.86.)

For the music of the 'free' atonal period (e.g. Schoenberg's works from op.11 to op.23), Perle (1962) coined the expression 'basic cell' (or 'intervallic cell') to denote a group of notes (or pitch classes: *see* PITCH-CLASS SET) from which the pitch content of a piece develops, e.g. the notes $b'–g\sharp'–g\natural'$ in op.11 no.1, the notes $a\flat–g–b\flat$ or the pitch classes F$\sharp$, A$\flat$ and A in op.23 no.1.

Combinatoriality. In the analysis of 12-note music, a property of a set which enables one part of it to be 'mapped' into another by one of the standard procedures in serial composition: transposition, inversion, retrograding. The term, borrowed from mathematics and first adopted in musical analysis by Babbitt (1955), is applied most often to unordered hexachords (the first six or last six elements of a set without regard to their internal order: *see* ORDERED SET). There are four types of hexachordal combinatoriality.
(i) Retrograde combinatoriality. A hexachord transposed by a certain interval maps into itself (trivially, all hexachords are retrogradally combinatorial under transposition by 0).
(ii) Retrograde inversional combinatoriality. The inversion of a hexachord, transposed by a certain interval, maps into itself ([0, 1, 3, 4, 6, 7] inverts to [0, 11, 9, 8, 6, 5] which, when transposed by 7, yields [7, 6, 4, 3, 1, 0]).
(iii) Prime combinatoriality. A hexachord transposed by a certain interval maps into its complement ([0, 1, 3, 4, 5, 8] transposed by 6 yields [6, 7, 9, 10, 11, 2]).
(iv) Inversional combinatoriality. The inversion of a hexachord, when transposed by a certain interval, maps into its complement ([0, 1, 3, 5, 7, 9] inverts to [0, 11, 9, 7, 5, 3] which, when transposed by 11, yields [11, 10, 8, 6, 4, 2]).
Certain hexachords possess all four forms of combinatoriality: these are said to be 'all-combinatorial'.

Complement. A term used in set-theory analysis to denote the set consisting of all pitch classes not in a given PITCH-CLASS SET; the former set is said to be the complement of the latter. Complementation is always taken with respect to a 'universal set' which, by convention, consists of the 12 pitch classes. Thus, for example, the complement of [0, 2, 6] is [1, 3, 4, 5, 7, 8, 9, 10, 11].

The set and its complement, when presented in their prime forms, will appear to have elements in common, since a PRIME FORM is always reckoned from 0. The prime form of the complement of [0, 2, 6], which is [0, 1, 2, 3, 4, 6, 7, 8, 10], actually includes the original set. Some six-element pitch-class sets, such as [0, 1, 2, 3, 4, 5] (the 'chromatic scale') and [0, 2, 4, 6, 8, 10] (the 'whole-tone scale'), are self-complementary: that is, the prime forms of these sets and their respective complements are identical.

Complex, set. *See* SET COMPLEX.

Composing-out. *See* AUSKOMPONIERUNG.

Consequent. *See* PERIOD.

Coupling. *See* KOPPELUNG.

Degree. *See* STUFE.

Descending register transfer. *See* TIEFERLEGUNG.

Developing variation. A term used by Schoenberg to describe the generation of material from a single idea or 'basic shape' (*see* GRUNDGESTALT), especially in tonal music after the period of Baroque polyphony. In that earlier period, musical development was achieved not so much by the reworking of ideas as by their being placed in new contexts (such as transposition, and inversion of voices in a contrapuntal texture). But between about 1750 and 1900, a period in which polyphony was conceived less in strictly contrapuntal terms, composers were obliged to develop musical material from their basic idea by the addition or deletion of material, and by alterations in rhythm, interval and contour, and harmony. Though Schoenberg did not specifically state that changes in dynamics, articulation and orchestration have a role to play in this process, it is possible that they may do so.

The principle of developing variation is frequently invoked by Schoenberg and others in connection with Brahms, whose development of musical material is freer and less symmetrical than, for instance, that of Wagner, whom Schoenberg saw as relying more heavily on literal repetition and sequence. His classic statements on, and illustrations of, developing variation in Brahms appear in the essays 'Criteria for the Evaluation of Music' and 'Brahms the Progressive' (both in Schoenberg, 1975), and have provided the cornerstone for further work in this area of analytical inquiry (see especially Frisch, 1984).

Diminution. In the terminology of Renaissance and Baroque performing practice (see Chapter II, §1), a type of ornamental variation. The term was used by Schenker in a general sense to denote the elaboration of musical material by methods of PROLONGA-TION to arrive at the contents of some LAYER of a piece; in his definitive statement he associated the term specifically with the foreground layer (1935, §§251–66). He viewed the process as more 'compositional' than 'analytical' because the complete piece is not the starting-point of the investigation but its end product. *See also* REDUCTION (i).

Divider. *See* TEILER.

Elision [Auslassung] (Ger.). In Riemann's theory of phrase structure (see Chapter IV, §5), the technique by which a regular phrase construction, consisting of alternating weak and strong elements, is made asymmetrical, either by the omission of one of the weak elements or by the overlapping of strong and weak elements of neighbouring constructions. Riemann normally used *Elision* in the former sense, to mean the suppression of the initial, unstressed 'growth' phase of a unit (e.g. the first element of a one-bar motif (*Taktmotiv*), the first motif of a two-bar group (*Zweitaktgruppe*)), which, when considered together with the next unit, results in a stress pattern of strong–weak–strong. The minuet of Mozart's String Quintet in G minor K516 provides an example (see fig.36, p.91). The first three three-bar phrases are understood as compressed four-bar units, the first bar of each having been omitted. This is indicated by the 'bar numbers' parenthesized below the violin part – '(2)', '(4)', '(6)', '(8)' and so on – from which the omission of '(1)' and '(5)' can be inferred.

In English-language writings, the word 'elision' generally approximates to Riemann's secondary meaning, indicating the superposition of the end of one phrase over the beginning of the next, for which Riemann preferred the term VERSCHRÄNKUNG.

Empty set. *See* INVARIANT SUBSET.

Equivalence (i). In the terminology of set theory, the property by which pitch-class sets can be reduced to the same form (*see* PITCH-CLASS SET). Two sets are 'transpositionally equivalent' if they are reducible to the same PRIME FORM (*see also* NORMAL ORDER). The sets representing *B–f–a* and *B♭–c″–f♯♯′* are transpositionally equivalent, as is demonstrated below:

	B–f–a	*B♭–c″–f♯*
initial order	[11,5,9]	[10,0,6]
ascending numerical order	[5,9,11]	[0,6,10]
normal order	[5,9,11]	[6,10,0]
prime form	[0,4,6]	[0,4,6]

Two sets are 'inversionally equivalent' if one set and the intervallic inversion of the other are reducible to the same prime form. In atonal music theory, inversion is taken with respect to the octave: 0 inverts to itself, 1 inverts to 11, 2 inverts to 10, and so on. The sets representing *B–f–g* and *B ♭–c″–f♯′* can be shown to be inversionally equivalent:

	B–f–g	*B♭–c″–f♯*
initial order	[11,5,7]	[10,0,6]
inversion of one set		[2,0,6]
ascending numerical order	[5,7,11]	[0,2,6]
normal order	[5,7,11]	[0,2,6]
prime form	[0,2,6,]	[0,2,6]

Equivalence (ii). In musical semiotics, identity with respect to function or context. Units that are materially dissimilar may nevertheless be 'equivalent' by virtue of always occupying the same context, for instance by being followed by the same unit (see Chapter IV, §7 and fig.39, p.96). The set of all elements defined as equivalent is said to form an 'equivalence class' (*see also* NIVEAU). Similarity of material (e.g. intervallic succession, rhythmic shape) or even musical identity is not in itself sufficient grounds for assigning the property of equivalence, but plays an important role in determining the initial partitioning (called SEGMENTATION) of the piece into units. Equivalence is sometimes used to define membership of a paradigm (*see* PARADIGMATIC AXIS), hence identity of syntactic function.

Esthésique (Fr.). *See* NIVEAU.

Fibonacci series. The sequence of whole numbers in which each element is the sum of the two previous elements, i.e. 0, 1, 1, 2, 3, 5, 8, 13, 21 and so on. The series, named after the 13th-century mathematician Leonardo of Pisa (nicknamed 'Fibonacci'), is important in the analysis of spatial proportions in music (*see* GOLDEN SECTION).

Figure. *See* MOTIF.

Foreground. *See* LAYER.

Function. A term used variously in mathematics, computing, psychology and other disciplines to denote a quantity or process which gives values to variables when operated upon them; a role within a structure. It has been adopted by musical analysts in a number of ways.

In Riemann's harmonic theory, function (Ger. *Funktion*) denotes the relationship of a chord to its tonal centre; this relationship is defined in terms solely of subdominant (S), dominant (D) and tonic (T), and chord progressions are viewed as combinations of these functions in various guises. Thus, for example, the chord of the supertonic is seen as having the function of subdominant; the supertonic is said to be the 'representative' (*Stellvertreter*) of the subdominant in such a case. In this, Riemann's theory differs sharply from Schenker's concept of Stufe and also from Schoenberg's harmonic theory. For Schoenberg (1954), structural function deals always with progressions, not with chords, and those progressions are considered in terms of their roots; function gives a sense of direction to a progression and determines its role within the scheme of regions which make up monotonality.

Function is central to Berry's analytical theory (1976), in which the term is used to denote the role of an event or succession in a structure, in particular as contributing to the expressive significance of a piece: tonal and linear functions may be ascribed to pitch; impulse and metric functions to rhythm; multiple functions to other events (which might thereby become functionally ambiguous).

In Keller's functional analysis (*MR*, 1957; 1985) the word has no role as an analytical term, but is used by analogy with physiology as it concerns 'the unifying "functions" of the living organism'.

Fundamental line. *See* Urlinie.

Fundamental structure. *See* Ursatz.

Gap-filling. A technique used in the process of Implication–Realization.

Generalauftakt (Ger.: 'general upbeat'). A term used by Riemann (see Chapter IV, §5) to denote a special category of upbeat that occurs at the beginning of a formal unit of two, four or eight bars (called *Zweitaktgruppe*, *Halbsatz* and *Periode*, respectively). Instead of being an upbeat merely to the first bar (*Taktmotiv*), it takes on the larger-scale function of an upbeat to the formal unit as a whole. The *Generalauftakt* is often marked *rallentando* or *ritenuto*, the return to a stricter tempo thereby tending to separate it from the first bar of the ensuing formal unit. In his analyses and 'phrase-structure editions' Riemann marked the *Generalauftakt* with a slur, open-ended at the right and followed by a dotted bar-line, as shown in his edition of Chopin's Nocturne in E♭ op.9 no.2 (ex.6; from Riemann and Fuchs, 1890, p.69); the local upbeat to the first bar of the new phrase is still present but has been compressed into a group of grace notes.

Ex.6

Golden section. A term used in analytic inquiry concerned with the relative lengths of sections in a musical work, and with the temporal distances between significant events in the work; this type of inquiry is commonly known as 'proportional analysis' (see Chapter III, §5). The golden section is, by definition, the division of a distance into two parts in such a way that the ratio of the smaller distance to the larger is the same as that of the larger to the whole. It is usually expressed as the ratio of the smaller distance to the larger, which can be determined algebraically by calculating for x in the equation: $\frac{x}{(1-x)} = \frac{1}{x}$. This yields a single positive value for x of $\frac{(\sqrt{5}-1)}{2}$, an irrational number which approximates to 0·618034.

In music, distance can be measured in a number of ways, even vertically (i.e. as the 'interval' between pitches in a chord, reckoned in semitones). But in most discussions of proportion in music, the golden section is applied to the time dimension, by counting the number of bars (or beats), or by reckoning the timings of performances, recorded or 'ideal' (the latter would take account of different bar lengths and metronomic markings).

It can be shown that the ratio of successive elements in a sequence of whole numbers formed by adding the previous two numbers together (e.g. the FIBONACCI SERIES) closely approximates to the golden section: that is, ratios such as 34:55, 89:144 and 144:233 (all numbers that occur in the Fibonacci series) are very close in value to 0·618034. This property makes it sensible for analysts to count bars, beats or smaller time values when ascertaining the existence of golden sections in music.

Group (Ger. *Gruppe*). In discussions of Classical sonata form and sonata-related forms, a term used for the totality of musical material by which a key centre in the exposition (or recapitulation) is established or affirmed, thus 'first group', 'second group'. The term *Gruppe* was used by Lobe (1850) and by other German writers regularly thereafter. For English analytical terminology, Tovey strongly advocated 'group' in place of 'subject' on the grounds that the standard expressions used in describing sonata forms ('first subject' and 'second subject') did not adequately reflect the variety of approach taken by Classical composers in the number and nature of the musical ideas contained in their works. Tovey understood his 'first group' and 'second group' as translations of the German *Hauptsatz* and *Seitensatz*, terms which had first been used by Marx (1837–47, iii); he thereby avoided misunderstandings that might otherwise have arisen in the analysis of a sonata movement whose exposition contains more than two distinct thematic ideas (as is typical of Mozart and Beethoven), or which uses the same musical idea as the starting-point for each part (Haydn's 'monothematicism'), or which uses the initial idea to round off the exposition.

Some writers refer to a 'closing group', i.e. that part of the exposition (repeated in the recapitulation) which allows time for the dissipation of harmonic tension established between the first and second groups; others (including Tovey) call it a 'cadence-theme', or 'cadence-phrase', and assign it a concluding place in the second group.

Grundgestalt (Ger.: 'basic shape'). A term originating with Schoenberg and taken up by other writers, such as Epstein (1979) and Frisch (1984), to denote the basic musical idea of a piece, the phrase which contains its essential material; the 'first creative thought' from which everything in the piece can be derived. This basic shape, normally two to three bars long, is made up of smaller elements called 'motifs', each containing features of interval and rhythm which 'are combined to produce a memorable shape or contour which usually implies an inherent harmony' (Schoenberg, 1967, p.8). All other motifs in the piece are ultimately referable to those in the basic shape. On the other side is the 'theme', a larger stretch of musical material built from the combination of the basic shape with repetitions, variants or variations of it (*see* PERIOD and SENTENCE).

Like the Schenkerian 'fundamental structure' (URSATZ), Schoenberg's 'basic shape' is significant for the overall design of a musical work, hence his emphasis of the principle 'the construction of the beginning determines the construction of the continuation' (ibid, pp.21 and 27). But in contrast to the fundamental structure, which can be inferred only by applying sophisticated techniques of reduction to a piece of music (*see* REDUCTION (ii)) and which, in any of its manifestations, is common to a large number of tonal pieces, the basic shape is actually perceived as part of the surface of a piece, and is unique to that piece.

Hexachord. In atonal theory, a Pitch-class set consisting of six elements; in the analysis of 12-note music in particular, the first six or last six elements of the basic set, considered as an unordered subset, from which the property of Combinatoriality can be determined. *See also* Z-relation.

Hintergrund (Ger.: 'background'). *See* Layer.

Höherlegung (Ger.). In Schenkerian analysis, the raising of a line into a higher octave, either by direct leap or in connection with one or more other methods of Prolongation (such as Arpeggiation and Übergreifen). Often it serves to set off one section of a piece from another; in the first movement of Mozart's Sonata in C k545, for instance, the second group begins on *d'''*, which lies an octave higher than the previous *d''* in bar 12 and which registrally governs the upper line in the second group (ex.7; after Schenker,

Ex.7

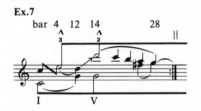

1935, fig.47/1). *Höherlegung* is usually rendered in English as 'ascending register transfer' or (less precisely) as 'register transfer' or 'octave transfer', terms that also apply to Tieferlegung. *See also* Koppelung.

Implication–realization. A pair of concepts brought together as a relational principle by Narmour (1977), extending the work of L. B. Meyer (1973) and in opposition to Schenkerian analysis. According to this principle, musical structure is understood in terms of initial material suggesting one or more possible continuations, rather than following some pre-ordained course determined ultimately by a set of immutable tonal laws (as embodied, for instance, by the Schenkerian Ursatz). Thus musical material 'implies' continuation in one or more ways. If these implications are to some extent 'realized', then some 'closure' is achieved. Implication and realization may take place over shorter or longer stretches of music. An implication may be only partly realized by the immediate continuation of the initial material; or the preliminary realization may set up new implications.

As the implication–realization model was set up as an alternative to the Schenkerian concepts of Prolongation and 'composing-out' (*see* Auskomponierung), the techniques first developed to illustrate it have been intended to highlight the differences between the two analytical approaches; hence they concentrate on two matters fundamental to the Schenkerian view of music, linear progression (*see* Zug) and Arpeggiation. According to Narmour, conjunct lines imply continuation in the same direction; in the key of C, for instance, the succession *e''–f''* implies a continuation to *g''* (for Schenker the return to *e''*, to form a neighbour-note figure, would have been just as plausible). Leaps similarly suggest triadic completion: for example, *g–b* implies a continuation to *d'*.

'Gap-filling', an important technique used in the implication–realization process, shows how arpeggiation and linear continuity are often interdependent: an initial leap implies the filling of the space between the boundary notes by linear movement in the opposite direction. Narmour (1977, ex.40) analysed the opening bars of the melody of

118

Beethoven's Bagatelle op.119 no.1 (see ex.8*a*), showing linear implication and realization at work on different levels; gap-filling is present on different levels and is seen both partly and fully achieved (see ex.8*b*, where 'NT' stands for 'neighbour tone'). At the highest level, the triadic movements *d″–f″* and *f″–d″* are aiming at *b♭″* and *b♭′*, respectively; these implications are not shown in the analysis, though one might understand subsequent events, such as the *b♭″* in bar 8 (thrown into relief by the striking harmonies supporting it: see ex.8*c*) and the *b♭′* in the last bar of the piece, as realizing these implications and thus providing closure.

Inclusion. A relation between two sets (*see* Pitch-class set) whereby either set is a Subset of the other.

Initial ascent. *See* Anstieg.

Interruption. *See* Unterbrechung.

119

Interval class. In the terminology of set theory, the class of all intervals equivalent to a given interval by octave complementation or compounding. In traditional terminology a minor 3rd is said to be equivalent to a major 6th, a minor 10th and so on; in integer terms, 3, 9 and 15 are said to belong to the same interval class. Interval classes are denoted by the whole number corresponding to the number of semitones contained by the smallest interval in that class: 0 = unison, octave etc; 1 = 1 semitone (minor 2nd, major 7th, minor 9th etc); 2 = 2 semitones (major 2nd, minor 7th etc); and so on. Augmented intervals are similarly reckoned in semitones: thus the diminished 4th belongs to the interval class 4, the augmented octave and diminished octave both belong to the interval class 1. Interval class is often referred to in the abbreviated form 'ic'.

Interval vector. In the terminology of set theory, a succession of digits describing the total interval content of a PITCH-CLASS SET, interval content being determined by measuring the interval between every pair of elements in the set and by adding up the number of occurrences of each INTERVAL CLASS. For the set [0,2,6], the interval content is computed from the following subtractions: 2 − 0 = 2; 6 − 0 = 6; 6 − 2 = 4. Thus the interval classes 2, 4 and 6 each occur once, the intervals 1, 3 and 5 do not occur at all.

To show the number of occurrences of each interval (or its non-occurrence), the interval vector is written as a succession of six digits enclosed in square brackets, whose first digit represents the number of times the interval 1 occurs, the second digit the number of occurrences of the interval 2 and so on. Thus the interval vector for [0,2,6] is [010101]. (Interval vectors are calculated only for sets containing different elements, i.e. without pitch-class repetitions. The interval class 0, which represents the unison (octave etc), does not appear and is not shown in the vector.)

The interval vector is not necessarily unique to a given pitch-class set. For instance, the sets [0,1,3,7] and [0,2,5,6] both have the interval vector [111111], as is demonstrated in Table 2:

TABLE 2

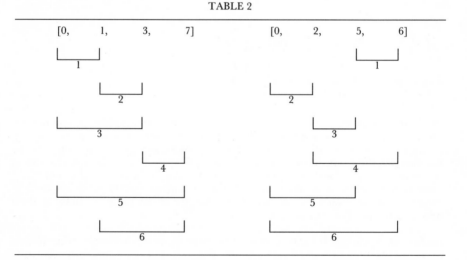

Such sets, which always occur in pairs, are said to be 'Z-related' (*see* Z-RELATION).

Invariant pitch class. In the terminology of set theory, a pitch class common to two

120

or more sets (*see* PITCH-CLASS SET). In mathematical terms, an 'invariant' element is one that belongs to the 'intersection' of those sets.

Invariant subset. The elements of a PITCH-CLASS SET that remain unchanged by an operation performed on that set, e.g. transposition or inversion. If the set [0,2,6] is transposed by 2, yielding [2,4,8], the invariant subset consists of the single element [2]. If it is transposed by 6, yielding [6,8,12] (which is simplified to [6,8,0]), the invariant subset consists of two elements, [0,6]. If it is transposed by 3, yielding [3,5,9], the invariant subset consists of no elements; this is called the 'empty set' or 'null set' (often written as [Φ]).

Sets also have invariants under inversion, or inversion followed by transposition. If, for instance, the set [0,2,6] is inverted, yielding [0,10,6], the invariant subset resulting from this operation contains two elements, [0,6]. If it is inverted and then transposed by 2, yielding [2,0,8], the invariant subset is a different two-element set, [0,2].

In computing transpositional and inversional invariance, pitch-class sets are taken as unordered, e.g. [2,0,8] and [0,2,8] are the 'same' set.

K. The symbol normally used for a SET COMPLEX; 'Kh' denotes the subcomplex.

Koppelung (Ger.: 'coupling'). In Schenkerian analysis, a method of PROLONGATION involving the linking of two registers separated by one or more octaves; hence also *Oktavkoppelung*. The two registers are not sounded simultaneously, but are 'coupled' by movement from one to another and back again. At a primary structural level, coupling reinforces movement in the prevailing or 'obligatory' register (OBLIGATE LAGE) of either the upper line or (rarely) the bass of the fundamental structure (URSATZ); coupling in the upper line is illustrated by Schenker's analysis of the first prelude from book 1 of Bach's *Das wohltemperirte Clavier* (Schenker, 1935, fig.49/1; see ex.10c, p.124). At later levels, i.e. towards the musical foreground, it enables the composer to abandon a register while fulfilling some other function elsewhere. A favourite example of Schenker's was the last six bars (bars 98–103) of the slow movement of Beethoven's Piano Sonata in D minor op.31 no.2: the *B♭′* at the beginning of this passage, which is picked up by the *B♭* at the end, is coupled to the *B♭* and *b♭′* in bars 100–102, which support a more delicate contrapuntal design (ibid, fig.108/2).

As *Koppelung* involves the linking of octave registers, it may be thought of as a synthesis of two closely related methods of prolongation, HÖHERLEGUNG and TIEFERLEGUNG, the transfer of a line into a higher or lower octave, respectively.

Layer [level, structural level] (Ger. *Schicht*). In Schenkerian analysis, one of a set of polyphonic representations of a tonal piece or movement in which only some of the harmonic and/or contrapuntal content of the piece is given; layers are hierarchical, so that each layer includes, and elaborates on, the content of the preceding one until the final layer – represented by the score of the piece itself – is reached.

The starting-point of a piece, working downwards in a typical Schenkerian graph, is called the background (Ger. *Hintergrund*) and is represented by the fundamental structure or URSATZ: this comprises the fundamental linear descent to the first note of the tonic triad (URLINIE), supported by the harmonic progression from the tonic to the dominant and back to the tonic, called the bass ARPEGGIATION. The layer whose representation most resembles the score of the piece itself, lacking only some detail, is called the foreground (Ger. *Vordergrund*); this is the only layer before the score itself that represents the rhythm and thus corresponds to the piece bar for bar. Between the background and the foreground lies the middleground (Ger. *Mittelgrund*), which is made up of one or more layers, often numbered '1. Schicht' (first layer), '2. Schicht' etc; the number of middleground layers depends upon the complexity of the piece and upon the detail of the analysis.

The analytical process is a reductive one, in which the piece is simplified to yield the foreground layer, and the foreground is in turn simplified to yield the middleground layers and ultimately the *Ursatz* (*see* REDUCTION (i)). But since analysis was, for Schenker, essentially the explanation of composition, he presented and discussed the layers in reverse order of their derivation, i.e. beginning with the *Ursatz*. In explaining the contents of a subsequent layer, it would then be necessary to illustrate with musical notation (or describe in words) the various methods of PROLONGATION used to achieve greater harmonic and contrapuntal complexity in the piece. The number of new prolongations increases as one approaches the foreground; for this reason the musical representation of the foreground and the accompanying verbal commentary (if present) are the longest. Most of Schenker's analyses end with some remarks on the piece itself, the layer beyond the foreground; Schenker called this the AUSFÜHRUNG ('realization').

For very short pieces, it is possible to align all the analytical layers vertically, so that the methods of prolongation used to get from one layer to the next may be conveniently studied. For pieces of moderate length, however, it is more practical for the foreground layer to be presented as a separate graph. (For examples of layer analyses, see figs.21–2, pp.50–51, and figs.29–30, pp.82–3.)

Level. *See* LAYER and NIVEAU.

Linear progression. *See* ZUG.

Liquidation. *See* REDUCTION (ii).

Middleground (Ger. *Mittelgrund*). *See* LAYER.

Monotonality. A term used by Schoenberg to denote the basic key of a piece of music. It could be argued that 'monotonality' means nothing more than Tovey's expression 'home key'; but whereas conventional harmonic analysis admits modulations to related or remote keys, for Schoenberg 'every digression from that tonic is still within the tonality, whether directly or indirectly, closely or remotely related' (1954, p.19). That is, instead of describing the progression to E♭ major in the exposition of a C minor sonata movement as 'modulation to the relative major', Schoenberg would have spoken of a move to the 'mediant region' (*see* REGION). Viewed in this way, Schoenberg's regions are, in principle, like Schenker's *Stufen* (*see* STUFE) in the background and middleground layers of a composition: a region is always relatable to the original tonality, as every harmonic deviation is 'subordinate to the central power of a tonic' (ibid).

Motif [motive] (Ger. *Motiv*). A term used in a variety of senses in thematic and phrase-structure analysis (see Chapter II, §2). It usually denotes a short utterance that retains its identity as a musical idea as it often 'appears in a characteristic and impressive manner at the beginning of a piece' (Schoenberg, 1967, p.8; *see also* GRUNDGESTALT and REDUCTION (ii)). It is usually thought of in melodic terms, and it is this conception that is sometimes rendered as 'figure'. Another term often encountered in the context of the melodic motif is CELL, which connotes a still smaller unit of melody, as in the opening theme of Beethoven's Piano Sonata in E op.109 (ex.9).

The rhythmic motif may be defined by analogy with the melodic type: a short, characteristic sequence of accented and unaccented (or short and long) articulations,

Ex.9

possibly including rests. Rhythmic motifs may be closely allied to melodic ideas (as in the first movement of Beethoven's Fifth Symphony), or they may exist as rhythmic ideas in themselves, with little melodic significance, for instance the Nibelungs' 'hammering' motif in the third scene of *Das Rheingold*. Harmonies or harmonic patterns, though seldom perceived independently of rhythmic figures or melodic contours, may nevertheless contribute powerfully to the perception of motifs, as they often do in the leitmotif of Wagnerian music drama.

In Riemann's theory of rhythm (see Chapter IV, §5), motif can take on a purely metric connotation: symmetry of phrase structure enables a four-bar phrase (Ger. *Halbsatz*) to be divided into two two-bar members (Ger. *Zweitaktgruppe*) and for each of these to be further divided into two 'motifs', each a bar long (Ger. *Motiv*, or *Taktmotiv*).

Motion from an inner voice. *See* UNTERGREIFEN.

Nexus set. *See* SET COMPLEX.

Niveau (Fr.: 'level'). A term used in musical semiotics. In the writings of Ruwet, it denotes each of a succession of processes of SEGMENTATION carried out on a piece. 'Niveau I' represents a first segmentation, based on preliminary observations of identity and difference. The elements obtained by this process are then further divided, yielding progressively smaller units at 'niveau II', perhaps 'niveau III' and so on. It is here that musically dissimilar units may nevertheless be deemed to have a common function and may thus be designated 'equivalent' (*see* EQUIVALENCE (ii)); the recognition of equivalence, in turn, enables the analyst to observe large-scale relations in the music and thus to arrive at segmentation on a higher level ('niveau 0').

Molino and Nattiez have used the term *niveau neutre* ('neutral level') to describe the level at which a work is understood on its own terms, without historical or interpretative conceptions. The *niveau neutre* occupies a central position among the various ways in which a work can be comprehended. It contrasts on the one hand with the *poiétique*, the realm of genesis in which historical, social and compositional considerations are taken into account (e.g. the prevailing political conditions, the composer's stylistic environment and musical education, the performers for whom the work was originally written, the written record of sketching and drafting); and on the other hand with the *esthésique*, the realm of reception in which the perception and judgment of a work by the individual may be taken into account, enabling the analyst to achieve a synthesis of his own perceptions with those of others (performances, critiques, other analyses, even transcriptions in the case of non-notated works).

Normal order [normal form]. In the terminology of set theory, that order of a PITCH-CLASS SET in which the interval between the first and last elements is the smallest possible. The normal order of the pitch-class set representing $B\flat$–c''–$f\sharp''$, [10,0,6,], for example, is determined by placing the elements in ascending numerical order, i.e. [0,6,10]; they are then 'rotated', i.e. rearranged with the first element placed at the end, yielding [0,6,10] → [6,10,0] → [10,0,6]. (To simplify the required calculations, 12 is added to each rotated element: [0,6,10] → [6,10,12] → [10,12,18].) For these permutations the intervals between the first and last elements are, respectively, 10, 6 and 8: thus the interval is smallest for [6,10,12] or, properly written, [6,10,0].

Sometimes a pitch-class set will have more than one normal order. The set representing the notes C–E–F–A♭, for instance, has normal orders [0,4,5,8] and [4,5,8,0], as the interval between the first and last elements is in both instances 8. In such cases the 'best normal order' is usually taken to be the one for which the interval between the first and second elements is the smallest; in the present example, this is [4,5,8,0].

Null set. *See* INVARIANT SUBSET.

Obligate Lage (Ger.: 'obligatory register'). In Schenkerian analysis, the register in which the fundamental line (URLINIE) makes its descent to the tonic from the 3rd, 5th or octave above. The term is sometimes also applied to the lower part of the fundamental structure, which presents the bass ARPEGGIATION.

'Obligatory register' is most often invoked in connection with a general principle (which Schenker called the 'Gesetz der obligaten Lage') which binds every primary elaboration (PROLONGATION) of the fundamental line and bass arpeggiation to the registers in which they unfold, and every secondary or subsequent prolongation to the respective register of the prolongation from which it is derived. The techniques most often encountered in the 'freeing' of lines from their obligatory registers involve the principle of octave transfer: HÖHERLEGUNG, the raising of a line into a higher octave; TIEFERLEGUNG, the lowering of a line by one or more octaves; and KOPPELUNG, the joining of two lines that are one or more octaves apart. In the first prelude from book 1 of Bach's *Das wohltemperirte Clavier*, for instance, the register of the fundamental line is determined by the *e″* established in bars 1–4 (ex.10*a*). This *e″* is brought down an octave to *e′* (bar 19), which resolves to *d′* (bar 24); the *d′* is then brought back to the higher octave (*d″* in bar 34) so that the last two bars of the prelude (ex.10*b*) can complete the descent of the fundamental line in its original, 'obligatory' register. The *Koppelung e″–e′/d′–d″* (ex.10*c*; after Schenker, 1935, fig.49/1, which shows the entire prelude at a higher level) thus serves to reinforce this register, as well as providing expansion in the lower octave.

Ex.10
(a) outline of bars 1–4   (b) bars 34–5

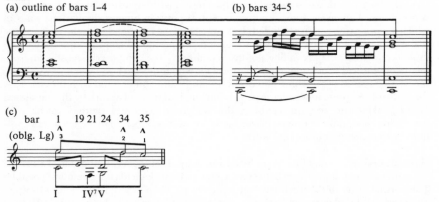

(c)   bar   1   19 21 24 34 35

Schenker argued that the law of obligatory register applied to both the fundamental line and the bass arpeggiation; but subsequent writings about long-range registral coherence both by Schenkerians (Oster, 1961) and non-Schenkerians (Rosen, 1971, pp.34f and 349), have mainly been concerned with examples of 'melodic' connections.

Paradigmatic axis

Octave transfer. In Schenkerian analysis, the raising of a line into a higher octave (*see* HÖHERLEGUNG) or the lowering of a line by one or more octaves (*see* TIEFERLEGUNG). *See also* KOPPELUNG.

Ordered set. A PITCH-CLASS SET in which the order of the integers (whole numbers) representing the pitch classes is significant. For example, if a set is intended to represent the succession of pitch classes in a single voice part (e.g. a 'melody'), then the set is ordered. Where the order of the pitch classes is of no significance, the set is said to be 'unordered'. The concept of unordered set allows analysts to compare sets more easily by rearranging the elements in them, for instance by placing them in NORMAL ORDER.

Overlapping. *See* ÜBERGREIFEN.

Paradigmatic axis. A term borrowed from linguistics, applied in musical semiotics; it signifies a notional vertical line along which a number of musical units that serve the same function within a given structure are assembled. These units are then said to be 'paradigmatically equivalent'. That relationship is, in practice, defined by the traits which successive elements have in common. In a semiotic layout the units belonging to a paradigm are aligned in their order of occurrence within the structure, so that the repetition and transformation of units may conveniently be studied. Nattiez (*Fondements*, 1975, p.334) analysed the opening bars of Debussy's *Syrinx* (ex.11: a key signature of five flats is understood), identifying 13 distinct units, most of which consist of three or four notes. In classifying these units according to their intervallic traits, he arrived at four

Ex.11

125

main paradigms for this part of the piece:

- A as represented by unit 1, a descending semitone followed by an ascending tone;
- B as represented by unit 3, a four-note descending figure comprising the intervals of semitone, semitone, augmented 2nd;
- C as represented by unit 4, an ascending tone followed by a descending semitone;
- D as represented by unit 7, a descending diminished 4th followed by an ascending semitone.

In this analysis, rhythmic shape is a much less significant factor than melodic contour in the SEGMENTATION of the musical line into units: units 1, 4 and 7 share the rhythm of dotted quaver plus two demisemiquavers, yet they are assigned to different paradigms; conversely, units 7, 8 and 9 are rhythmically different, but are assigned to the same paradigm by virtue of their melodic contour.

Units that meet some, but not all, of the criteria for membership in a paradigm are placed off-centre in relation to the column used for that paradigm; thus unit 10, whose last three notes correspond to the falling shape of unit 3, is placed off-centre in the column for Paradigm B.

In some cases, the analysis may suggest other possible groupings of notes to form units. Thus, for instance, Nattiez divided the third bar of *Syrinx* into a three-note figure (unit 4) plus a held $b\flat''$ (unit 5); alternatively, the entire bar could be regarded as the single unit 6. Similarly, the six notes making up units 8 and 9 may be regrouped as a single note plus a five-note figure (units 11 and 12, respectively).

Period. In phrase-structure and formal analysis (see Chapter II, §2), a term used to describe a section of a musical work (usually a tonal piece from after the era of Baroque polyphony) that makes a complete thematic and harmonic statement. Neither German theorists of the Classical era nor modern analysts agree on a definition or set of definitions for 'period' (Ger. *Periode*) or such related terms as 'sentence' (Ger. *Satz*) and 'phrase' (Ger. *Abschnitt, Einschnitt, Rhythmus* etc); even individual authors are sometimes inconsistent. That such theorists as Sulzer (1771–4) and Koch (*Musikalisches Lexikon*, 1802) actually complained of a lack of uniformity in nomenclature might perhaps be taken as evidence that Classical phraseology and thematic construction defy straightforward definition.

Schoenberg (1967) distinguished 'period' from 'sentence' in the following way: a sentence begins with a short 'motif' which is immediately repeated (transposition or slight variation is permitted) before the music is continued further (see ex.13, p.129); thus sentence construction emphasizes development from a single starting-point. The period, on the other hand, consists of two balanced phrases, called 'antecedent' and 'consequent', each of which begins with a statement of the opening motif. Thus the first eight bars of Mozart's Piano Sonata in A K331/300*i* constitute a classic example of a period. Schoenberg did not require that a period begin and end in the same tonal area: in his analysis of the first part of the theme from the variation movement of Mozart's Piano Sonata in D K284/205*b* (1967, ex.45*f*) the perfect cadence on the dominant (A major) marks the end of a period.

Koch (1782–93) also used the term *Hauptperiode* for each of the sections in a large-scale form (e.g. exposition, development and recapitulation in sonata form). Wagner's conscious extension of the concept of period to large-scale musical and dramatic units led Lorenz (1924–33) to his monumental analyses of the mature stage works (see Chapter III, §2).

Pitch-class set. A collection of pitch classes, a pitch class being the name given to all notes of the same pitch irrespective of the octave register in which they are written or sounded. In analysing atonal music with the aid of set theory, it is appropriate to regard enharmonically equivalent notes as identical (thus all F♯s and G♭s belong to the same pitch class) and to represent pitch classes not by their traditional letter names – C, C♯/D♭ etc – but by integers, i.e. whole numbers. By general agreement C = 0, C♯/D♭ = 1 and so on up to B/C♭ = 11. Thus, for example, the pitch-class set representing the succession of notes B♭–c″–f♯′ is [10,0,6]. The term is often used in the abbreviated form 'pc set'. *See also* ORDERED SET.

Poiétique (Fr.). *See* NIVEAU.

Prime cell. *See* CELL.

Prime form. In the terminology of set theory, and as a provisional definition, the NORMAL ORDER (or 'best normal order') of a PITCH-CLASS SET transposed so that its first element is 0. (Transposing a pitch-class set involves adding the same integer to each of its elements and then simplifying the result by subtracting 12 from all numbers larger than 11.) The prime form of the set representing B♭–c″–f♯′, [10,0,6], for example, is calculated first by arranging the elements in ascending numerical order: [0,6,10]; finding the normal order: [6,10,0]; and, in this case, adding 6 to each element: [12,16,6] or simply [0,4,6].

At this point an additional convention is introduced. As 'inversionally equivalent' pitch-class sets are considered to be very closely related to one another (*see* EQUIVALENCE (i)), theorists identify them with one another by assigning them to the same prime form. This requires finding a 'better' prime form for a set and its inversion. For example the prime form of [10,0,6] is [0,4,6]; the prime form of its inversion is [0,2,6]. The interval between the first and last elements is the same for both sets; but the set [0,2,6] is preferred because the interval between the first two elements is smaller. And for practical purposes, [0,2,6] is called the 'prime form' of the sets representing B♭–c″–f♯′ and all other sets that are transpositionally or inversionally equivalent to it.

Progression, linear. *See* ZUG.

Prolongation. In Schenkerian analysis, the generation of the substance of a tonal piece by the linear elaboration of its fundamental structure (URSATZ). Methods of prolongation may be applied to the upper voice or to the bass, or to one of the middle voices arising from early stages of elaboration; they may also link a middle voice to an outer one, or the two outer voices to each other.

In the main Allegro theme of the first movement of Haydn's Symphony no.104 in D, the fundamental structure (ex.12*a*, overleaf) is 'prolonged' by an interruption (UNTERBRECHUNG) after the arrival of $\hat{2}$ on the dominant, which necessitates a return of the opening $\hat{3}$ over the tonic and the eventual completion of the motion $\hat{3}$–$\hat{2}$–$\hat{1}$ in the second half of the theme (see ex.12*b*). To reach the next stage (ex.12*c*; after Schenker, 1935, fig.95*a*/5, which shows only the first eight bars), the first bass note *d* is brought into a higher octave (*d'*) by an ascending register transfer (HÖHERLEGUNG). This *d'* initiates a linear progression (ZUG) through the interval of an octave which returns to the original *d* before proceeding to the dominant. The upper part imitates the octave progression with a linear progression of its own, beginning on *d″* and proceeding in 10ths with the bass until it, too, regains its starting-note *f♯′*. This 6th-progression is preceded by an unfolding of the tonic chord (*f♯′–a′–d″*), called an ARPEGGIATION. The arrival on the dominant in bar 8 is delayed by a 6-4/5-3 suspension.

127

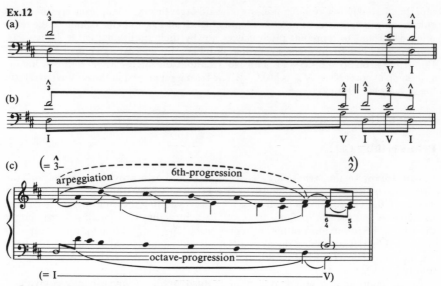

Other methods of prolongation include ANSTIEG, AUSFALTUNG, KOPPELUNG, TIEFER-LEGUNG, ÜBERGREIFEN and UNTERGREIFEN.

Proportional analysis. *See* GOLDEN SECTION.

R_0, R_1, R_2, R_p. *See* SIMILARITY RELATION.

Reaching over. *See* ÜBERGREIFEN.

Realization. *See* AUSFÜHRUNG.

Reduction (i). In Schenkerian analysis, a term used to describe the process by which the piece is understood in increasingly simpler terms as represented by its various layers: a piece is 'reduced' first to its foreground, then to its middleground and ultimately to its background (*see* LAYER). Schenker himself did not use this term: he presented his layer analyses in 'reverse' direction (i.e. from background to foreground) and called the process of growth from one layer to the next DIMINUTION.

Reduction (ii). In the theoretical terminology of Schoenberg, the paring down of a theme or 'basic shape' (GRUNDGESTALT) to a smaller figure in order to give the effect of rhythmic animation or to concentrate interest in only part of the theme at a time. In the opening of Beethoven's Piano Sonata in F minor op.2 no.1 (ex.13; after Schoenberg, 1967, ex.52*a*), the reduction of the basic shape in bars 1–2 to half its length in bar 5 creates the rhythmic animation that effectively pushes the music towards the half-close in bar 8; bars 3–4 are similarly reduced in bar 6.

Although Schoenberg described these reductions in terms of motif, i.e. the transformation of (a) + (b) into (b), and of (a^1) + (b^1) into (b^1), the grace notes in bars 5–6 enable the listener to hear the initial interval in each of these bars as a collapsing of the arpeggio figures (a) and (a^1), rather than their omission altogether. The application of this technique in its extreme form, i.e. the reducing of a musical idea to its limiting

Ex.13

Ex.14

(a)

(b)

129

position, is called 'liquidation', examples of which are illustrated by the opening of Beethoven's Piano Sonata in D op.10 no.3. In ex.14*a* (first movement, bars 1–10) the initial four-note descent (motif (a)) is shown as one of three elements of the basic shape given in bars 1–4; the consequent phrase begins with a reduction of the basic shape to a sequence of motif (a). In ex.14*b* (bars 83–93) liquidation may be observed in the incessant repetition of motif (a), which eventually gives way to an unbroken stepwise descent in crotchets (bars 85–91). This can be understood as a single extension of the statement of motif (a) in bar 85 (with its upbeat): it would make little musical sense to view it as seven consecutive statements of the motif.

Region. In Schoenberg's later theory of harmonic function, a term used to describe a tonal area of a piece of music as it is related to the original key of the piece (its MONOTONALITY). A region can be merely touched on, as in a progression through a secondary dominant chord to a closely related harmonic function: thus Schoenberg would have described the opening bars of Beethoven's First Symphony as moving through the subdominant, tonic and dominant regions before finally settling in the tonic

Ex.15

region in bars 5ff (ex.15). A region can also be more remotely related to the monotonality: the Neapolitan region, for example, is prominent in Beethoven's op.57, op.59 no.2 and op.95, all middle-period works in minor keys. Every deviation in tonality should be thought of not as a move to an independent key, but as a region: thus second groups in the expositions of standard Classical sonata movements are properly understood as being not in the key of the dominant (or relative major) but in the dominant (or mediant) region.

The relative proximity or remoteness of a region is shown by Schoenberg's 'charts of the regions' (1954, tabulated on pp.20, 30). Those regions whose relation to the tonic is 'close and direct' – dominant, subdominant, parallel minor/major and relative major/minor – form a central cross with the tonic. Those whose relationship is indirect, remote or very remote (Schoenberg: 'distant') are placed on either side of the cross, in accordance with their degree of relatedness. The Neapolitan region is placed below the chart of the regions and in oblique alignment to it; it is, appropriately, placed nearer the central cross of the chart of the regions in minor.

Register transfer. In Schenkerian analysis, the raising of a line into a higher octave (*see* HÖHERLEGUNG) or the lowering of a line by one or more octaves (*see* TIEFERLEGUNG). *See also* KOPPELUNG.

Scale step. *See* STUFE.

Schicht (Ger.). *See* LAYER.

Segmentation. In musical semiotics, the division of a piece into smaller components, called 'units' (or 'unities'), by a process involving no previous assumptions about form. The search for units is based on repetition, making use (where possible) of such natural markers as rests, double bars and relatively long note values as additional criteria. Although based in principle on literal repetition, it can make use of the notion of 'equivalence' to recognize non-literal repetition, i.e. variation, development, similarity (*see* EQUIVALENCE (ii)).

Segmentation typically takes place on a number of levels (*see* NIVEAU): the initial procedure may perhaps rely solely on literal repetition, with subsequent procedures allowing equivalence to play an increasing role. In this way, the process feels its way forward towards a segmentation of the piece under examination, excluding as far as possible preconceived ideas. The forms of variation specific to the piece gradually emerge, as equivalence is given greater scope; in this way each segmentation is intuitively tailor-made to the piece. (For an illustration of segmentation, see Chapter IV, §7 and fig.39, p.96. *See also* PARADIGMATIC AXIS.)

Segmentation is also used more generally in other methods of analysis, notably that of set theory (see Chapter IV, §9), to mean the division of musical material into units of more manageable size, for example phrases, motifs or chords.

Sentence. In Schoenbergian analysis, a thematic statement whose shape is determined by the immediate repetition or variation of an initial recognizable motif or basic idea, for instance by the juxtaposition of its 'tonic form' and 'dominant form' (see ex.13, p.129). The thematic construction of a sentence contrasts with that of a PERIOD, in which statement and repetition are placed at the beginning of each of two complementary phrases.

Set. A term borrowed from mathematics and logic to denote a collection of objects or elements classified together according to a given rule. It is applied in music to a PITCH-CLASS SET.

Set complex. A term used in set-theory analysis (see Chapter IV, §9) to denote a particular grouping of pitch-class sets about a given, referential set. The set complex about a given PITCH-CLASS SET consists of all sets which are related by inclusion to the given set or its COMPLEMENT; that is, each set in the complex is either a SUBSET or a SUPERSET of the given set or its complement. This referential set is called the 'nexus set'. The symbol normally used for the set complex is K.

Set complexes tend to be quite large and thus of limited significance as analytical tools. A more useful group, called a 'subcomplex', comprises only those sets which are related by inclusion both to the nexus set and to its complement. The conventional symbol for the subcomplex is Kh.

Similarity relation. In set-theory analysis (see Chapter IV, §9), a relation between pairs of sets of the same cardinality (i.e. having the same number of elements) based on the correspondence between either their pitch classes (*see* PITCH-CLASS SET) or between their respective interval vectors (*see* INTERVAL CLASS and INTERVAL VECTOR). Several such relationships are recognized as of potential significance.

(1) Two sets are said to have 'maximal similarity with respect to pitch class' if they have all but one pitch class in common. For example, the five-element pitch-class sets [B♭,C♯,E,E♭,C] and [B♭,C♯,E,E♭,B] are maximally similar because they have in common the four-element SUBSET [B♭,C♯,E,E♭]. The symbol for this relationship is R_p.

In atonal music, one often finds this relationship explicitly demonstrated by, say, two groups of notes with only one different pitch class in each, as is the case with the two sets given above. In such cases R_p is said to be 'strongly represented', because the common pitch classes are clearly perceivable. However, the common subset is sometimes more deeply embedded in the structure of both sets and is not immediately recognizable because the actual pitch classes are different. For instance, the sets [G,F,E,E♭] and [D,B,C♯,G♯] have no common pitch classes, but the subsets comprising the first three elements of each, [G,F,E] and [D,B,C♯] respectively, are reducible to the same PRIME FORM, which can be represented numerically as [0,1,3]. In such cases R_p is said to be 'weakly represented'.

(2) Two sets are said to have 'maximal similarity with respect to interval class' if, when their respective interval vectors are compared, four of the six numbers match in size and position. For example, the pitch-class sets [0,1,2,5] and [0,1,3,7] have the respective interval vectors [211110] and [111111], from which it can be seen that the tallies of interval classes 2 (major 2nd), 3 (minor 3rd), 4 (major 3rd) and 5 (perfect 4th) are the same for both sets.

Certain pairs of sets that are maximally similar with respect to interval have the additional property that the remaining tallies of interval class are the same but in the wrong position. This is the case for the sets [0,2,3,6] and [0,2,5,8], whose interval vectors

$$\downarrow \qquad \qquad \downarrow$$

are, respectively, [112101] and [012111]. This property, illustrated by the arrows above

$$\uparrow \qquad \qquad \uparrow$$

and below the first and fifth positions in the vectors, is called the 'interchange feature' and serves to distinguish a more limited number of related sets, hence a stronger relation. The symbol R_1 signifies the relationship of maximal similarity with respect to interval class with the interchange feature; without the interchange feature, the symbol is R_2.

(3) Two sets having no matching numbers in their respective interval vectors are said to have 'minimal similarity with respect to interval class', for which the symbol is R_0.

While these similarity relations are sometimes useful in themselves, they gain in significance when combined with one another. A large number of pairs of sets are maximally similar as regards pitch class (R_p), but fewer are also maximally similar as regards interval class (either R_1 or R_2); still fewer of these pairs enjoy this relationship with the 'interchange feature' (R_1 only). These dual relationships are indicated by a pair of brackets preceded by a dot; for either/or relationships the dot is omitted. (The relationships described here are accordingly written $\cdot(R_p,(R_1,R_2))$ and $\cdot(R_p,R_1)$, respectively.)

Pairs of sets may also be interestingly related by combining opposing similarity features: for instance they may be maximally similar as regards pitch class, but minimally similar as regards interval class, i.e. $\cdot(R_p,R_0)$. Or they may be maximally similar with regard to interval class, but not have maximal pitch-class similarity; this relationship is written $\cdot R(+(R_1,R_2),-R_p)$. The purpose of dual relationships is to weed out pairs of sets whose similarities are not very distinctive, i.e. to reduce the number of similar pairs in order to arrive at a smaller quantity of more specifically – and hence more significantly – related pairs.

Structural level. *See* LAYER.

Stufe (Ger.: 'step', 'degree'). In Schenkerian analysis, a harmony of structural significance; the degree (scale step) on which that harmony is based. The term first appeared in Schenker's *Harmonielehre* (1906), where it was used to distinguish basic harmonic occurrences from chords of secondary significance, or those based on purely harmonic procedure. In the ritornello of the aria 'Buss und Reu' from Bach's *St Matthew Passion* (ex.16; after Schenker, 1906, fig.153), each of the notes in the supposed 'dominant'

Ex.16

V – I – IV – VII –

III – VI * (IV) V – I

chord (marked with an asterisk) can be explained in purely contrapuntal terms, without reference to harmonic meaning: *c♯* is a passing note in the bass, *e♯″* an unprepared lower auxiliary embellishing the suspension resolution *g″–f♯″* in the upper voice, and *g♯′* the result of the middle voice moving in parallel 6ths with the upper voice.

In the subsequent development of Schenker's theories, *Stufe*, like all other musical phenomena, is defined in terms of structural levels (*see* LAYER). In his analyses from the mid-1920s he described the basic harmonic structure of a piece as a progression of *Stufen* entirely within a single tonality (*Tonalität*). At later levels in the analysis, these would be expanded into harmonic regions, or keys, in their own right (*Stufen der Tonalität als Tonarten*) (see figs.21–2, p.50).

This view of tonality and modulation need not be applied only to large stretches of music: in a song or self-contained theme the harmonies can also be interpreted differently at different structural levels. Schenker (1935, §277 and fig.39/3) illustrated this in his analysis of the 'Emperor Hymn' from Haydn's String Quartet op.76 no.3 (ex.17):

> The *Stufen* at levels a), b) and c) can be distinguished very precisely. In a) they govern the entire song; in b) they serve the entire initial ascent (*Anstieg*) from *g′* to *d″*; in c) they serve only a part of that ascent, from *a′* to *d″*. Thus the D major resulting from this last elaboration is only an illusory key (*Scheintonart*).

Ex.17

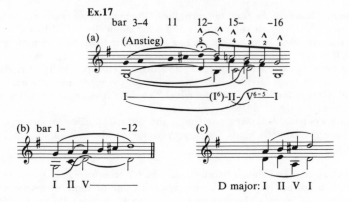

The term *Stufe* has been rendered in English – not wholly adequately – as 'scale step', 'harmonic degree' or simply 'degree'.

Subcomplex. *See* SET COMPLEX.

Subject. *See* GROUP.

Subset. In set-theory analysis, a term applied to a PITCH-CLASS SET when each of its elements is contained in another set; the former set is said to be a subset of the latter. A 'proper subset' contains at least one element of, but fewer elements than, the other set. *See also* INVARIANT SUBSET.

Superposition. *See* ÜBERGREIFEN.

Superset. In set-theory analysis, a term applied to a PITCH-CLASS SET when each of the elements in some other set is contained in it; the former set is said to be a superset of the latter. A 'proper superset' contains at least one more element than the other set.

Syntagmatic axis. A term borrowed from linguistics, applied in musical semiotics; it signifies the notional horizontal line showing the succession of functions of a musical structure. Successive musical 'units', taken as representatives of these functions, are placed next to one another along the syntagmatic axis to show their respective syntactic functions, for instance as the beginning of a phrase or as a cadence figure. *See also* PARADIGMATIC AXIS.

Teiler (Ger.: 'divider'). In Schenkerian analysis, the first occurrence of the dominant in a complete tonal statement (*see* PERIOD) that marks a temporary resting point on the way to a full close; hence also *Quintteiler*, *Oberquintteiler* and, most precisely, *teilende Dominante* ('dividing dominant'). For works in the minor mode, the divider is normally the minor dominant, whose third is raised when required 'for cadential purposes' (Schenker, 1935, §89).

The concept of divider is closely connected with interruption (UNTERBRECHUNG): Schenker definitively used *Teiler* to mean the first dominant in a fundamental structure that is interrupted, i.e. the dominant immediately preceding the double lines:

$$\hat{3}\ \hat{2}\ \|\ \hat{3}\ \hat{2}\ \hat{1}$$
$$\text{I V}\ \|\ \text{I V I}$$

More frequently, however, he used the term for a dominant of lesser structural importance: for instance, the dominant at the end of a harmonically 'open' first group in a movement in sonata form, which is clearly of a lower order than the dominant reached at the end of the exposition. This meaning of divider is illustrated by analyses of C major sonata movements by Mozart (K279/189*d*) and Beethoven (op.2 no.3) (ibid, fig.154/ 1–2). Used in either sense, 'divider' is an alternative for the more conventional 'imperfect cadence' (Ger. *Halbschluss*), a term of which Schenker disapproved because it misleadingly implies closure (ibid, §89).

In his early analyses, Schenker often used the term *Oberquintteiler* for 'secondary dominant'; one occasionally finds *Unterquintteiler* for a subdominant of special significance.

Tieferlegung (Ger.). In Schenkerian analysis, the lowering of a line by one or more octaves, either by direct leap or in connection with one or more other methods of PROLONGATION. In Chopin's Mazurka in E minor op.41 no.2 (ex.18; after Schenker, 1935, fig.75), the bass line is brought down from *e* to *E* in the cadential progression in bars 1–4, so that the first true tonic chord in the piece can be emphasized more than the

Ex.18

E minor: V⁷/IV   IV   V   I

V⁷/IV with which it opens. *Tieferlegung* is usually rendered in English as 'descending register transfer', or (less precisely) as 'register transfer' or 'octave transfer', terms that also apply to HÖHERLEGUNG; the two procedures can be used conjunctly to produce KOPPELUNG, the 'coupling' of voices in different octaves.

Tonicization (Ger. *Tonikalisierung*). The act of establishing a new key centre, or of giving a scale step other than the first the temporary role of tonic. This is accomplished by emphasizing the critical properties of that tonic: in particular, its leading note and the fourth scale step above it, both of which appear in the dominant 7th chord. Thus, for example, the opening chord of Haydn's String Quartet op.74 no.1, though not a tonic chord itself, 'tonicizes' the home key of C major. At the beginning of the slow movement of Mozart's String Quartet in E♭ κ160/159*a* (ex.19), the first chord tonicizes B♭ major and so helps to delay the clear arrival of the home key of A♭.

Ex.19   **Un poco adagio**

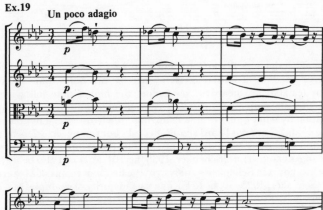

Übergreifen

The term *Tonikalisierung* originates in the second part of Schenker's *Harmonielehre* (1906, Chapters 2–3), where examples of tonicization are used to show how one diatonic collection can be musically enriched by the implication of another (through the presence of a single foreign note) and how the concept of STUFE (i.e. a significant harmony identified with a particular scale step) is more useful than the notion of transitory modulation. The term 'tonicization' is sometimes used by non-Schenkerian writers to characterize modulation at a low level, where a new key is touched on only briefly.

Übergreifen (Ger.). In Schenkerian analysis, the juxtaposition of two or more descending lines (in rare instances, leaps) in such a way that the resultant line appears to climb from an inner voice to a higher one; each of the descending lines is called an *Übergreifzug*.

Ex.20

The opening of Beethoven's Piano Sonata in C op.2 no.3 (ex.20*a*) serves to demonstrate *Übergreifen* as a method of PROLONGATION whereby two notes that are conceptually simultaneous (ex.20*b*) are heard in succession, the higher note following the lower (ex.20*c*). In this, its simplest form, *Übergreifen* enables the upper voice to regain its original position by what is, in effect, a changing-note figure (i.e. a double neighbour): in ex.20*c* the *d'* and *f'* are not heard simultaneously but can nevertheless be understood as a middle and upper voice of a dominant 7th. The procedure can be extended to give the effect of an ARPEGGIATION (Schenker, 1935, fig.101/5); it can also be used to change tonal centre, as shown in Schenker's analysis of the first movement of Mozart's G minor Symphony (Schenker, 1925–30, ii, 121). The vast majority of examples of *Übergreifen* in the Schenkerian literature show that the *Übergreifzüge* descend, and do so by step. However, leaps may sometimes be employed (1935, fig.101/3).

Several English terms for *Übergreifen* have been used. In the glossary compiled for the English version (1969) of Schenker's *Fünf Urlinie-Tafeln* (1932), Salzer defined it as a 'technique of shifting tones (often from an inner voice) above the upper voice', by analogy with *Übergreifen*, the German word for 'shifting' in string playing. The term is translated as 'superposition' in Salzer's *Structural Hearing* (1952) and in essays that have appeared in *The Music Forum*; as 'reaching over' in Oster's translation (1979) of *Der freie Satz* (1935); and as 'overlapping' in Forte's and Gilbert's *Introduction to Schenkerian Analysis* (1982).

Unfolding. A term used generally to denote the presentation or elaboration of some structural feature (e.g. 'the unfolding of the bass', 'the linear unfolding of the tonic chord'); more specifically, the English equivalent of the Schenkerian concept of AUSFALTUNG. *See also* PROLONGATION.

Unit [unity]. *See* SEGMENTATION.

Universal set. *See* COMPLEMENT.

Unordered set. *See* ORDERED SET.

Unterbrechung (Ger.: 'interruption'). In Schenkerian analysis, the principal method of PROLONGATION applied to the fundamental structure (URSATZ) of a tonal piece, achieved by 'interrupting' its progress after the first arrival on the dominant; this interruption requires a return to the starting-point of the fundamental structure. The symbol for an interruption is a double stroke on the same line as the capped arabic numbers representing the melodic scale steps of the fundamental line (URLINIE), as shown in ex.21. The dominant that immediately precedes the interruption is called the 'divider' (TEILER).

Ex.21

When the fundamental line encompasses a 3rd (as in ex.21) or a 5th, the interruption occurs after the arrival on $\hat{2}$. When it covers a full octave, however, a true interruption is impossible: for if it were to take place after either $\hat{7}$ or $\hat{2}$, the return to the octave would create the impression of an upper or lower neighbour (in C major, C–B–C or C–D–C); and if it occurred after $\hat{5}$, the subsequent return to $\hat{8}$ would produce consecutive octaves. It is possible, however, to divide the fundamental line at $\hat{5}$ by having the bass return to the tonic while the $\hat{5}$ is tied over (ex.22); this is the nearest equivalent to interruption when the fundamental line encompasses an octave (Schenker, 1935, §§76 and 100).

Ex.22

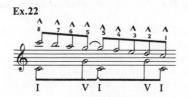

As a method of prolongation, interruption is of utmost significance for musical form, providing the structural basis of two-part song form and, by extension, of sonata form: the return to the starting-point of the fundamental structure corresponds to the beginning of the recapitulation in the musical foreground.

Untergreifen (Ger.). In Schenkerian analysis, a method of PROLONGATION whereby motion in the upper voice is temporarily halted by an ascending line from an inner voice leading up to it; this line is called an *Untergreifzug*. The simplest function the line can perform is to delay the motion of the upper voice in the opposite direction (i.e. descend-

Ex.23

Untergreifzug

Untergreifzug

ing), as shown in the first eight bars of Mozart's String Quartet in A к464 (ex.23). Elsewhere it may serve to reinforce a neighbour note that embellishes the fundamental line (URLINIE), as illustrated by Schenker's analyses of Chopin's Study in A minor op.10 no.2 and the *St Antony Chorale* (Schenker, 1935, fig.42/1–2). No single English word can convey the meaning of *Untergreifen*; the term is now usually translated as 'motion from an inner voice'.

Although a work cannot begin with *Untergreifen* (because no structurally important note has yet been established), one often encounters a line which ascends to the first note of the fundamental line; Schenker called this an ANSTIEG.

Urlinie (Ger.: 'fundamental line'). In Schenkerian analysis, the diatonic stepwise descent to the tonic from the 3rd, 5th or octave, which conceptually spans the upper voice of an entire piece. The interval encompassed by the *Urlinie* and the register in which it appears are determined by the analysis of the piece. As the upper voice of the basic contrapuntal design of the piece (called the URSATZ), the fundamental line can be considered to encapsulate its melody. Because *Urlinie* was the first term Schenker coined in connection with his new analytical method, it became the word most closely identified with this method, as well as the one whose meaning changed most significantly in the course of his development as a theorist. Hence it is probably the source of most misunderstandings, and misgivings, about his theories.

Schenker mentioned and described the *Urlinie* for the first time in the foreword to the *Erläuterungsausgabe* of Beethoven's Piano Sonata in A op.101 (see Chapter III, §1 and fig.17, p.42). Yet it is clear from his analysis of op.101, and from the essays in his next series of publications (*Der Tonwille*, 1921–4), that the *Urlinie* was at first understood not as an archetypal melodic line, but rather as a reduction of the surface of the piece that left the phrase structure and broad melodic and harmonic outlines intact. The *Urlinie* of one of these earlier analyses is not only polyphonic but often preserves the bar-lines of the piece under investigation. Thus the original meaning of the term corresponds more closely to what Schenker was eventually to call the 'foreground' (*see* LAYER), and explains why he continued to use the expression *Urlinie-Tafel* for the musical representation of the foreground layer in his analyses.

Ursatz (Ger.: 'fundamental structure'). In Schenkerian analysis, the basic contrapuntal design that underlies the entire structure of a piece; the final result of successive 'reductions' in a LAYER analysis of a tonal piece and thus the representation of the 'background' of the piece.

The upper voice of the fundamental structure, called the 'fundamental line' (UR-LINIE), consists of a diatonic stepwise descent to the tonic from the 3rd, 5th or octave; the interval it encompasses and the register in which it appears depend on the analysis, i.e. the content of the previous layers and, ultimately, of the piece itself. The lower voice, which encapsulates the harmonic motion of the piece, consists of a tonic, followed by a dominant and a return to the tonic; this is called the ARPEGGIATION of the bass (Ger. *Bassbrechung*) since it involves movement between two elements of the tonic triad. Thus the upper and lower parts of the fundamental structure both exhibit a 'horizontal' unfolding of the tonic. Two common forms of the fundamental structure in C major are given in ex.24.

Ex.24

While the fundamental structure can, from an analytical point of view, be regarded as a reduction of a tonal piece to its simplest polyphonic terms, it may also be understood compositionally as the initial elaboration of the tonic triad, and thus the starting-point for the explanation of pieces in terms of growth and development. It is for this reason that 'fundamental structure' is the first concept developed in Schenker's *Der freie Satz* (1935), and also the starting-point – both graphically and verbally – of all his analyses. In the course of his development as a theorist, the meaning of *Ursatz* changed. Initially it denoted something a little more elaborate: ex.25 shows the *Ursatz* of the first movement of Mozart's G minor Symphony according to Schenker's analysis of 1926. By the time of the 'Eroica' analysis (1930), this level of elaboration would have been called the '1. Schicht' or 'first layer' of the middleground.

Ex.25

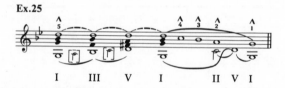

Verschränkung (Ger.: 'crossing', 'folding' [e.g. of limbs]). In Riemann's theory of phrase structure (see Chapter IV, §5), the interlocking of two consecutive phrases whereby the initial, unstressed 'growth' phase of the second is superimposed over the beginning of the final, stressed 'decay' phase of the first. In practical terms this means that the last bar of, say, an eight-bar phrase also marks the beginning of the next phrase. In the first movement of Mozart's Piano Concerto in G K453 (ex.26, overleaf), the varied repetition of the principal second-group theme begins at the cadence point of the initial statement and thus offers a typical illustration of *Verschränkung* in Classical phraseology. (In the repeat, the soloist's echoes of the woodwind phrase in the second half of bars 2 and 4 are examples of 'annexed motifs' in the form of a feminine ending; *see* ANSCHLUSS-MOTIV.)

The sign for *Verschränkung* is an overlapping, or 'crossing', of slurs above the musical text. In his more tersely illustrated analyses, which dispense with slurs, Riemann used the bracketed bar-number symbol (8 = 1) to denote *Verschränkung*. (For the sake of clarity, both types of symbol are given in ex.26.)

Because the superposition of stressed and unstressed elements effectively means the abandonment of regular phrase structure by a process of contraction, Riemann placed the concept of *Verschränkung* under the general heading of ELISION.

Verschränkung

Ex.26

(2)   (4)

Vordergrund (Ger.: 'foreground'). *See* LAYER.

Z-relation. In set-theory analysis (see Chapter IV, §9), an association between one PITCH-CLASS SET and another which, though they are not reducible to the same PRIME FORM, nevertheless have the same interval vector. (For an illustration of a Z-relation between two sets, *see* INTERVAL VECTOR, Table 2.)

Z-related pairs often have special properties, especially those consisting of six pitch classes (which are sometimes called Z-hexachords). For instance, a Z-hexachord is always the COMPLEMENT of the other hexachord in the pair; it follows from this that any SET COMPLEX or subcomplex about a Z-hexachord is identical with the complex (subcomplex) about its corresponding Z-hexachord. For this reason Z-related pairs of hexachords, even though they consist in reality of different sets, are often counted as one set (e.g. when tallying the total number of sets in a complex or subcomplex).

Zug (Ger.: 'pull', 'stress', 'procession', 'progression'). In Schenkerian analysis, a diatonic stepwise progression encompassing a certain interval, by which movement from one pitch, register or voice to another is established; having this function, it is one of the chief methods of PROLONGATION or elaboration of a basic musical structure. The term is usually translated as 'progression' or, more precisely, 'linear progression'. In identifying these progressions in analytical writings, the interval usually forms part of the name, thus *Terzzug, Quartzug, Quintzug, Sextzug, Septzug, Oktavzug* ('3rd-progression', '4th-progression', etc).

At the most basic LAYER of an analysis, the function of a linear progression is to connect the fundamental line (URLINIE) with a middle part. In ex.27a, for instance, the

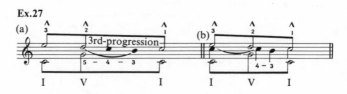

Ex.27

3rd-progression $d''–c''–b'$ interrupts the linear motion from e'' ($\hat{3}$) to c'' ($\hat{1}$) by passing through c'' on the way to the leading note b'; by this 3rd-progression an inner part is implied, as indicated by the crotchets in ex.27*b*. Because this line embellishes a note in the fundamental line, it is called a *Terzzug erster Ordnung* ('3rd-progression of the first order'). At other structural levels, a linear progression outlines movement within a voice (or between voices) in one direction. In the Scherzo from Beethoven's String Quartet in

Ex.28

F op.18 no.1 (ex.28), the first six bars of the first violin part can be represented by an ascending 5th-progression ($f'–c''$), which is extended to a 7th-progression by $d''–e''$ in bars 7–8. The thrust of the first ten bars considered as a single phrase can, however, also be represented by the descending 4th-progression $f'–(e'–)d'–c'$ (shown with downward stems in ex.28), in which e' is implied from the e'' in bar 8.

Schenker occasionally used the term *Zug* with a secondary meaning of 'trait', 'feature' or 'characteristic', on which he often punned. Thus *Stimmführungszüge* may be taken to mean the various linear progressions that make up a contrapuntal design or simply 'the characteristics of voice-leading'.

Bibliography

The bibliography is ordered alphabetically by author's surname; within a given author it is chronological by date of publication, and within a given year it is alphabetical by first word of title. Works of joint authorship are entered at the end of the first-named author's list.

To allow secondary literature (writings about particular theorists) to be placed adjacent to relative primary literature (writings by those theorists), subsections have been created within the main alphabetical list; these are shown by indentation. Where an item of secondary literature relates substantively to several theorists (e.g. Federhofer writing on Kurth, Riemann and Schenker), it is fully cited only under its author, and is cross-referred from those of the theorists who have their own sections.

Since Schenkerian methods are employed, and have been extended, by many analysts, yet are associated with their originator by name (unlike set-theoretical analysts, for example), Schenker has been treated as a special case. The entry for Schenker is fourfold: (i) primary; (ii) Schenkerian theory by other writers and extensions of Schenkerian theory; (iii) bibliography; and (iv) secondary. The effects of this are, first, that the analytical writings of any wholly Schenkerian analyst are placed solely under Schenker (ii), with a cross-reference from that author's name if appropriate; and second, that the writings of an analyst only part of whose work is Schenkerian are placed partly under Schenker (ii) and partly under that author's name, with cross-reference.

L. U. Abraham: 'Trivialität und Persiflage in Beethovens Diabelli-Variationen'; 'Zur Harmonik in Gustav Mahlers Vierter Symphonie', *Neue Wege der musikalischen Analyse*, ed. R. Stephan (Berlin, 1967), 7, 43

G. Adler: 'Umfang, Methode und Ziel der Musikwissenschaft', *VMw*, i (1885), 5

——: 'Die Wiederholung und Nachahmung in der Mehrstimmigkeit', *VMw*, ii (1886), 271

——: *Wagner-Vorlesungen* (Leipzig, 1904)

——: *Der Stil in der Musik*, i: *Prinzipien und Arten des musikalischen Stils* (Leipzig, 1911, 2/1929/ R1973) [ii, on style in historical periods, never issued, but i expanded as *Methode der Musikgeschichte*, 1919/R1971]

T. W. Adorno: 'On the Problem of Musical Analysis', *MusA*, i (1982), 169 [Ger. orig. 'Zum Probleme der musikalischen Analyse', lecture 1969]

P. Aldrich: 'An Approach to the Analysis of Renaissance Music', *MR*, xxx (1969), 1

B. Alphonce: 'The Invariance Matrix as an Analytical Tool', *IMSCR*, xi *Copenhagen 1972*, i, 228

——: *The Invariance Matrix* (diss., Yale U., 1974)

G. Altmann: *Musikalische Formenlehre: Beispiele und Analysen* (Berlin, 1960, 2/1968)

P. Andraschke: *Gustav Mahlers IX Symphonie: Kompositionsprozess und Analyse* (Wiesbaden, 1976)

——: 'Struktur und Gehalt im ersten Satz von Gustav Mahlers Sechster Symphonie', *AMw*, xxxv (1978), 275

S. Anheisser: 'Das Vorspiel zu "Tristan und Isolde" und seine Motivik: ein Beitrag zur Hermeneutik des Musikdramas Wagners', *ZMw*, iii (1920–21), 257–303

E. Ansermet: *Les fondements de la musique dans la conscience humaine* (Neuchâtel, 1961)

M. Philippot: 'Ansermet's Phenomenological Metamorphoses', *PNM*, ii/2 (1964), 129

B. Archibald: 'The Harmony of Berg's "Reigen"', *PNM*, vi/2 (1969), 73

M. Arend: 'Harmonische Analyse des Tristanvorspiels', *BB*, xxiv (1901), 160

Bibliography

S. Arom: 'Essai d'une notation des monodies à des fins d'analyse', *RdM*, lv (1969), 175

B. F. Asaf'yev: *Muzikal'naya forma kak protsess* [Musical form as process] (Moscow, 1930–47, 2/1963 ed. E. Orlova, 3/1971; Cz. trans., 1965; Ger. trans., 1976; Eng. trans. by J. Tull, 1977)

C. Ayrey: 'Berg's "Scheideweg": Analytical Issues in op.2/ii', *MusA*, i (1982), 189

M. Babbitt: 'Some Aspects of Twelve-tone Composition', *The Score and IMA Magazine*, xii (1955), 53

——: 'Twelve-tone Invariants as Compositional Determinants', *MQ*, xlvi (1960), 246; also pubd in *Problems of Modern Music*, ed. P. H. Lang (New York, 1960), 108

——: 'Set Structure as a Compositional Determinant', *JMT*, v (1961), 72; also pubd in *Perspectives on Contemporary Music Theory*, ed. B. Boretz and E. T. Cone (New York, 1972), 129

——: 'Remarks on Recent Stravinsky', *PNM*, ii/2 (1964), 35

——: 'The Structure and Functions of Music Theory', *College Music Symposium*, v (1965), 49

——: 'The Use of Computers in Musicological Research', *PNM*, iii/2 (1965), 74

——: 'Contemporary Music Composition and Music Theory as Contemporary Intellectual History', *Perspectives in Musicology*, ed. B. S. Brook (New York, 1972), 151–84

——: see also Schenker (ii) [review of Salzer, 1952]

R. Bailey: 'The Structure of the "Ring" and its Evolution', *19th Century Music*, i (1977–8), 48

J. M. Baker: *Alexander Scriabin: the Transition from Tonality to Atonality* (diss., Yale U., 1977)

——: 'Scriabin's Implicit Tonality', *MTS*, ii (1980), 1

——: 'Coherence in Webern's Six Pieces for Orchestra, op.6', *MTS*, iv (1982), 1

——: *The Music of Alexander Scriabin* (New Haven, 1986)

——: see also Schenker (ii)

P. Barbaud: *La musique, discipline scientifique: introduction élémentaire à l'étude des structures musicales* (Paris, 1968)

C. K. Baron: 'Varèse's Explications of Debussy's "Syrinx" in "Density 21.5" and an Analysis of Varèse's Composition: a Secret Model Revealed', *MR*, xlii (1982), 121

M. Baroni: 'Sulla nozione di grammatica musicale', *RIM*, xvi (1981), 240–79; Eng. trans. as 'The Concept of Musical Grammar', *MusA*, ii (1983), 175–208

—— and C. Jacoboni: 'Analysis and Generation of Bach's Chorale Melodies', *Ier congrès internationale de sémiotique musicale: Belgrade 1973*, 125

——: *Proposal for a Grammar of Melody: the Bach Chorales* (Montreal, 1978)

——, eds.: *Musical Grammars and Computer Analysis: Modena 1982*, esp. Baroni and others: 'A Grammar for Melody: Relationships between Melody and Harmony', 201

—— and C. Jacoboni: 'Computer Generation and Melodies: Further Proposals', *CHum*, xvii (1983), 1

D. Bartha: 'Liedform-probleme', *Festskrift Jens Peter Larsen* (Copenhagen, 1972)

R. Barthes: *Image–Music–Text* (London, 1977)

P. Batstone: 'Musical Analysis as Phenomenology', *PNM*, vii/2 (1969), 94

D. Baumann: *Die dreistimmige italienische Lied-Satztechnik im Trecento* (Baden-Baden, 1979)

J. Baur: 'Über Weberns "Bagatellen für Streichquartett"', *Neue Wege der musikalischen Analyse*, ed. R. Stephan (Berlin, 1967), 62

D. W. Beach: 'The Origins of Harmonic Analysis', *JMT*, xviii (1974), 274–307

——: 'Pitch Structure and the Analytic Process in Atonal Music: an Interpretation of the Theory of Sets', *MTS*, i (1979), 7

——: see also Schenker (ii)

——, D. Mintz and R. Palmer: 'Analysis Symposium', *JMT*, xiii (1969), 186–217

C. Bean: *Information Theory Applied to the Analysis of a Particular Formal Process in Tonal Music* (diss., U. of Illinois, 1961)

H. Beck: 'Zur musikalischen Analyse', *GfMKB, Kassel 1962*, 291

——: *Methoden der Werkanalyse in Musikgeschichte und Gegenwart* (Wilhelmshaven, 1974)

G. Becking: '"Hören" und "Analysieren" (über Riemanns Beethoven-Analysen)', *ZMw*, i (1918–19), 587

——: *Studien zu Beethovens Personalstil: das Scherzothema* (Leipzig, 1921)

——: 'Über ein dänisches Schul-Liederbuch: über Mitbewegungen und Gestaltanalyse',

144

ZMw, vi (1923–4), 100

——: *Der musikalische Rhythmus als Erkenntnisquelle* (Augsburg, 1928)

——: 'Der musikalische Bau des Montenegrischen Volksepos', *1st International Congress of Phonetic Sciences: Amsterdam 1932* [*Archives néerlandaises de phonétique expérimentale*, viii–ix (1933)], 144

——: *Gustav Becking zum Gedächtnis: eine Auswahl seiner Schriften und Beiträge seiner Schüler*, ed. A. Kramolisch (Tutzing, 1957)

See Seidl (1975)

R. A. Beeson: 'Background and Model: a Concept in Musical Analysis', *MR*, xxxii (1971), 349

P. Benary: *Die deutsche Kompositionslehre des 18. Jahrhunderts* (Leipzig, 1961)

——: 'Musikalische Werkbetrachtung in metrischer Sicht', *Mf*, xiv (1961), 2

I. Bengtsson: 'On Relationships between Tonal and Rhythmic Structures in Western Multipart Music', *STMf*, xliii (1961), 49

——: 'On Melody-registration and "Mona"', *Elektronische Datenverarbeitung in der Musikwissenschaft*, ed. H. Heckmann (Regensburg, 1967), 136

W. E. Benjamin: '"Pour les sixtes": an Analysis', *JMT*, xxii (1978), 253–90

——: 'Ideas of Order in Motivic Music', *MTS*, i (1979), 23

——: 'Pitch-class Counterpoint in Tonal Music', *Music Theory: Special Topics*, ed. R. Browne (New York, 1981), 1–32

——: 'Models of Underlying Tonal Structure: How Can They be Abstract, and How Should They be Abstract?', *MTS*, iv (1982), 28

——: 'A Theory of Musical Meter', *Music Perception*, i (1984), 355–413

——: see also R. P. Morgan

I. D. Bent: 'Current Methods in Stylistic Analysis', *IMSCR*, xi *Copenhagen 1972*, i, 43

——: 'The Terminology of Silence', *IMSCR*, xii *Berkeley 1977*, 797

——: 'Analytical Thinking in the First Half of the Nineteenth Century', *Modern Musical Scholarship*, ed. E. Olleson (Stocksfield, 1980), 151

——: 'The "Compositional Process" in Music Theory 1713–1850', *MusA*, iii (1984), 29

—— and J. Morehen: 'Computers in the Analysis of Music', *PRMA*, civ (1977–8), 30

S. Bérard: *Musique, langage vivant: analyse d'oeuvres musicales des XVIIᵉ et XVIIIᵉ siècles* (Paris, 1981)

A. Berger: 'Problems of Pitch Organization in Stravinsky', *PNM*, ii/1 (1963), 11

K. Berger: 'Tonality and Atonality in the Prologue to Orlando di Lasso's *Prophetiae Sibyllarum*: some Methodological Problems in Analysis of Sixteenth-century Music', *MQ*, lxvi (1980), 484

W. Berger: 'Structuri sonore şi aspectele lor armonice', *Muzica*, xix (1969), no.9, p.10; no.10, p.8

P. Bergquist: see Schenker (ii)

G. Berlind, ed.: *Writings on the Use of Computers in Music* (New York, 1966)

H. Berlioz: [reviews of Beethoven's symphonies], *Revue et gazette musicale de Paris*, iv (1837), 121 [no.3]; v (1838), 33 [nos.1, 2, 4 and 5], 47 [no.6], 64 [no.7], 75 [no.8], 96 [no.9]; all repr. in *A travers chants* (Paris, 1862; Eng. trans. by E. Evans, 1913–18; Eng. trans. by R. de Sola, 1975), 17–62

J. W. Bernard: 'Pitch/Register in the Music of Edgard Varèse', *MTS*, iii (1981), 1

——: 'Spatial Sets in Recent Music of Elliott Carter', *MusA*, ii (1983), 5

L. Bernstein: *The Unanswered Question: Six Talks at Harvard* (Cambridge, Mass., 1976) [review by A. Keiler, *MQ*, lxiv (1978), 195]

W. Berry: *Form in Music: an Examination of Traditional Techniques of Musical Structure and their Application in Historical and Contemporary Styles* (Englewood Cliffs, 1966)

——: *Structural Functions in Music* (Englewood Cliffs, 1976)

——: 'Rhythmic Accelerations in Beethoven', *JMT*, xxii (1978), 177–236

——: 'On Structural Levels in Music', *MTS*, ii (1980), 19–45

——: 'Metric and Rhythmic Articulation in Music', *MTS*, vii (1985), 7

—— and A. Forte: 'Analysis Symposium: Brahms, Alto Rhapsody', *JMT*, xxvii (1983), 223–71

—— and others: 'Analysis Symposium: Mozart Symphony no.40', *ITO*, i/7 (1975), 8

Bibliography

H. Besseler: 'Grundfragen des musikalischen Hörens', *JbMP 1925*, 35

J. B. H. Birnbach: *Der vollkommene Komponist* (Berlin, 1832–46)

J. Blacking: 'Deep and Surface Structures in Venda Music', *YIFMC*, ii (1971), 91

——: 'Towards a Theory of Musical Competence', *Man: Anthropological Essays Presented to O. F. Raum* (Cape Town, 1971), 19

C. von Blumröder: 'Gruppe, Gruppenkomposition' and 'Offene Form', *HMT*

H. Boatwright and E. Oster: 'Analysis Symposium', *JMT*, x (1966), 18–53 [on Mozart: Menuetto in D, κ355]

P. Bogatyrev: 'La chanson populaire du point de vue fonctionnel', *Travaux du Cercle linguistique de Prague*, vi (1936), 222

N. Böker-Heil: 'DODEK – eine Computerdemonstration', *Zeitschrift für Musiktheorie*, ii (1971), 2

——: 'Ein algebraisches Modell des Durmoll tonalen Systems', *1. Internationaler Kongress für Musiktheorie: Stuttgart 1971*, 64–104

——: 'Musikalisches Stilanalyse und Computer: einige grundsätzliche Erwägungen', *IMSCR*, xi *Copenhagen 1972*, i, 45, 108

——: 'Computer-Simulation eines musikalischen Verstehensprozesses', *IMSCR*, xii *Berkeley 1977*, 324

B. Boretz: 'Meta-variations: Studies in the Foundations of Musical Thought (I)', *PNM*, viii/1 (1969), 1–74; 'II: Sketch of a Musical System', viii/2 (1970), 49–111; 'III: Analytic Fallout (I)', xi/1 (1972), 146–223; 'IV: Analytic Fallout (II)', xi/2 (1973), 156–203

——: 'The Construction of a Musical Syntax', *PNM*, ix/1 (1970), 23; ix/2–x/1 (1971), 232–70

S. Borris: 'Probleme der traditionellen Harmonielehre', *Probleme des musiktheoretischen Unterrichts*, ed. R. Stephan (Berlin, 1967), 23

P. Boulez: *Penser la musique aujourd'hui* (Paris, 1964; Eng. trans., 1971)

——: *Relevés d'apprenti*, ed. P. Thévenin (Paris, 1966; Eng. trans., 1966)

W. Bright: 'Language and Music: Areas for Co-operation', *EM*, vii (1963), 26

J. Brincker: 'Statistical Analysis of Music: an Application of Information Theory', *STMf*, lii (1970), 53

A. R. Brinkman: *Johann Sebastian Bach's 'Orgelbüchlein': a Computer-assisted Study of the Melodic Influence of the Cantus Firmus on the Contrapuntal Voices* (diss., U. of Rochester, 1978)

——: 'The Melodic Process in Johann Sebastian Bach's "Orgelbüchlein"', *MTS*, ii (1980), 46

R. Brinkman: *Arnold Schönberg: Drei Klavierstücke Op.11: Studien zur frühen Atonalität bei Schönberg* (Wiesbaden, 1969)

H. A. Brockhaus: 'Probleme der musikalischen Analyse', *Musik und Gesellschaft*, xvii (1967), 433

——: 'Probleme des Kategoriensystems', *BMw*, xi (1969), 245

——: 'Bemerkungen zur Verbalisierung des Musikalischen im Prozess der Analyse', *IMSCR*, xi *Copenhagen 1972*, i, 309

M. E. Brockhoff: 'Zur Methodik der musikwissenschaftlichen Analyse', *IMSCR*, iv *Basel 1949*, 80

J. L. Broeckx and W. Landrieu: 'Comparative Computer Study of Style, Based on Five Liedmelodies', *Interface*, i (1972), 29–92

B. H. Bronson: 'Mechanical Help in the Study of Folksong', *Journal of American Folklore*, lxii (1949), 81

B. S. Brook, ed.: *Musicology and the Computer: Musicology 1966–2000: a Practical Program, Three Symposia* (New York, 1970) [i and iii on analysis and cataloguing; ii on music input languages]

R. Browne, ed.: *Music Theory: Special Topics* (New York, 1981)

R. Browne: 'Tonal Implications of the Diatonic Set', *ITO*, v/6–7 (1981), 3

——: 'The Dialectic of Good Continuation in Tonal Music', *MusA*, iv (1985), 5

M. Broyles: 'Organic Form and the Binary Repeat', *MQ*, lxvi (1980), 339

E. Bücken: 'Der galante Stil: eine Skizze seiner Entwicklung', *ZMw*, vi (1923–4), 418

—— and P. Mies: 'Grundlagen, Methoden und Aufgaben der musikalischen Stilkunde',

ZMw, v (1922–3), 219

E. Budde: *Anton Weberns Lieder op.3: Untersuchungen zur frühen Atonalität bei Webern* (Wiesbaden, 1971)

——: 'Arnold Schoenbergs Monodram "Erwartung": Versuch einer Analyse des ersten Satzes', *AMw*, xxxvi (1979), 1

G. J. Buelow: 'Music, Rhetoric and the Concept of the Affections: a Selective Bibliography', *Notes*, xxx (1973–4), 250

——: 'Rhetoric and Music', *Grove 6*

——: see also Mattheson

J. Burmeister: *Hypomnematum musicae* (Rostock, 1599)

——: *Musica autoschediastike* (Rostock, 1601)

——: *Musica poetica* (Rostock, 1606/R1955)

    M. Ruhnke: *Joachim Burmeister: ein Beitrag zur Musiklehre um 1600* (Kassel, 1955)

H. B. Buys: 'Gestallensymboliek en diminutietechniek', *Mens en melodie*, iv (1950), 321

G. Capellen: 'Harmonik und Melodik bei R. Wagner', *BB*, xxv (1902), 3

W. E. Caplin: *Theories of Harmonic–Metric Relationships from Rameau to Riemann* (diss., U. of Chicago, 1981)

——: 'Tonal Function and Metrical Accent: a Historical Perspective', *MTS*, v (1983), 1

P. Carpenter: 'The Musical Object', *CMc*, no.5 (1967), 56–87 [response by L. Treitler, 87]

F. Cassirer: *Beethoven und die Gestalt: ein Kommentar* (Stuttgart, 1925)

P. Cerone: *El melopeo y maestro* (Naples, 1613/R)

J. Chailley: 'Essai sur les structures mélodiques', *RdM*, xliv (1959), 139–75

——: *Traité historique d'analyse musicale* (Paris, 1964)

A. C. Chandola: 'Some System of Musical Scales and Linguistic Principles', *Semiotica*, ii (1970), 135

A. Chapman: 'Some Intervallic Aspects of Pitch-class Set Relations', *JMT*, xxv (1981), 275

V. Chenoweth: *Melodic Perception and Analysis: a Manual on Ethnic Melody* (Ukarumpa, Papua New Guinea, 1972)

G. Chew: 'The Spice of Music: Towards a Theory of the Leading Note', *MusA*, ii (1983), 35

H. Chiarucci: 'Essai d'analyse structurale d'oeuvres musicales', *Mj*, no.12 (1973), 11–44

M. Chop: *Ludwig van Beethovens Symphonien: geschichtlich und musikalisch Analysiert* (Leipzig, 1910)

R. Chrisman: *A Theory of Axis-tonality for Twentieth-century Music* (diss., Yale U., 1969)

——: 'Identification and Correlation of Pitch-sets', *JMT*, xv (1971), 58

——: 'Describing Structural Aspects of Pitch-sets using Successive-interval Arrays', *JMT*, xxi (1977), 1

——: 'Anton Webern's "Six Bagatelles for String Quartet", op.9: the Unfolding of Intervallic Successions', *JMT*, xxiii (1979), 81–122

A. Clarkson and E. Laufer: 'Analysis Symposium: Brahms op.105/1', *JMT*, xv (1971), 2–57

T. Clifton: 'An Application of Goethe's Concept of *Steigerung* to the Morphonology of Diminution', *JMT*, xiv (1970), 166

——: *Music as Heard: a Study in Applied Phenomenology* (New Haven, 1983)

M. W. Cobin: ' "Musicology and the Computer": a Plenary Session at the 1966 Annual Meeting of the American Musicological Society, in New Orleans', *CHum*, i (1967), 131

R. D. Cogan: 'Tone Colour: the New Understanding', *Sonus*, i/1 (1980), 3

——: 'Stravinsky's Sound: a Phonological View: Stravinsky the Progressive', *Sonus*, ii/2 (1982), 4

——: *New Images of Musical Sound* (Cambridge, Mass., 1984)

—— and Pozzi Escot: *Sonic Design: the Nature of Sound and Music* (Englewood Cliffs, 1976)

——: *Sonic Design: Practice and Problems* (Englewood Cliffs, 1981)

A. Cohen and D. White: *Anthology of Music for Analysis* (New York, 1965)

D. Cohen: 'Palestrina Counterpoint: a Musical Expression of Unexcited Speech', *JMT*, xv (1971), 84

J. E. Cohen: 'Information Theory and Music', *Behavioural Science*, vii (1962), 137

P. Coindreau: *Analyse des dix-sept quatuors de Beethoven* (Paris, 1910)

Bibliography

M. S. Cole: 'Sonata-rondo: the Formulation of a Theoretical Concept in the 18th and 19th Centuries', *MQ*, lv (1969), 180

E. T. Cone: 'Analysis Today', *MQ*, xlvi (1960), 172

——: 'Beyond Analysis', *PNM*, vi/1 (1967), 33 [see also response by D. Lewin, vii/2 (1969), 59 and response by Cone, 70]

——: *Musical Form and Musical Performance* (New York, 1968) [see also commentary by Cone, *MTS*, vii (1985), 149]

——: *The Composer's Voice* (Berkeley, 1974)

——: 'Berlioz's Divine Comedy: the "Grande Messe des morts"', *19th Century Music*, iv (1980–81), 3

D. Cooke: *The Language of Music* (London, 1959)

——: 'The Unity of Beethoven's Late Quartets', *MR*, xxiv (1963), 30

E. Coons and D. Kraehenbuehl: 'Information as a Measure of Structure in Music', *JMT*, ii (1958), 127–61

G. W. Cooper: *An Introduction to the Analysis of Certain Contemporary Harmonic Practices* (diss., Harvard U., 1939)

—— and L. B. Meyer: *The Rhythmic Structure of Music* (Chicago, 1960)

R. Cooper: 'Propositions pour un modèle transformationnel de description musicale', *Mj*, no.10 (1973), 70

R. Court: 'Langage verbale et langages esthétiques', *Mj*, no.2 (1971), 14

——: 'Musique, mythe, langage', *Mj*, no.12 (1973), 45

F. B. Crane: *A Study of Theoretical Writings on Musical Form to ca. 1460* (diss., U. of Iowa, 1960)

M. van Crevel, ed.: *Jacobus Obrecht: Missa 'Sub tuum praesidium'*, Opera omnia, i/6 (Amsterdam, 1959); *Missa 'Maria zart'*, Opera omnia, i/7 (Amsterdam, 1964)

L. Crickmore: 'The Musical Gestalt', *MR*, xxxiii (1972), 285

R. Crocker: *A History of Musical Style* (New York, 1966)

L. Cross, ed.: 'Colloquium: Can Analysis be Taught?', *MusA*, iv (1985), 183

M. Curti: 'J. S. Bach's Chaconne in D minor: a Study in Coherence and Contrast', *MR*, xxxvii (1976), 249

C. Czerny, ed.: *Vollständiges Lehrbuch der musikalischen Composition . . . von A. Reicha* (Vienna, 1834) [trans. of Reicha, 1814, ?1816–18, 1824–6]

C. Czerny: *School of Practical Composition* (London, ?1849/R1979; Ger. orig., ?1849–50 as *Schule der praktischen Tonsetzung*)

——: see also Reicha (1833)

See Bent (1980, 1984), Cole (1969), Moyer (1969), Ritzel (1969) and Stevens (1974)

C. Dahlhaus: 'Zur Kritik musiktheoretischer Allgemeinprinzipien', *Musikalische Zeitfragen*, ix (1960), 68

——: 'Über das Analysieren neuer Musik: zu Schönbergs Klavierstücken Op.11, 1 und Op.33a: Fortschritt und Rückbildung in der deutschen Musikerziehung', *Vorträge der 6. Bundesschulmusikwoche: Bonn 1965*, 224

——: 'Analyse', *RiemannL 12*

——: 'Gefühlsästhetik und musikalische Formenlehre', *Deutsche Vierteljahrsschrift für Literaturwissenschaft und Geistesgeschichte*, xli (1967), 505

——: *Grundlagen der Musikgeschichte* (Cologne, 1967; Eng. trans. by J. B. Robinson, 1983 as *Foundations of Music History*)

——: *Musikästhetik* (Cologne, 1967; Eng. trans. by W. W. Austin, 1982 as *Esthetics of Music*)

——: 'Was ist musikalischer Rhythmus?', *Probleme des musiktheoretischen Unterrichts*, ed. R. Stephan (Berlin, 1967), 16

——: 'Zur Rhythmik in Beethovens Diabelli-Variationen'; 'Schönbergs Lied "Streng ist uns das Glück und Spröde"', *Neue Wege der musikalischen Analyse*, ed. R. Stephan (Berlin, 1967), 18, 45

——: 'Analyse und Werturteil, Musikpädagogik', *Forschung und Lehre*, viii, ed. S. Abel-Struth (Mainz, 1970)

——: 'Hermann von Helmholtz und der Wissenschaftscharakter der Musiktheorie', *Über Musiktheorie: Arbeitstagung Berlin 1970*, 49

——: 'Wagners dramatisch-musikalischer Formbegriff', *AnMc*, no.11 (1972), 290

——: 'Schoenberg and Schenker', *PRMA*, c (1973–4), 209

Bibliography

——, ed.: *Beiträge zur musikalischen Hermeneutik* (Regensburg, 1975), esp. 159–72

——: 'Some Models of Unity in Musical Form', *JMT*, xix (1975), 2

——: 'Polemisches zur Theorie der musikalischen Rhythmik und Metrik', *Mf*, xxix (1976), 183

——: 'Zur Theorie der musikalischen Form', *AMw*, xxiv (1977), 20

——: 'Satz und Periode: zur Theorie der musikalischen Syntax', *Zeitschrift für Musiktheorie*, ix (1978), 16

——: 'Cantabile und thematischer Prozess: der Übergang zum Spätwerk in Beethovens Klaviersonaten', *AMw*, xxxvii (1980), 81

——: 'Harmony', 'Tonality', *Grove 6*

——: 'Über das System der musiktheoretischen Disziplinen im klassisch-romantischen Zeitalter', *Ars musica, musica scientia: Festschrift Heinrich Hüschen*, ed. D. Altenburg (Cologne, 1980), 76

——: *Die Musiktheorie im 18. und 19. Jahrhundert*, i: *Grundzüge einer Systematik*, Geschichte der Musiktheorie, x (Darmstadt, 1984)

——: see also H. C. Koch, and D. de la Motte (1968)

C. Wintle: 'Issues in Dahlhaus', *MusA*, i (1982), 341

J. le R. D'Alembert: *Elémens de musique théorique et pratique suivant les principes de M. Rameau* (Paris, 1752/*R*1966, 2/1762, 3/1772; Ger. trans. by F. W. Marpurg, 1757 as *Systematische Einleitung in die musikalische Setzkunst*)

W. Danckert: 'Stil als Gesinnung', *Bärenreiter-Jb*, v (1929), 24

——: *Personal Typen des Melodiestils* (Kassel, 1931, enlarged 2/1932 as *Ursymbole melodischer Gestaltung: Beiträge zur Typologie der Personalstile aus sechs Jahrhunderten der abendländischen Musikgeschichte*)

——: *Beitrag zur Bach-Kritik* (Kassel, 1934)

A. Daniélou: *Sémantique musicale (essai de psychologie auditive)* (Paris, 1967)

J. N. David: *Die Jupiter-Symphonie: eine Studie über die thematisch-melodischen Zusammenhänge* (Göttingen, 1953, 4/1960)

——: *Die zweistimmigen Inventionen von Johann Sebastian Bach* (Göttingen, 1957)

——: *Die dreistimmigen Inventionen von Johann Sebastian Bach* (Göttingen, 1959)

——: *Das wohltemperierte Klavier: versuch einer Synopsis* (Göttingen, 1962)

——: *Der musikalische Satz im Spiegel der Zeit* (Graz, 1963)

H. Federhofer: 'Johann Nepomuk Davids Analysen von Werken Johann Sebastian Bachs', *AMw*, xix–xx (1962–3), 147

R. Klein: 'Von der Kunstwahrheit in den Analysen von Johann Nepomuk David', *ÖMz*, xxv (1970), 165

L. Davidson: 'The Structure of Lassus' Motets a2 (1577)', *Sonus*, ii/2 (1982), 71

C. T. Davie: *Musical Structure and Design* (London, 1953/*R*1966)

H. Degen: *Handbuch der Formenlehre* (Regensburg, 1957)

F. Delalande: 'L'analyse des musiques électro-acoustiques', *Mj*, no.8 (1972), 50

C. Deliège: 'La musicologie devant le structuralisme', *L'arc*, no.26 (1965), 45

——: 'Approche d'une sémantique de la musique', *RBM*, xx (1966), 21

E. Derr: 'The Two-part Inventions: Bach's Composer's Vademecum', *MTS*, iii (1981), 26

G. S. Dickinson: *A Handbook of Style in Music* (New York, 1969)

A. Dommel-Dieny: *L'analyse harmonique en exemples de J. S. Bach à Debussy* (Neuchâtel, 1967)

R. Donington: *Wagner's 'Ring' and its Symbols: the Music and the Myth* (London, 1963, 3/1974)

W. Drabkin: 'Character, Key Relations and Tonal Structure in "Il trovatore"', *MusA*, i (1982), 143

——: 'Beethoven and the Open String', *MusA*, iv (1985), 15

G. Dressler: *Praecepta musicae poeticae* (1563–4); ed. B. Engelke: *Geschichte-Blätter für Stadt und Land Magdeburg*, xlix–1 (1914–15), 213–50

J. Dunsby: *Structural Ambiguity in Brahms: Analytical Approaches to Four Works* (diss., U. of Leeds, 1976; Ann Arbor, 1981)

——: 'Schoenberg's "Premonition", op.22, no.4, in Retrospect', *JASI*, i (1976–7), 137

——: 'Schoenberg and the Writings of Schenker', *JASI*, ii (1977–8), 26

——: 'A Bagatelle on Beethoven's WoO 60', *MusA*, iii (1984), 57

—— and J. Stopford: 'The Case for a Schenkerian Semiotic', *MTS*, iii (1981), 49

——: see also Schoenberg

F. L. S. Dürenberg: *Die Symphonien Beethovens und anderer berühmter Meister ... analysiert und zum Verständnisse erläutert* (Leipzig, 1863)

W. Dürr and others: 'Rhythm', *Grove 6*

U. Eco: *La struttura assente* (Milan, 1968; Fr. trans., 1972; enlarged Eng. trans. by D. Osmond-Smith, 1976 as *A Theory of Semiotics*)

H. H. Eggebrecht: 'Figuren, musikalisch-rhetorische', *RiemannL 12*

——: 'Zur Methode der musikalischen Analyse', *Erich Doflein Festschrift* (Mainz, 1972), 67

C. von Ehrenfels: 'Die musikalische Architektonik', *BB*, xix (1896), 257

——: *Richard Wagner und seine Apostaten* (Vienna and Leipzig, 1913)

H. Eimert: 'Debussy's "Jeux"', *Die Reihe*, no.5 (1959), 3; Eng. trans. in *Die Reihe*, no.5 (1961), 3

E. von Elterlein [E. Gottschald]: *Beethoven's Symphonien nach ihrem idealen Gehalt mit besonderer Rücksicht auf Haydn's und Mozart's Symphonien* (Dresden, 1854, 3/1870; Eng. trans. by F. Weber, ?1893)

——: *Beethoven's Clavier-Sonaten, für Freunde der Tonkunst erläutert* (Leipzig, 1856, 4/1885; Eng. trans. by E. Hill, 1875)

H. Engel: 'Thematische Satzverbindungen zyklischer Werke bis zur Klassik', *Musa-mens-musici: im Gedenken an Walther Vetter* (Leipzig, 1969), 109

W. Engelsmann: 'Die Sonatenform Beethovens: Probleme in der Klaviersonate As-dur opus 110', *Neue-Musikzeitung*, xlvi (1925), 203, 222

——: *Beethovens Kompositionspläne* (Augsburg, 1931)

G. Epperson: *The Musical Symbol: a Study of the Philosophical Theory of Music* (Ames, Iowa, 1967)

D. Epstein: *Beyond Orpheus: Studies in Musical Structure* (Cambridge, Mass., 1979)

——: 'Tempo Relations: a Cross-cultural Study', *MTS*, vii (1985), 34–71

E. Ergo: 'Über Wagners Melodik und Harmonik', *BB*, xxx (1907), 125, 181, 270; xxxi (1908), 33

R. Erickson: *Sound Structure in Music* (Berkeley, 1975)

——: *The Structure of Music: a Listener's Guide: a Study in Terms of Melody and Counterpoint* (Westport, Conn., 1977)

R. F. Erickson: 'Musical Analysis and the Computer', *JMT*, xii (1968), 240

——: 'Musical Analysis and the Computer: a Report on some Current Approaches and the Outlook for the Future', *CHum*, iii (1968), 87

——: 'A General-purpose System for Computer Aided Musical Studies', *JMT*, xiii (1969), 276

——: *Rhythmic Problems and Melodic Structure in Organum purum: a Computer-assisted Study* (diss., Yale U., 1970)

A. Ernst: 'Die Uebereinstimmung der einzelnen Szenen in den Dramen Wagners', *BB*, xvii (1894), 234

H. Erpf: *Der Begriff der musikalischen Form* (Stuttgart, 1914)

——: 'Analyse', *MGG*

——: *Form und Struktur in der Musik* (Mainz, 1967)

P. Faltin: 'Musikalische Syntaxis: ein Beitrag zum Problem des musikalischen Sinngehalts', *AMw*, xxiv (1977), 1

——: *Phänomenologie der musikalischen Form: eine experimental-psychologische Untersuchung zur Wahrnehmung des musikalischen Materials und der musikalischen Syntax* (Wiesbaden, 1979)

—— and H. P. Reinecke: *Musik und Verstehen: Aufsätze zur semiotischen Theorie, Ästhetik und Soziologie der musikalischen Rezeption* (Cologne, 1974)

T. Fay: 'Context Analysis of Musical Gestures', *JMT*, xviii (1974), 124

H. Federhofer: *Beiträge zur musikalischen Gestaltanalyse* (Graz, 1950)

——: 'Die Funktionstheorie H. Riemanns und die Schichtenlehre H. Schenkers', *IMSCR, vii Cologne 1958*, 183

——: 'J. J. Fux und J. Mattheson im Urteil L. Chr. Mizlers', *Speculum musicae artis: Festgabe für Heinrich Husmann* (Munich, 1970), 111

——: *Akkord und Stimmführung in den musiktheoretischen Systemen von Hugo Riemann, Ernst Kurth und Heinrich Schenker* (Vienna, 1981)

———: 'Fux's "Gradus ad Parnassum" as Viewed by Heinrich Schenker', *MTS*, iv (1982), 66

A. Feil: *Satztechnische Fragen in den Kompositionslehren von F. E. Niedt, J. Riepel und H. Chr. Koch* (Heidelberg, 1955)

———: 'Abmessung (und Art) der Einschnitte: Rhythmus in Beethovens Satzbau', *GfMKB, Bonn 1970*, 33

K. G. Fellerer: *Klang und Struktur in der abendlaendischen Musik* (Cologne, 1967)

D. N. Ferguson: *Music as Metaphor: the Elements of Expression* (Minneapolis, 1960)

———: *Image and Structure in Chamber Music* (Minneapolis, 1964/*R*1977)

———: *A History of Musical Thought* (Westport, Conn., 1975)

L. Ferrara: 'Phenomenology as a Tool for Musical Analysis', *MQ*, lxx (1984), 355

F.-J. Fétis: 'Beethoven (Louis Van)', *Biographie universelle des musiciens*, ii (Paris, 1835, 2/1860/ *R*1963)

See Vertrees (1974)

R. von Ficker: 'Primäre Klangformen', *JbMP 1929*, 21

M. Fink: *Music Analysis: an Annotated Bibliography* (Los Alamitos, 1972)

J. Finscher: 'Thesen zu Analyse und Interpretation', *IMSCR, xi Copenhagen 1972*, i, 54

K. von Fischer: *Die Beziehung von Form und Motiv in Beethovens Instrumentalwerken* (Strasbourg and Zurich, 1948, enlarged 2/1972)

W. Fischer: *Zur Entwicklungsgeschichte des Wiener Klassischen Stils* (Habilitationsschrift, U. of Vienna, 1915); extracts in *SMw*, iii (1915), 24–84

P. Fontaine: *Basic Formal Structures in Music* (New York, 1967)

A. Forte: *Contemporary Tone Structures* (New York, 1955)

———: 'Context and Continuity in an Atonal Work: a Set-theoretic Approach', *PNM*, i/2 (1963), 72

———: 'A Theory of Set-complexes for Music', *JMT*, viii (1964), 136–83; see also ix (1965), 163, 173

———: 'The Domain and Relations of Set-complex Theory', *JMT*, ix (1965), 173

———: 'A Program for the Analytic Reading of Scores', *JMT*, x (1966), 330–64

———: 'Computer-implemented Analysis of Musical Structure', *West Virginia University Conference on Computer Applications in Music: Morgantown 1966*, 29

———: 'Music and Computing: the Present Situation', *Proceedings of the Fall Joint Computer Conference: Anaheim, California, 1967*; also in *CHum*, ii (1967–8), 32

———: 'Sets and Nonsets in Schoenberg's Atonal Music', *PNM*, xi/1 (1972), 43

———: 'The Basic Interval Patterns', *JMT*, xvii (1973), 234–72

———: *The Structure of Atonal Music* (New Haven and London, 1973) [see reviews by W. E. Benjamin and E. Regener, *PNM*, xiii/1 (1974), 170, 191; R. A. Browne, *JMT*, xviii (1974), 390]

———: 'Theory', *Dictionary of Contemporary Music*, ed. J. Vinton (New York, 1974)

———: 'Schoenberg's Creative Evolution: the Path to Atonality', *MQ*, lxiv (1978), 133–76

———: *The Harmonic Organization of 'The Rite of Spring'* (New Haven and London, 1978)

———: 'Aspects of Rhythm in Webern's Atonal Music', *MTS*, ii (1980), 90

———: 'The Magical Kaleidoscope: Schoenberg's First Atonal Masterwork, Opus 11, No.1', *JASI*, v (1981), 127–68

———: 'Foreground Rhythm in Early Twentieth-century Music', *MusA*, ii (1983), 239

———: 'Motivic Design and Structural Levels in the First Movement of Brahms's String Quartet in C Minor', *MQ*, lxix (1983), 471–502

———: 'Middleground Motives in the Adagietto of Mahler's Fifth Symphony', *19th Century Music*, viii (1984–5), 153

———: 'Pitch-class Set Theory Today', *MusA*, iv (1985), 29

———: see also Schenker (ii) and (iv)

——— and S. E. Gilbert: *Introduction to Schenkerian Analysis* (New York, 1982) [see also *Instructors Manual for Introduction to Schenkerian Analysis* (New York, 1982)]

R. Francès: *La perception de la musique* (Paris, 1958)

W. Frisch: see Schoenberg

W. Frisius: 'Musik-Sprache', *Musik und Bildung*, iv (1972), 575

Bibliography

W. Frobenius: 'Polyphony', *Grove 6*

W. Fucks: *Mathematische Analyse der Formalstruktur von Musik* (Cologne and Opladen, 1958)

——: 'Über formale Struktureigenschaften musikalischer Partituren', *Experimentelle Musik: Raum-Musik, Visuelle Musik*, ed. F. Winckel (Berlin, 1970), 33

—— and J. Lauter: *Exaktwissenschaftliche Musikanalyse* (Cologne and Opladen, 1965)

J. J. Fux: *Gradus ad Parnassum* (Vienna, 1725, 2/1742/*R*1974; partial Eng. trans., 1943 as *Steps to Parnassus: the Study of Counterpoint*, rev. 2/1965 as *The Study of Counterpoint*)

 H. Federhofer: 'J. J. Fux als Musiktheoretiker', *Hans Albrecht in Memoriam* (Kassel, 1962), 109

 See also Federhofer (1970, 1982)

A. Gabaud: *Guide pratique d'analyse musicale* (Paris, 1940)

K. Gabura: *Music Style Analysis by Computer* (diss., U. of Toronto, 1967)

H. Gál: 'Die Stileigentümlichkeiten des jungen Beethoven', *SMw*, iv (1916), 58–115

F. Galeazzi: *Elementi teorico-pratici di musica* (Rome, 1791–6; Eng. trans. of vol.i, ed. A. Frascarelli, 1969)

 B. Churgin: 'Francesco Galeazzi's Description (1796) of Sonata Form', *JAMS*, xxi (1968), 181

 See also Schmalzriedt (1984)

R. Gauldin: 'Wagner's Parody Technique: "Träume" and the "Tristan" Love Duet', *MTS*, i (1979), 35

F. Gennrich: *Grundriss einer Formenlehre des mittelalterlichen Liedes als Grundlage einer musikalischen Formenlehre des Liedes* (Halle, 1932/*R*1970)

G. George: *Tonality and Musical Structure* (New York, 1970)

G. Geowey and J. Kucaba: *Understanding Musical Form* (Dubuque, 1962)

S. Gilbert: *The Trichord: an Analytic Outlook for Twentieth-century Music* (diss., Yale U., 1970)

——: 'An Introduction to Trichordal Analysis', *JMT*, xviii (1974), 338

A. Goehr: see Schoenberg

P. Goetschius: *Lessons in Music Form: a Manual of Analysis* (New York, 1893/*R*1970)

——: *Models of the Principal Musical Forms* (Boston, 1895)

H. Goldschmidt: 'Zur Methodologie der musikalischen Analysen', *BMw*, iii/4 (1961), 3

A. J. Goodrich: *Complete Musical Analysis* (Cincinnati, 1887)

P. Gossett: *'Anna Bolena' and the Artistic Maturity of Gaetano Donizetti* (Oxford, 1985)

H. Grabner: *Lehrbuch der musikalischen Analyse* (Leipzig, 1925)

——: *Musikalische Werkbetrachtung* (Stuttgart, 1950)

F. K. Grave: ' "Rhythmic Harmony" in Mozart', *MR*, xli (1980), 87

——: 'Common-time Displacement in Mozart', *JMus*, iii (1984), 423

D. M. Green: *Form in Tonal Music: an Introduction to Analysis* (New York, 1965, 2/1979)

R. Groth: *Die französische Kompositionslehre des 19. Jahrhunderts* (Wiesbaden, 1983)

G. Grove: *Beethoven and his Nine Symphonies* (London, 1896)

K. Grunsky: 'Wagner als Sinfoniker', *Wagner-Jb*, i (1906), 242

——: 'Das Vorspiel und der erste Akt von "Tristan und Isolde" ', *Richard Wagner-Jb*, ii (1907), 207–84

R. Guldenstein: 'Synthetische Analyse', *SMz*, xcvi (1956), 205

D. Gwilt: 'Sonata-Allegro Revisited', *ITO*, vii/5–6 (1984), 3

W. H. Hadow: *Studies in Modern Music* (London, 1893–5)

——: *Sonata Form* (London, 1896, 2/1912/*R*1975)

E. von Hagen: *Beiträge zur Einsicht in das Wesen der Wagnerschen Kunst: gesammelte Aufsätze* (Berlin, 1883)

R. A. Hall: 'La struttura della musica e del linguaggio', *NRMI*, vii (1973), 206

A. O. Halm: *Die Symphonie Anton Bruckners* (Munich, 1913, 2/1923)

——: 'Über den Wert musikalischer Analysen', *Die Musik*, xxi (1928–9), 481

——: *Von Form und Sinn der Musik: gesammelte Aufsätze*, ed. S. Schmalzriedt (Wiesbaden, 1978)

F. E. Hansen: 'Musikalsk analyse ved hjaelp af modeller', *STMf*, lii (1970), 50

E. Hanslick: *Vom musikalisch-Schönen* (Leipzig, 1854, 7/1885; Eng. trans. by G. Cohen, 1957 as *The Beautiful in Music*)

Bibliography

H. Hanson: *Harmonic Materials of Modern Music: Resources of the Tempered Scale* (New York,1960)

J. L. Hanson: *An Operational Approach to Theory of Rhythm* (diss., Yale U., 1969)

R. Hanson: 'Webern's Chromatic Organization', *MusA*, ii (1983), 135

W. G. Harbinson: 'Rhythmic Structure in Schoenberg's "Jane Grey"', *JASI*, vii (1983), 222

R. Harweg: 'Sprache und Musik', *Poetica*, i (1967) 390 [see also ibid, p.556 and ii (1968), 433]; Eng. trans. of orig. article in *Foundations of Language*, iv (1968), 270; Fr. trans., *Mj*, no.5 (1971), 19

C. Hasty: 'Segmentation and Process in Post-tonal Music', *MTS*, iii (1981), 54

M. Hauptmann: *Erläuterungen zu Johann Sebastian Bach's 'Kunst der Fuge'* (Leipzig, 1841, 2/1861)

——: *Die Natur der Harmonik und der Metrik: zur Theorie der Musik* (Leipzig, 1853, 2/1873; Eng. trans., 1888)

——: *Die Lehre von der Harmonik* (Leipzig, 1868, 2/1873)

    W. E. Caplan: 'Moritz Hauptmann and the Theory of Suspensions', *JMT*, xxviii (1984), 251

    P. Rummenhöller: *Moritz Hauptmann als Theoretiker: eine Studie zum erkenntniskritischen Theoriebegriff in der Musik* (diss., U. of Göttingen, 1963; Wiesbaden, 1963)

    ——: 'Der dialektische Theoriebegriff: zur Verwirklichung Hegelschen Denkens in Moritz Hauptmanns Musiktheorie', *GfMKB, Leipzig 1966*, 387

    ——: 'Moritz Hauptmann: der Begründer einer transzendental-dialektischen Musiktheorie', *Beiträge zur Musiktheorie des 19. Jahrhunderts*, ed. M. Vogel (Regensburg, 1966), 11

    ——: 'Der dialektische Begriff Moritz Hauptmanns', *Musiktheoretisches Denken im 19. Jahrhundert*, ed. P. Rummenhöller (Regensburg, 1967), 39

    W. Seidl: 'Moritz Hauptmanns organische Lehre: Tradition, Inhalt und Geltung ihrer Prämisse', *IRASM*, ii (1971), 243

G. Hausswald: *Musikalische Stilkunde* (Wilhelmshaven, 1973)

D. Headlam: 'A Rhythmic Study of the Exposition in the Second Movement of Beethoven's Quartet op.59, no.1', *MTS*, vii (1985), 114

H. Heckmann: 'Neue Methoden der Verarbeitung musikalischer Daten', *Mf*, xvii (1964), 381

——, ed.: *Elektronische Datenverarbeitung in der Musikwissenschaft* (Regensburg, 1967)

——: *Musikwissenschaft und Computer* (Leipzig, 1972)

J. D. Heinichen: *Der General-Bass in der Composition, oder: Neue und gründliche Anweisung* (Dresden, 1728)

E. Helm: 'The "Hamlet" Fantasy and the Literary Elements in C. P. E. Bach's Music', *MQ*, lviii (1972), 277

T. Helm: *Beethovens Streichquartette: versuch einer technischen Analyse dieser Werke* (Leipzig, 1885, 3/1921)

G. Hennenberg: *Theorien zur Rhythmik und Metrik* (Tutzing, 1974)

M. Henze: *Studien zu den Messenkompositionen Johannes Ockeghems* (diss., Freie U. Berlin, 1964; Berlin, 1968)

J. F. Herbart: *Psychologische Bemerkungen zur Tonlehre* (Königsberg, 1811)

R. Hermann: 'Luciano Berio's "Circles", First Movement', *Sonus*, iv/2 (1984), 26

L. A. Hiller: *On the Use of a High-speed Electronic Digital Computer for Musical Composition* (diss., U. of Illinois, 1958)

——: 'Informationstheorie und Musik', *Darmstädter Beiträge zur neuen Musik*, viii (1964), 7

—— and C. Bean: 'Information Theory Analyses of Four Sonata Expositions', *JMT*, x (1966), 96–137

—— and L. M. Isaacson: *Experimental Music: Composition with an Electronic Computer* (New York, 1959/R1981) [incl. material from diss.]

—— and B. Levy: 'General System Theory as Applied to Music Analysis: Part I', *Musical Grammars and Computer Analysis: Modena 1982*, 295

P. Hindemith: *Unterweisung im Tonsatz* (Mainz, 1937, 2/1940; Eng. trans., 1942 as *The Craft of Musical Composition*)

153

Bibliography

H. R. Hensel: *On Paul Hindemith's Fluctuation Theory* (diss., U. of Illinois, 1964)

V. Landau: 'Paul Hindemith: a Case Study in Theory and Practice', *MR*, xxi (1960), 38

J.-H. Lederer: 'Zu Hindemiths Idee einer Rhythmen- und Formenlehre', *Mf*, xxix (1976), 21

G. Schubert: 'Vorgeschichte und Entstehung der "Unterweisung im Tonsatz, theoretischer Teil"', *Hindemith-Jahrbuch*, ix (1980), 16–64

C. Taylor: 'The Hindemith Theories: a Revaluation of Premise and Purpose', *MR*, xliv (1980), 246

W. Thomson: 'Hindemith's Contribution to Music Theory', *JMT*, ix (1965), 54

J. Hirshberg: 'Formal and Dramatic Aspects of Sonata Form in Mozart's "Idomeneo"', *MR*, xxxviii (1977), 192

E. T. A. Hoffman: [Review of Beethoven's Fifth Symphony], *AMZ*, xii (1809–10), cols. 630, 652; partial Eng. trans. in *Beethoven: Symphony no.5 in C minor*, ed. E. Forbes (New York, 1971), 150

C. Dahlhaus: 'E. T. A. Hoffmans Beethoven-Kritik und die Aesthetik der Erhabenen', *AMw*, xxxviii (1981), 79

O. Hostinský: *Das Musikalisch-Schöne und das Gesamtkunstwerk vom Standpunkte der formalen Ästhetik* (Leipzig, 1877)

B. Hough: 'Schoenberg's "Herzgewächse" and the "Blaue Reiter" Almanach', *JASI*, vii (1983), 197

R. Howat: 'Bartók, Lendvai and the Principles of Proportional Analysis', *MusA*, ii (1983), 69; response by Lendvai, iii (1984), 255

——: *Debussy in Proportion: a Musical Analysis* (Cambridge, 1983)

J. Hunkemöller: 'Bartók analysiert seine "Musik für Saiteninstrumente, Schlagzeug und Celesta"', *AMw*, xl (1983), 147

J. T. Hutcheson: *Musical Form and Analysis: a Programmed Course* (Boston, 1972)

M. H. Hyde: 'A Theory of Twelve-tone Meter', *MTS*, vi (1984), 14–51

——: 'Musical Form and the Development of Schoenberg's Twelve-tone Method', *JMT*, xxix (1985), 85–143

C. Hynais: *Die Harmonik Richard Wagners in Bezug auf die Fundamentaltheorie Sechters* (Vienna, 1901)

M. Imberty: *Entendre la musique: sémantique psychologique de la musique* (Paris, 1979)

R. Jackendoff and F. Lerdahl: 'Generative Music Theory and its Relation to Psychology', *JMT*, xxv (1981), 45–90

——: see also Lerdahl and Jackendoff

R. Jackson: 'Music Theory: a Single or Multiple View?', *College Music Symposium*, xiii (1973), 65

R. L. Jacobs: 'Gestalt Psychologists on Music: a Discussion of the Article on Gestalt Psychology in Grove V', *MR*, xvii (1956), 185

S. Jadassohn: *Musikalische Kompositions-Lehre* (Leipzig, 1883–9)

R. Jakobson: 'Musikwissenschaft und Linguistik', *Prager Presse* (7 Dec 1932); Eng. trans. in *Selected Writings*, ii (The Hague, 1971)

K. Jeppesen: *Palastrinastil med särligt henblik paa dissonansbehandlingen* (Copenhagen, 1923; Ger. trans., 1925; Eng. trans., 1927, 2/1946/R1971 as *The Style of Palestrina and the Dissonance*)

——: 'Zur Kritik der Klassischen Harmonielehre', *IMSCR*, iv Basel 1949, 23

J. Jiránek: 'Observations on the Theory and Historical and Contemporary Practice of Musical Analysis', *HV*, xiii (1976), 106

——: 'Semantische Analyse der Musik', *AMw*, xxxvii (1980), 187

——: 'Janáčeks Klavierkompositionen vom Standpunkt ihres dramatischen Charakters: Versuch einer semantischen Analyse', *AMw*, xxxix (1982), 179

P. Johnson: 'Symmetrical Sets in Webern's op.10, no.4', *PNM*, xvii/1 (1978), 219

O. Jonas: see Schenker (ii)

G. T. Jones: 'Symbols used in Music Analysis: a Progress Report', *Council for Research in Music Education Bulletin*, no.2 (1964), 9; no.16 (1968), 68

C. M. Joseph: 'Structural Coherence in Stravinsky's "Piano-Rag-Music"', *MTS*, iv (1982), 76

Bibliography

T. Kabisch: 'Struktur und Form im Spätwerk Franz Liszts: das Klavierstück "Unstern" (1886)', *AMw*, xlii (1985), 178

G. Kähler: *Studien zur Entstehung der Formenlehre in der Musiktheorie* (diss., U. of Heidelberg, 1958)

E. Karkoschka: 'Musik und Semantik', *Melos*, xxxii (1962), 252

——: 'Zur musikalischen Form und Formanalyse', *Probleme des musiktheoretischen Unterrichts*, ed. R. Stephan (Berlin, 1967), 40

——: 'Über Exaktheit in Musikanalyse', *Zeitschrift für Musiktheorie*, iv/2 (1973), 3

T. Karp: 'A Test for Melodic Borrowings among Notre Dame "Organa dupla"', *The Computer and Music*, ed. H. B. Lincoln (Ithaca, NY, and London, 1970), 293

W. Karthaus: 'Die musikalische Analyse', *Die Musik*, xxi (1928–9), 264

J. Kasem-Bek: 'Informationstheorie und Analyse musikalischer Werke', *AMw*, xxxv (1978), 62

J. C. Kassler: *The Science of Music in Britain, 1714–1830* (New York, 1979)

M. Kassler: 'A Sketch of the Formalized Use of Languages for the Assertion of Music', *PNM*, i/2 (1963), 83

——: *A Trinity of Essays: toward a Theory that is the Twelve-note Class System; toward Development of a Constructive Tonality Theory based on Writing by Heinrich Schenker; toward a Simple Programming Language for Musical Information Retrieval* (diss., Princeton U., 1967)

A. T. Katz: see Schenker (ii)

H. Kaufmann: 'Struktur in Schönbergs Georgeliedern'; 'Figur in Weberns erster Bagatelle', *Neue Wege der musikalischen Analyse*, ed. R. Stephan (Berlin, 1967), 53, 69

——: 'Zur Problematik der Werkgestalt in der Musik des 18. Jahrhunderts', *NZM*, cxxx (1969), 290

S. Keil: 'Zum Begriff "Struktur" in der Musik', *Musica*, xxviii (1974), 324

A. Keiler: 'The Syntax of Prolongation I', *ITO*, iii/5 (1977), 3; see also M. A. Guck: 'The Functional Relations of Chords: a Theory of Musical Intuitions', *ITO*, iv/5 (1978), 29

——: 'Bernstein's "The Unanswered Question" and the Problem of Musical Competence', *MQ*, lxiv (1978), 195

Hans Keller: 'KV503: the Unity of Contrasting Themes and Movements', *MR*, xvii (1956), 48, 120

——: 'A Slip of Mozart's: its Analytical Significance', *Tempo*, no.42 (1956–7), 2

——: 'Functional Analysis: its Pure Application', *MR*, xviii (1957), 202; see also xxi (1960), 73, 237

——: 'Knowing Things Backwards', *Tempo*, no.46 (1957), 14

——: 'The Musical Analysis of Music', *The Listener*, lviii (29 Aug 1957), 326

——: 'Wordless Analysis', *Musical Events*, xii (1957), Dec, 26

——: 'The Home-coming of Musical Analysis', *MT*, xcix (1958), 657

——: 'Wordless Functional Analysis: the First Year', *MR*, xix (1958), 192

——: 'The Principles of Composition (I)', *The Score and the IMA Magazine*, no.26 (1960), 35

——: 'Wordless Functional Analysis: the Second Year and Beyond', *MR*, xxi (1960), 73, 237

——: 'Schoenberg's Return to Tonality', *JASI*, v (1981), 2

——: 'Epi/Prologue: Criticism and Analysis', *MusA*, i (1982), 9

——: 'Functional Analysis of Mozart's G minor Quintet', *MusA*, iv (1985), 73 [introduction and score]

——: *The Great Haydn Quartets: their Interpretation* (London, 1986)

    P. Barford: 'Wordless Functional Analysis', *MMR*, lxxxviii (1958), 44

    D. Cooke: 'In Defence of Functional Analysis', *MT*, c (1959), 456

    See also Beeson (1971)

Hermann Keller: *Das Wohltemperierte Klavier von J. S. Bach* (Kassel, 1965; Eng. trans. by L. Gerdine, 1976)

R. Kelterborn: *Zum Beispiel Mozart: Beitrag zur musikalischen Analyse* (Basle, 1981)

J. Kerman: 'A Profile for Musicology', *JAMS*, xviii (1965), 61; correspondence, 222, 426

——: 'Verdi's Use of Recurring Themes', *Studies in Music History: Essays for Oliver Strunk* (Princeton, 1968), 496

155

Bibliography

——: *The Masses and Motets of William Byrd* (Berkeley, 1981)
——: *Contemplating Music* (Cambridge, Mass., 1985; as *Musicology*, London, 1985)
——: see also Tovey
W. Kindermann: 'Dramatic Recapitulation in Wagner's "Götterdämmerung"', *19th Century Music*, iv (1980–81), 101
——: 'Das "Geheimnis der Form" in Wagners "Tristan und Isolde"', *AMw*, xl (1983), 174
J. P. Kirnberger: *Der allezeit fertige Polonoisen- und Menuettencomponist* (Berlin, 1757; Fr. trans., 1757)
——: *Die Kunst des reinen Satzes in der Musik aus sicheren Grundsätzen hergeleitet* (Berlin, 1771–9/ R1968, 2/1793; Eng. trans. of i and ii/1 by D. W. Beach and J. Thym, 1982)
——: *Die wahren Grundsätze zum Gebrauch der Harmonie . . . als ein Zusatz zu der Kunst des reinen Satzes in der Musik* (Berlin, 1773/R1974, 2/1793; Eng. trans. in *JMT*, xxiii, 1979) [written by J. A. P. Schulz under Kirnberger's supervision]
——: see also Sulzer
    J. Mainka: 'Frühe Analysen zweier Stücke aus dem "Wohltemperierten Klavier"', *Musa–mens–musici: im Gedenken an Walther Vetter* (Leipzig, 1969), 177 [essays by J. A. P. Schulz, 1773]
    W. S. Newman: 'Kirnberger's "Method for Tossing Off Sonatas"', *MQ*, xlvii (1961), 517
    See also Wason (1981, 1983)
H. Kirschenbaum: 'Music Analysis by Computer', *Music Educators Journal*, liii/6 (1967), 94
P. Kivy: *The Corded Shell: Reflections on Musical Expression* (Princeton, 1980)
——: *Sound and Semblance: Reflections on Musical Representation* (Princeton, 1984)
R. Klein: 'Vom Sinn der Analyse', *ÖMz*, xx (1965), 37
V. L. Kliewer: *The Concept of Organic Unity in Music Criticism and Analysis* (diss., Indiana U., 1961)
R. Kluge: 'Definition der Begriffe Gestalt und Intonation', *BMw*, vi (1964), 85
——: 'Volksliedanalyse und -systematisierung mit Hilfe eines Rechenautomaten', *GfMKB, Leipzig 1966*, 458
——: 'Typ, Funktion, Bedeutung: Bemerkungen zur semantischen Analytik musikalischer Typen', *BMw*, ix (1967), 98
——: 'Zur automatischen quantitativen Bestimmung musikalischer Ähnlichkeit', *IMSCR, x Ljubljana 1967*, 450
R. Knapp: 'The Tonal Structure of "Tristan und Isolde": a Sketch', *JASI*, xlv (1984), 11
T. Kneif: 'Bedeutung, Struktur, Gegenfigur: zur Theorie des musikalischen "Meinens"', *IRASM*, ii (1971), 213
L. Knopoff: 'Some Technological Advances in Musical Analysis', *SM*, vii (1965), 301
H. C. Koch: *Versuch einer Anleitung zur Composition* (Leipzig and Rudolstadt, 1782–93/R1969; Eng. trans. of ii, 342–464 and iii by N. K. Baker, 1983 as *Introductory Essay on Composition: the Mechanical Rules of Melody, Sections 3 and 4*)
    N. K. Baker: 'Heinrich Koch and the Theory of Melody', *JMT*, xx (1976), 1–48
——: 'The Aesthetic Theories of Heinrich Christoph Koch', *IRASM*, viii (1977), 183
    C. Dahlhaus: 'Der rhetorische Formbegriff H. Chr. Kochs und die Theorie der Sonatenform', *AMw*, xxxv (1978), 155
    S. Davis: 'H. C. Koch, the Classic Concerto, and the Sonata-form Retransition', *JMus*, iii (1983), 45
    G. Henneberg: 'Heinrich Christoph Kochs Analysen von Instrumentalwerken Joseph Haydns', *Haydn-Studien*, iv (1978), 105
    G. Jones: *Heinrich Christoph Koch's Description of the Symphony and a Comparison with Selected Symphonies of C. P. E. Bach and Haydn* (diss., UCLA, 1973)
    E. R. Sisman: 'Small and Expanded Forms: Koch's Model and Haydn's Music', *MQ*, lxviii (1982), 444–75
    G. Wagner: 'Anmerkungen zur Formtheorie Heinrich Christoph Kochs', *AMw*, xli (1984), 86
    See also Bent (1984) and Feil (1955)
W. Koch: 'Inhaltliche oder formale Analyse?: zur Krise des musikalischen Hörens', *Musica*, i (1947), 192

156

Bibliography

F. Koegel: 'Der Bau des Tristandramas', *BB*, xv (1892), 257

V. Kofi Agawu: 'The Musical Language of "Kindertotenlieder" no.2', *JMus*, ii (1983), 81

——: 'Structural "Highpoints" in Schumann's "Dichterliebe"', *MusA*, iii (1984), 159

E. B. Kohs: *Musical Form: Studies in Analysis and Synthesis* (Boston, 1976)

A. Kollmann: *An Essay on Musical Harmony* (London, 1796, 2/1817)

——: *An Essay on Practical Musical Composition* (London, 1799/R1973), rev. 2/1812)

——: *A New Theory of Musical Harmony* (London, 1806, rev. 2/1823)

M. Kassler: 'Transferring a Tonality to a Computer', *IMSCR*, xii *Berkeley 1977*, 339

J. P. Lambert: 'Eighteenth-century Harmonic Theory in Concept and Practice: Kollmann's Analysis of J. S. Bach's Chromatic Fantasy', *ITO*, viii/3 (1984), 11

W. Kolneder: 'Visuelle und auditive Analyse', *Veröffentlichungen des Instituts für Neue Musik und Musikerziehung Darmstadt*, iii (1962, 2/1965), 57

——: 'Zur Geschichte der Analyse musikalischer Kunstwerke', *SMz*, cv (1965), 68

A. J. Komar: *Theory of Suspensions: a Study of Metrical and Pitch Relations in Tonal Music* (Princeton, 1971)

S. M. Kostka: *A Bibliography of Computer Applications in Music* (Hackensack, 1974)

D. Kraehenbuehl and E. Coons: 'Information as a Measure of Experience in Music', *Journal of Aesthetics and Art Criticism*, xvii (1958–9), 510

—— and others: 'The Professional Music Theorist: his Habits and Training – a Forum', *JMT*, iv (1960), 62

J. Kramer: 'The Fibonacci Series in Twentieth-century Music', *JMT*, xvii (1973), 111–48

——: 'Studies of Time and Music: a Bibliography', *MTS*, vii (1985), 72–106

L. Kramer: 'The Mirror of Tonality: Transitional Features of Nineteenth-century Harmony', *19th Century Music*, iv (1980–81), 191

J. Kresky: *Tonal Music: Twelve Analytic Studies* (Bloomington, 1977)

H. Kretzschmar: *Führer durch den Konzertsaal*, i (Leipzig, 1887, 7/1932); ii (Leipzig, 1888, 5/1921); iii (Leipzig, 1890, 5/1939)

——: 'Anregungen zur Förderung musikalischer Hermeneutik', *JbMP 1902*, 47; *1905*, 75; also in *Gesammelte Aufsätze aus den Jahrbüchern der Musikbibliothek Peters* (Leipzig, 1911), i, 168; ii, 280

W. Braun: 'Kretzschmars Hermeneutik', *Beiträge zur musikalischen Hermeneutik*, ed. C. Dahlhaus (Regensburg, 1975), 33

I. Krohn: 'Über die Methode der musikalischen Analyse', *IMusSCR*, iv *London 1911*, 250

K. Kropfinger: 'Zur thematischen Funktion der langsamen Einleitung bei Beethoven', *Colloquium amicorum: Joseph Schmidt-Görg* (Bonn, 1967), 197

E. Kurth: 'Die Jugendopern Glucks bis Orfeo', *SMw*, i (1913), 193–277

——: *Die Voraussetzungen der theoretischen Harmonik und der tonalen Darstellungssysteme* (Berne, 1913/R1973)

——: *Die Grundlagen des linearen Kontrapunkts: Einführung in Stil und Technik von Bachs melodischer Polyphonie* (Berne, 1917, 5/1956/R1977)

——: 'Zur Motivbildung Bachs', *BJb*, xiv (1917), 80–136

——: *Romantische Harmonik und ihre Krise in Wagners 'Tristan'* (Berne and Leipzig, 1920/R1968, 3/1923)

——: *Bruckner* (Berlin, 1925/R1971)

——: *Musikpsychologie* (Berlin, 1931/R1969, 2/1947)

D. M. Hsu: 'Ernst Kurth and his Concept of Music as Motion', *JMT*, x (1966), 2

P. McCreless: 'Ernst Kurth and the Analysis of the Chromatic Music of the Late Nineteenth Century', *MTS*, v (1983), 56

L. A. Rothfarb: *Ernst Kurth as Theorist and Analyst* (diss., Yale U., 1985)

See also Dahlhaus (1977) and Federhofer (1981)

A. Labussière: *Codage des structures rythmo-mélodiques à partir de créations vocales* (Paris, 1973)

R. Lach: 'Der Inhaltsproblem in der Musikästhetik: ein Beitrag der musikalischen Hermeneutik', *Festschrift Hermann Kretzschmar* (Leipzig, 1918/R1973), 74

P. Lansky and G. Perle: 'Atonality', 'Set', *Grove 6*

J. LaRue: 'A System of Symbols for Formal Analysis', *JAMS*, x (1957), 25; see also xix (1966), 403

——: 'On Style Analysis', *JMT*, vi (1962), 91

157

Bibliography

——: 'Two Problems in Musical Analysis: the Computer Lends a Hand', *Computers in Humanistic Research: Readings and Perspectives*, ed. E. A. Bowles (Englewood Cliffs, 1967), 194

——: 'Fundamental Considerations in Style Analysis', *Notes*, xxv (1968–9), 447

——: *Guidelines for Style Analysis* (New York, 1970; see also *College Music Symposium*, xxi (1981), 40)

O. E. Laske: 'An Acoulogical Performance Model for Music', *Electronic Music Reports*, no.4 (1971), 31–64

——: 'On Musical Strategies with a View to a Generative Theory of Music', *Interface*, i (1972), 111

——: *Introduction to a Generative Theory of Music* (Utrecht, 1973)

——: 'Verification and Sociological Interpretation in Musicology', *IRASM*, viii (1977), 211

——: *Music and Mind: an Artificial Intelligence Perspective* (Boston, 1981)

——: 'KEITH: a Rule-system for Making Music-analytical Discoveries', *Musical Grammars and Computer Analysis: Modena 1982*, 165–99

——: 'Understanding Musical Listening Procedurally', *Sonus*, v/1 (1984), 61

D. Leech-Wilkinson: *Compositional Procedure in the Four-part Isorhythmic Works of Philippe de Vitry and his Contemporaries* (diss., U. of Cambridge, 1983)

——: 'Machaut's "Rose, lis" and the Problem of Early Music Analysis', *MusA*, iii (1984), 9

H. Lefebvre: 'Musique et sémiologie', *Mj*, no.4 (1971), 52

G. Lefkoff: 'Computers and the Study of Musical Style', *West Virginia University Conference on Computer Applications in Music: Morgantown 1966*, 43

P. G. Le Huray and J. Day, eds.: *Music and Aesthetics in the Eighteenth and Early-nineteenth Centuries* (Cambridge, 1981)

H. Leichtentritt: *Musikalische Formenlehre* (Leipzig, 1911, enlarged 2/1927; Eng. trans., 1951)

H. Lemacher and H. Schröder: *Formenlehre der Musik* (Cologne, 1962, 2/1968; Eng. trans., 1967)

E. Lendvai: *Bartók stilusa* [Bartók's style] (Budapest, 1955; rev. Eng. trans., 1971 as *Béla Bartók: an Analysis of his Music*)

——: *The Workshop of Bartók and Kodály* (Budapest, 1983)

——: 'Remarks on Roy Howat's "Principles of Proportional Analysis" ', *MusA*, iii (1984), 255 [see Howat, 1983]

W. von Lenz: *Beethoven et ses trois styles: analyses des sonates de piano, suivis de l'essai d'un catalogue critique, chronologique et anecdotique de l'oeuvre de Beethoven* (St Petersburg, 1852); ed. M. D. Calvocoressi (Paris, 1909/R1980)

F. Lerdahl and R. Jackendoff: 'Toward a Formal Theory of Tonal Music', *JMT*, xxi (1977), 111–71

——: 'On the Theory of Grouping and Meter', *MQ*, lxvii (1981), 479

——: *A Generative Theory of Tonal Music* (Cambridge, Mass., 1983) [review and responses, *JMT*, xxviii (1984), 271; xxix (1985), 145, 161]

——: see also Jackendoff and Lerdahl

J. Lester: 'Articulation of Tonal Structures as a Criterion for Analytic Choice', *MTS*, i (1979), 67

——: 'Simultaneity Structures and Harmonic Functions', *ITO*, v/5 (1980), 3

S. Levarie: *Mozart's Le nozze di Figaro: a Critical Analysis* (Chicago, 1952/R1977)

——: 'Tonal Relations in Verdi's "Un Ballo in maschera" ', *19th Century Music*, ii (1978–9), 143

——: 'Once More: the Slow Introduction to Beethoven's First Symphony', *MR*, xl (1979), 168

C. Lévi-Strauss: *Le cru et le cuit* (Paris, 1964; Eng. trans., 1970 as *The Raw and the Cooked*), esp. 14–32

  See Nattiez (1973) and Osmond-Smith (1985)

D. B. Levy: *Early Performances of Beethoven's Ninth Symphony: a Documentary Study of Five Cities* (diss., U. of Rochester, 1980)

D. Lewin: 'Intervallic Relations between Two Collections of Notes', *JMT*, iii (1959), 298

——: 'The Intervallic Content of a Collection of Notes', *JMT*, iv (1960), 98

Bibliography

——: 'Forte's Interval Vector, my Interval Function, and Regener's Common-note Function', *JMT*, xxi (1977), 194–237

——: 'Some New Constructs involving Abstract PCsets, and Probabilistic Applications', 'A Response to a Response: on PCset Relatedness', *PNM*, xviii/1–2 (1979–80), 433, 498

——: 'On Generalized Intervals and Transformations', *JMT*, xxiv (1980), 243

——: 'On Harmony and Meter in Brahms's op.76, no.8', *19th Century Music*, iv (1980–81), 261

——: 'A Way into Schoenberg's Opus 15, Number 7', *ITO*, vi/1 (1981), 3

——: 'Some Investigations into Foreground Rhythmic and Metric Patterning', *Music Theory: Special Topics*, ed. R. Browne (New York, 1981), 101–37

——: 'A Formal Theory of Generalized Tonal Functions', *JMT*, xxvi (1982), 23–60

——: 'On Extended Z-Triples', 'An Example of Serial Technique in Early Webern', *TP*, vii/1 (1982), 38, 40

——: 'Vocal Meter in Schoenberg's Atonal Music, with a Note on a Serial Hauptstimme', *ITO*, vi/4 (1982), 12

——: 'Schubert: "Auf dem Flusse" ', *19th Century Music*, vi (1982–3), 47

——: 'An Interesting Global Rule for Species Counterpoint', *ITO*, vi/8 (1983), 19

C. Lewis: 'Tonal Focus in Atonal Music: Berg's op.5/3', *MTS*, iii (1981), 84

D. Lidov: *On Musical Phrase* (Montreal, 1975)

H. B. Lincoln: 'The Computer and Music Research: Prospects and Problems', *Council for Research in Music Education Bulletin*, xviii (1969), 1

——, ed.: *The Computer and Music* (Ithaca, NY, and London, 1970), esp. 115–295

B. Lindblom and J. Sundberg: 'Towards a Generative Theory of Melody', *Speech Transmission Laboratory Quarterly Progress and Status Report*, iv (1969), 53–86

——: 'Towards a Generative Theory of Melody', *STMf*, lii (1970), 71

P. Linke: *Grundfragen der Wahrnehmungslehre* (Munich, 1918)

D. Linthicum: 'Verdi's "Falstaff" and Classical Sonata Form', *MR*, xxxix (1978), 39

J. Lippius: *Synopsis musicae novae* (Strasbourg, 1612)

Z. Lissa: 'Hegel und das Problem der Formintegration in der Musik', *Festschrift für Walter Wiora* (Kassel, 1967), 112

S. Łobaczewska: *Die Analyse des musikalischen Kunstwerks als Problem der Musikwissenschaft* (Vienna, 1956)

J. C. Lobe: *Compositions-Lehre oder umfassende Theorie von der thematischen Arbeit* (Weimar, 1844)

——: *Lehrbuch der musikalischen Komposition*, i: *Von der ersten Elementen der Harmonielehre an bis zur vollständigen Komposition des Streichquartetts und aller Arten von Klavierwerken* (Leipzig, 1850, 6/1900 ed. H. Kretzschmar; Fr. trans., 1889); ii: *Die Lehre von der Instrumentation* (Leipzig, 1855, 3/1878); iii: *Lehre von der Fuge, dem Kanon und dem doppelten Kontrapunkte* (Leipzig, 1860, 2/1875); iv: *Die Oper* (Leipzig, 1867, 2/1887)

——: *Katechismus der Compositionslehre* (Leipzig, 1862, Eng. trans., 1868; rev. 8/1914)
  See Bent (1984)

L. Lockwood: 'A Stylistic Investigation of the Masses of Josquin Desprez with the Aid of the Computer: a Progress Report', *Musicology and the Computer*, ed. B. S. Brook (New York, 1970), 19

——: 'The Autograph of the First Movement of Beethoven's Sonata for Violoncello and Pianoforte, Opus 69', *Music Forum*, ii (1970), 1–109

D. Loeb: 'Mathematical Aspects of Music', *Music Forum*, ii (1970), 110

——: see also Schenker (ii)

G. W. Logemann: 'The Canons in the Musical Offering of J. S. Bach: an Example of Computational Musicology', *Elektronische Datenverarbeitung in der Musikwissenschaft*, ed. H. Heckmann (Regensburg, 1967), 63

J. B. Logier: *System der Musik-Wissenschaft und der praktischen Komposition* (Berlin, 1827; Eng. trans., 1827/R1976 as *A System of the Science of Music and Practical Composition*; rev., enlarged C. Stein, 1888/R1976 as *Logier's Comprehensive Course in Music, Harmony, and Practical Composition*)

A. Lomax: *Folk Song Style and Culture* (Washington, DC, 1968)

H. C. Longuet-Higgins: 'Perception of Melodies', *Nature*, cclxiii (1976), 646

——: 'The Perception of Music', *Interdisciplinary Science Review*, iii (1978), 143
—— and M. Steedman: 'On Interpreting Bach', *Machine Intelligence*, vi (1971), 221
A. Lönn and E. Kjellberg, eds.: *Analytica: Studies in the Description and Analysis of Music* (Stockholm, 1985)
A. B. Lord: *The Singer of Tales* (Cambridge, Mass., 1960)
C. Lord: 'Intervallic Similarity Relations in Atonal Set Analysis', *JMT*, xxv (1981), 91
A. O. Lorenz: *Gedanken und Studien zur musikalischen Formgebung in R. Wagners 'Ring des Nibelungen'* (diss., U. of Frankfurt am Main, 1922)
——: 'Die formale Gestaltung des Vorspiels zu Tristan und Isolde', *ZMw*, v (1922–3), 546
——: 'Betrachtungen über Beethovens Eroica-Skizzen', *ZMw*, vii (1924–5), 409
——: *Das Geheimnis der Form bei Richard Wagner*, i: *Der musikalische Aufbau des Bühnenfestspieles Der Ring des Nibelungen* (Berlin, 1924/R1966); ii: *Der musikalische Aufbau von Richard Wagners 'Tristan und Isolde'* (Berlin, 1926/R1966); iii: *Der musikalische Aufbau von Richard Wagners 'Die Meistersinger von Nürnberg'* (Berlin, 1930/R1966); iv: *Der musikalische Aufbau von Richard Wagners 'Parsifal'* (Berlin, 1933/R1966)
——: 'Das Finale in Mozarts Meisteropern', *Die Musik*, xix (1927), 621
See Dahlhaus (1977) and Kindermann (1983)
M. Lussy: *Traité de l'expression musicale: accents, nuances et mouvements dans la musique vocale et instrumentale* (Paris, ?1870, 8/1904; Eng. trans. by M. E. von Glehn, 1885)
——: *Le rythme musical: son origine, sa fonction et son accentuation* (Paris, 1883, 4/1911; abridged Eng. trans., ed. E. Dutoit as *A Short Treatise on Musical Rhythm*, 1908; Sp. trans. by P. Quaratino, Buenos Aires, 1945)
——: *L'anacrouse dans la musique moderne: grammaire de l'exécution musicale* (Paris, 1903)
——: *La sonate pathétique de L. van Beethoven, op.13, édition rythmée et annotée* (Paris, 1912)
F. B. Mâche: 'Connaissance des structures sonores', *ReM*, no.244 (1959), 17
——: 'Méthodes linguistiques et musicologie', *Mj*, no.5 (1971), 75
M. McLean: 'A New Method of Melodic Interval Analysis as Applied to Maori Chant', *EM*, x (1966), 174
M. McMullin: 'The Symbolic Analysis of Music', *MR*, viii (1947), 25
——: 'Musical Analysis and Appreciation: a Critique of "Pure Music" ', *MR*, xlv (1984), 47
A. McNamee: 'Bitonality, Mode, and Interval in the Music of Karol Szymanowski', *JMT*, xxix (1985), 61
S. Macpherson: *Form in Music with Special Reference to the Designs of Instrumental Music* (London, 1908, 2/1912 with appx, rev. 1915)
G. Madell: 'Thematic Unity and the Language of Music', *MR*, xxiii (1962), 30
J. Mainwaring: ' "Gestalt" Psychology', *Grove 5*
N. Malmendier: *Grundlagen der statistischen Teste und die Möglichkeiten ihrer Anwendung bei der Analyse der Formalstruktur von Werken der Sprache und Musik* (diss., Technische Hochschule, Aachen, 1966)
J.-E. Marie: 'Inverse Function: Differentiation and Integration in Messiaen and Boulez', *Sonus*, ii/1 (1981), 26; v/1 (1984), 36
F. W. Marpurg: *Systematische Einleitung in die musikalische Setzkunst, nach den Lehrsätzen des Herrn Rameau* (Leipzig, 1757) [trans. of D'Alembert, 1752]
C. Marti: 'Zur Kompositionstechnik von Igor Strawinsky: das *Petit concert* aus der *Histoire du soldat*', *AMw*, xxxviii (1981), 93
D. Martino: 'The Source Set and its Aggregate Formations', *JMT*, v (1961), 224–73
E. W. Marvin: 'The Structural Role of Complementation in Webern's "Orchestral Pieces (1913)" ', *MTS*, v (1983), 76
A. B. Marx: *Die Lehre von der musikalischen Komposition, praktisch-theoretisch*, i: (Leipzig, 1837, rev. 9/1887, 10/1903; Eng. trans. of 3rd edn. by H. Saroni, New York, 1851; Eng. trans. of 4th edn. by A. Wehrhan, London, 1852); ii: *Die freie Komposition* (Leipzig, 1837, rev. 7/1890); iii: (Leipzig, 1845, 5/1879); iv: (Leipzig, 1847, rev. 5/1888) [revs. of 1887–90 by H. Riemann]
——: *Die alte Musiklehre im Streit mit unserer Zeit* (Leipzig, 1841)
——: *Die Musik des neunzehnten Jahrhunderts und ihre Pflege: Methode der Musik* (Leipzig, 1855, 2/1873; Eng. trans. by A. H. Wehrhan and N. C. MacFarren, 1855)

——: *Ludwig van Beethoven: Leben und Schaffen* (Berlin, 1859, 7/1907–10)

——: *Anleitung zum Vortrag Beethovenscher Klavierwerke* (Berlin, 1863, 4/1912; Eng. trans. by F. L. Gwinner, 1895)

——: *Musikalische Schriften über Tondichter und Tonkunst*, ed. L. Hirschberg (Hildburghausen, 1912–22) [collection of most of Marx's important contributions to *Berliner allgemeine musikalische Zeitung*]

C. Dahlhaus: 'Formenlehre und Gattungstheorie bei A. B. Marx', *Heinrich Sievers zum 70. Geburtstag* (Tutzing, 1978), 29

——: 'Aesthetische Prämissen der "Sonatenform" bei Adolf Bernhard Marx', *AMw*, xli (1984), 73

A. Edler: 'Zur Musikanschauung von Adolf Bernhard Marx', *Beiträge zur Geschichte der Musikanschauung im 19. Jahrhundert*, ed. W. Salmen (Regensburg, 1965), 103

K.-E. Eicke: *Der Streit zwischen A. B. Marx und G. W. Fink um die Kompositionslehre* (diss., U. of Cologne, 1966; Regensburg, 1966)

See also Moyer (1969), Nielsen (1971) and Ritzel (1969)

R. M. Mason: 'An Encoding Algorithm and Tables for the Digital Analysis of Harmony', *JRME*, xvii (1969), 286, 369

D. Mast: *Struktur und Form bei Alexander N. Skrjabin* (Munich, 1981)

J. Mattheson: *Das neu-eröffnete Orchestre, oder Universelle und gründliche Anleitung* (Hamburg, 1713)

——: *Kern melodischer Wissenschaft* (Hamburg, 1737/R1976)

——: *Der vollkommene Capellmeister* (Hamburg, 1739/R1954; Eng. trans., ed. E. C. Harris, 1969, rev. 1981)

W. Arlt: 'Zur Handhabung der "inventio" in der deutschen Musiklehre des frühen achtzehnten Jahrhunderts', *New Mattheson Studies*, ed. G. J. Buelow and H. J. Marx (Cambridge, 1983), 371

W. Braun: *Johann Mattheson und die Aufklärung* (diss., Martin Luther U., 1952)

——: 'Musiktheorie im 17./18. Jahrhundert als "öffentliche" Angelegenheit', *Über Musiktheorie*, ed. F. Zaminer (Cologne, 1970), 37

G. J. Buelow: 'The Concept of "Melodielehre": a Key to Classic Style', *MJb 1978–9*, 182

——: 'Johann Mattheson and the Invention of the "Affektenlehre"', *New Mattheson Studies*, ed. G. J. Buelow and H. J. Marx (Cambridge, 1983), 393

P. Kivy: 'What Mattheson Said', *MR*, xxxiv (1973), 132

——: 'Mattheson as Philosopher of Art', *MQ*, lxx (1984), 248

H. Lenneberg: 'Johann Mattheson on Affect and Rhetoric in Music', *JMT*, ii (1958), 47, 193

C. V. Palisca: 'The Genesis of Mattheson's Style Classification', *New Mattheson Studies*, ed. G. J. Buelow and H. J. Marx (Cambridge, 1983), 409

W. Schenkman: 'Mattheson's "Forty-eight" and their Commentaries', *MR*, xlii (1981), 9

See also Bent (1984), Federhofer (1970) and Kivy (1980)

C. Mayrberger: 'Die Harmonik Richard Wagner's an den Leitmotiven des Vorspieles zu "Tristan und Isolde" erläutert', *BB*, iv (1881), 169

See Wason (1981, 1983)

R. Mayrhofer: *Psychologie des Klanges und die daraus hervorgehende, theoretisch-praktische Harmonielehre* (Leipzig, 1907)

——: *Die organische Harmonielehre* (Berlin, 1908)

L. Mazel: 'Ästhetik und Analyse von Musikwerken', *Kunst und Literatur*, xv (1967), 489

A. Mendel and T. Hall: 'Princeton Computer Tools for Music Research', *Informatique et sciences humaines*, xix (Dec 1973), 41, 61

H. Mersmann: *Beethoven: die Synthese der Stile* (Berlin, 1922)

——: 'Versuch einer Phänomenologie der Musik', *ZMw*, v (1922–3), 226–69

——: *Musikhören* (Potsdam and Berlin, 1938, 2/1952)

O. Messiaen: *Technique de mon langage musicale* (Paris, 1944; Eng. trans., 1956)

K. Mey: *Musik als tönende Weltidee* (Leipzig, 1901)

H. Meyer: 'Analytische und/oder hermeneutische Werkbetrachtung', *Musica*, xxiv (1970), 346

Bibliography

L. B. Meyer: *Emotion and Meaning in Music* (Chicago, 1956)

——: 'Meaning in Music and Information Theory', *Journal of Aesthetics and Art Criticism*, xv (1956–7), 412; repr. in *Music, the Arts and Ideas* (Chicago, 1967), chap.1

——: 'On Rehearing Music', *JAMS*, xiv (1961), 257; repr. in *Music, the Arts and Ideas* (Chicago, 1967), chap.3

——: *Music, the Arts and Ideas: Patterns and Predictions in Twentieth-century Music* (Chicago, 1967)

——: *Explaining Music: Essays and Explorations* (Berkeley, 1973/R1978)

——: 'Process and Morphology in the Music of Mozart', *JMus*, i (1982), 67

W. Meyer-Eppler: *Grundlagen und Anwendungen der Informationstheorie* (Berlin, 1959)

——: 'Informationstheoretische Probleme der musikalischen Kommunikationen', *Die Reihe*, no.8 (1962), 7; Eng. trans. in *Die Reihe*, no.8 (1968), 7

C. Miereanu: ' "Textkomposition": voie zéro de l'écriture musicale', *Mj*, no.13 (1973), 49

P. Mies: *Die Bedeutung der Skizzen Beethovens zur Erkenntnis seines Stiles* (Leipzig, 1925; Eng. trans., 1929)

J. W. Mitchell: *A History of Theories of Functional Harmonic Progression* (diss., Indiana U., 1963)

R. Mix: *Die Entropieabnahme bei Abhängigkeit zwischen mehreren simultanen Informationsquellen und bei Übergang zu Markoff-Ketten höherer Ordnung, untersucht an musikalischen Beispielen* (Cologne and Opladen, 1967)

A. A. Moles: 'Informationstheorie der Musik', *Nachrichtentechnische Fachberichte*, iii (1956), 47

——: *Théorie de l'information et perception esthétique* (Paris, 1958; Eng. trans., 1966)

J. Molino: 'Fait musical et sémiologie de la musique', *Mj*, no.17 (1975), 37

J.-J. de Momigny: *Cours complet d'harmonie et de composition* (Paris, 1803–6)

——: *La seule vraie théorie de la musique* (Paris, 1821)

    M. Cole: 'Momigny's Analysis of Haydn's Symphony no.103', *MR*, xxx (1969), 261

    A. Palm: *J. J. de Momigny: Leben und Werk* (diss., U. of Tübingen, 1957; Cologne, 1969)

    ——: 'Mozart und Haydn in der Interpretation Momignys', *GfMKB, Kassel 1962*, 187

    ——: 'Mozarts Streichquartett d-moll, KV 421, in der Interpretation Momignys', *MJb 1962–3*, 256

    See also Groth (1983)

J. A. Moorer: *On the Segmentation and Analysis of Continuous Musical Sound by Digital Computer* (diss., Stanford U., 1975)

R. P. Morgan: *The Delayed Structural Downbeat and its Effect on the Tonal and Rhythmic Structure of Sonata Form Recapitulation* (diss., Princeton U., 1969)

——: 'Dissonant Prolongation: Theoretical and Compositional Precedents', *JMT*, xx (1976), 49–91; see also W. E. Benjamin: 'Tonality with Fifths: Remarks on the First Movement of Stravinsky's Concerto for Piano and Wind Instruments', *ITO*, ii/11–12 (1977), 53; iii/2 (1977), 9; W. E. Benjamin: 'Dissonant Prolongations, Perfect Fifths, and Major Thirds in Stravinsky's Piano Concerto', *ITO*, iv/4 (1978), 3

——: 'The Theory and Analysis of Tonal Rhythm', *MQ*, lxiv (1978), 435–73

E. Morin: *Essai stylistique comparé: les variations de William Byrd et John Tomkins sur 'John come kiss me now'* (Montreal, 1979)

R. O. Morris: *The Structure of Music: an Outline for Students* (London, 1935)

D. de la Motte: 'Reform der Formenlehre?', *Probleme des musiktheoretischen Unterrichts*, ed. R. Stephan (Berlin, 1967), 30

——: *Musikalische Analyse* (Kassel, 1968, 2/1972) [with critical commentary by C. Dahlhaus]

H. de la Motte-Haber: 'Typologien musikalischen Verhaltens: ein Überblick', *Musica*, xxiv (1970), 136

N. Moutard: 'L'articulation en musique', *La linguistique*, vii/2 (1971), 5; viii/1 (1972), 25

B. P. V. Moyer: *Concepts of Musical Form in the Nineteenth Century with Special Reference to A. B. Marx and Sonata Form* (diss., Stanford U., 1969)

H. Mühe: *Musikanalyse: Methode, Übung, Anwendung* (Leipzig, 1978)

D. R. Murray: 'Major Analytical Approaches to Wagner's Musical Style: a Critique', *MR*, xxxix (1978), 211

M. Musgrave: 'Brahms's First Symphony: Thematic Coherence and its Secret Origin',

MusA, ii (1983), 117

E. Narmour: *Beyond Schenkerism: the Need for Alternatives in Musical Analysis* (Chicago, 1977)

——: 'Toward an Analytical Symbology: the Melodic, Harmonic and Durational Functions of Implication and Realization', *Musical Grammars and Computer Analysis: Modena 1982*, 83–114

J.-J. Nattiez: 'Lexique des termes linguistiques', *Mj*, no.5 (1971), 93 [incl. bibliography of musical semiotics]

——: 'Situation de la sémiologie musicale', *Mj*, no.5 (1971), 3

——: 'Is a Descriptive Semiotics of Music Possible?', *Language Sciences*, no.23 (1972), 1

——: 'La linguistique: voie nouvelle pour l'analyse musicale?', *Cahiers canadiens de musique*, iv (1972), 101; Eng. trans. in *IRASM*, iv (1973), 56 .

——: 'Analyse musicale et sémiologie: le structuralisme de Lévi-Strauss', *Mj*, no.12 (1973), 59

——: 'Linguistics: a New Approach for Musical Analysis', *IRASM*, iv (1973), 53

——: 'Rencontre avec Lévi-Strauss: le plaisir et la structure', *Mj*, no.12 (1973), 3

——: 'Sémiologie et sémiographie musicales', *Mj*, no.13 (1973), 78

——: 'Trois modèles linguistiques pour l'analyse musicale', *Mj*, no.10 (1973), 3

——: '*Densité 21.5' de Varèse: essai d'analyse sémiologique* (Montreal, 1975; Eng. trans. in *MusA*, i (1982), 243–340)

——: *Fondements d'une sémiologie de la musique* (Paris, 1975)

——: *Tétralogies: Wagner, Boulez, Chéreau* (Paris, 1983)

——: 'The Concepts of Plot and Seriation Process in Music Analysis', *MusA*, iv (1985), 107

—— and L. Hirbour-Paquette: 'Analyse musicale et sémiologie: à propos du Prélude de "Pelléas"', *Mj*, no.10 (1973), 42

J. Dunsby: 'Music and Semiotics: the Nattiez Phase', *MQ*, lxix (1983), 27

O. Neighbour: *The Consort and Keyboard Music of William Byrd* (London, 1978)

C. B. Nelson: 'Programmed Analyses of Musical Works: an Experimental Evaluation', *Bulletin of the Council for Research in Music Education*, xiv (1968), 11

B. Nettl: 'Some Linguistic Approaches to Musical Analysis', *JIFMC*, x (1958), 37

F. Neumann: *Musikalische Syntaxis und Form im Liederzyklus 'Die schöne Müllerin' von Franz Schubert: eine morphologische Studie* (Tutzing, 1978)

D. Neumeyer: 'Organic Structure and the Song Cycle: another Look at Schumann's "Dichterliebe"', *MTS*, iv (1982), 76

B. Newbould: 'A New Analysis of Brahms's Intermezzo in B minor, op.119 no.1', *MR*, xxxviii (1977), 33

W. S. Newman: 'Yet Another Major Beethoven Forgery by Schindler?', *JMus*, iii (1984), 397

P. Nielsen: *Den musikalske formanalyse fra A. B. Marx 'Kompositionslehre' til vore dages strukturanalyse* (Copenhagen, 1971)

Q. R. Nordgren: 'A Measure of Textural Patterns and Strengths', *JMT*, iv (1960), 19

J. Nordmark: 'New Theories of Form and the Problem of Thematic Identities', *JMT*, iv (1960), 210

F. R. Noske: *Forma formans: een struucturanalytische methode toegepast op de instrumentale muziek van Jan Pieterszoon Sweelinck* (Amsterdam, 1969)

G. Nottebohm: *Ein Skizzenbuch von Beethoven* (Leipzig, 1865, 2/1924/R1970)

——: *Beethoveniana* (Leipzig, 1872, 2/1925/R1970)

——: *Ein Skizzenbuch von Beethoven aus dem Jahre 1803* (Leipzig, 1880, 2/1924/R1970)

——: *Zweite Beethoveniana*, ed. E. Mandyczewski (Leipzig, 1887, 2/1925/R1970)

W. Ogden: 'How Tonality Functions in Schoenberg's Opus 11, Number 1', *JASI*, v (1981), 169

M. d'Ollone: *Le langage musicale* (Paris and Geneva, 1954)

D. Osmond-Smith: 'Music as Communication: Semiology or Morphology?', *IRASM*, ii (1971), 108

——: *Playing on Words: a Guide to Luciano Berio's 'Sinfonia'* (London, 1985)

E. Oster: see Schenker (i) and (ii)

C. V. Palisca: 'Theory, Theorists', *Grove 6*

G. D. Parish: 'Tonality: a Multi-levelled System', *MR*, xli (1980), 52

163

Bibliography

R. Parker: 'The Dramatic Structure of "Il trovatore" ', *MusA*, i (1982), 155

R. S. Parks: 'Pitch Organization in Debussy: Unordered Sets in "Brouillards" ', *MTS*, ii (1980), 119

——: 'Harmonic Resources in Bartók's "Fourths" ', *JMT*, xxv (1981), 245

——: 'Tonal Analogues as Atonal Resources and their Relation to Form in Debussy's Chromatic Etude', *JMus*, xxix (1985), 33

R. Pascall: 'Organicist Meditations', *MusA*, i (1982), 112

J. Pasler: 'Debussy, "Jeux" ', *19th Century Music*, vi (1982–3), 60

G. Perle: *Serial Composition and Atonality: an Introduction to the Music of Schoenberg, Berg and Webern* (Los Angeles and London, 1962, 4/1978)

——: *Twelve-tone Tonality* (Berkeley, 1977)

——: *The Operas of Alban Berg*, i: *Wozzeck* (Berkeley, 1980); ii: *Lulu* (Berkeley, 1985)

——: 'Scriabin's Self-Analyses', *MusA*, iii (1984), 101

P. Petrobelli: 'Per un'esegesi della struttura drammatica del "Trovatore" ', *3° congresso internazionale di studi verdiani: Milano 1972*, 387; Eng. trans. in *MusA*, i (1982), 129

——, W. Drabkin and R. Parker: 'Verdi's "Il trovatore": a Symposium', *MusA*, i (1982), 125–67

E. R. Phillips: 'Pitch Structures in a Selected Repertoire of Early German Chorale Melodies', *MTS*, iii (1981), 98

P. S. Phillips: 'The Enigma of "Variations": a Study of Stravinsky's Final Work for Orchestra', *MusA*, iii (1984), 69

G. H. Phipps: 'Tonality in Webern's Cantata 1', *MusA*, iii (1984), 125–58

C. Pieper: *Musikalische Analyse: eine musikalische Formenlehre in der Form von Musteranalysen klassischer Tonstücke* (Cologne, 1925)

A. A. Pierce: *The Analysis of Rhythm in Tonal Music* (diss., Brandeis U., 1968)

A. Pike: *A Phenomenological Analysis of Musical Experience and Other Related Essays* (New York, 1970)

——: 'The Perceptual Aspects of Motivic Structure in Music', *Journal of Aesthetics and Art Criticism*, xxx (1971–2), 79

R. C. Pinkerton: 'Information Theory and Melody', *Scientific American*, cxciv (1956), 77

M. Piszczalski and B. A. Galler: 'Computer Analysis and Transcription of Performed Music: a Project Report', *CHum*, xiii (1979), 195

P. Pontio: *Ragionamento di musica* (Parma, 1588)

A. Pople: 'Skryabin's Prelude, op.67, no.1: Sets and Structure', *MusA*, ii (1983), 151

M. Porten: *Zum Problem der Form bei Debussy: Untersuchungen am Beispiel der Klavierwerke* (Munich, 1974)

H. Pousseur: *Fragments théoriques*, i: *Sur la musique expérimentale* (Brussels, 1970)

——: *Musique, sémantique, société* (Paris, 1972)

H. Powers: Panel contribution, *IMSCR*, xi *Copenhagen 1972*, i, 58

Pozzi Escot: 'Towards a Theoretical Concept: Non-linearity in Webern's opus 11, no.1', *Sonus*, iii/1 (1982), 18

——: 'Gothic Cathedral and Hidden Geometry of St. Hildegard', *Sonus*, v/1 (1984), 14

——: see also Cogan

M. Praetorius: *Syntagma musicum*, iii (Wolfenbüttel, 1618, 2/1619/R1958 and 1976)

J.-G. Prod'homme: *Les symphonies de Beethoven* (Paris, 1906, 5/1949)

——: *Les sonates pour piano de Beethoven* (Paris, 1937)

E. Prout: *Musical Form* (London, 1893–7/R1971)

——: *Applied Forms* (London, 1895)

——: *Analysis of J. S. Bach's Forty-eight Fugues (Das Wohltemperirte Clavier)* (London, 1910)

G. Rabson and C. Rabson: 'The National Tune Index: a Systems Overview', *CHum*, xv (1981), 129

J. Rahn: 'Logic, Set Theory, Music Theory', *College Music Symposium*, xix (1979), 114

——: 'Relating Sets', *PNM*, xviii/1–2 (1979–80), 483

——: *Basic Atonal Theory* (New York, 1980)

——: 'Ockeghem's Three-section Motet "Salve Regina": Problems in Coordinating Pitch and Time Constructs', *MTS*, iii (1981), 117

——: 'Teorie su alcuni mottetti dell'ars antiqua, con relative considerazioni metodologis-

Bibliography

tiche', *Musical Grammars and Computer Analysis: Modena 1982*, 39

J.-P. Rameau: *Traité de l'harmonie réduite à ses principes naturels* (Paris, 1722; Eng. trans., 1737; ed. and Eng. trans. by P. Gossett, New York, 1971)

——: *Génération harmonique ou Traité de musique théorique et pratique* (Paris, 1737); ed. and trans. in D. Hayes: *Rameau's Theory of Harmonic Generation* (diss., Stanford U., 1974)

D. Hayes: 'Rameau's "Nouvelle méthode"', *JAMS*, xxvii (1974), 61

A. R. Keiler: 'Music as Metalanguage: Rameau's Fundamental Bass', *Music Theory: Special Topics*, ed. R. Browne (New York, 1981), 83

J. W. Krehbiel: *Harmonic Principles of J.-Ph. Rameau and his Contemporaries* (diss., Indiana U., 1964)

D. Lewin: 'Two Interesting Passages in Rameau's "Traité de l'harmonie"', *ITO*, iv/3 (1978), 3

C. B. Paul: *Rameau's Musical Theories and the Age of Reason* (diss., U. of California, Berkeley, 1966)

E. C. Verba: 'The Development of Rameau's Thoughts on Modulation and Chromatics', *JAMS*, xxvi (1973), 69

——: 'Rameau's Views on Modulation and their Background in French Theory', *JAMS*, xxxi (1978), 467

J. K. Randall: 'Haydn: String Quartet in D Major, op.76, no.5', *MR*, xxii (1960), 94

L. S. Rappoport, A. Sokhor and Yu. Kholopov, eds.: *Teoreticheskiye problemï muzïkal'nïkh form i zhanrov* [Theoretical problems of musical form and genre] (Moscow, 1971–2)

R. Rastall: 'Vocal Range and Tessitura in Music from York Play 45', *MusA*, iii (1984), 181

L. G. Ratner: *Harmonic Aspects of Classic Form* (diss., U. of California, Berkeley, 1947); see also *JAMS*, ii (1949), 159

——: 'Eighteenth-century Theories of Musical Period Structure', *MQ*, xlii (1956), 439

——: *Music: the Listener's Art* (New York, 1957, 3/1977)

——: *Harmony, Structure and Style* (New York, 1962)

——: '*Ars combinatoria*: Chance and Choice in Eighteenth-century Music', *Studies in Eighteenth-century Music: a Tribute to Karl Geiringer* (New York and London, 1970)

——: *Classic Music: Expression, Form and Style* (New York, 1979)

E. Ratz: *Einführung in die musikalische Formenlehre: über Formprinzipien in den Inventionen und Fugen J. S. Bachs und ihre Bedeutung für die Kompositionstechnik Beethovens* (Vienna, 1951, 3/1968)

——: *Probleme der muskalischen Formenlehre* (Vienna, 1953)

——: 'Zum Formproblem bei Gustav Mahler: eine Analyse des ersten Satzes der IX. Symphonie', *Mf*, viii (1955), 169

——: 'Zum Formproblem bei Gustav Mahler: eine Analyse des Finales der VI. Symphonie', *Mf*, ix (1956), 156

——: 'Über die Bedeutung der funktionellen Formenlehre für die Erkenntnis des Wohltemperierten Klaviers', *Mf*, xxi (1968), 17

——: 'Analyse und Hermeneutik in ihrer Bedeutung für die Interpretation Beethovens', *ÖMz*, xxv (1970), 756; Eng. trans. in *MusA*, iii (1984), 243

F. Reckow: 'Unendliche Melodie', *HMT*

W. Reckziegel: 'Die Notenschrift im Computer dargestellt', *SM*, ix (1967), 395

——: 'Musikanalyse: eine exakte Wissenschaft?', *Elektronische Datenverarbeitung in der Musikwissenschaft*, ed. H. Heckmann (Regensburg, 1967), 203

——: 'Musikanalyse und Wissenschaft', *SM*, ix (1967), 163

——: *Theorien zur Formalanalyse mehrstimmiger Musik* (Cologne and Opladen, 1967)

——: 'Musik im Datenspeicher', *Mf*, xxi (1968), 427

A. A. Reformastky: 'Rech'i musïka v penii' [Musical speech in song], *Vosprosï kul'turï rech'i*, ed. S. I. Ozegov (Moscow, 1955), i, 173

E. Regener: 'A Multi-pass Transcription and a System for Music Analysis by Computer', *Elektronische Datenverarbeitung in der Musikwissenschaft*, ed. H. Heckmann (Regensburg, 1967), 89

——: 'Layered Music-theoretic Systems', *PNM*, vi/1 (1967), 52

A. Reicha: *Practische Beispiele: ein Beitrag zur Geistescultur des Tonsetzers* (Vienna, 1803)

——: *Traité de mélodie* (Paris, 1814, 2/1832; Ger. trans. in Czerny, 1834; Eng. trans., 1893)

165

Bibliography

——: *Cours de composition musicale ou traité complet et raisonné d'harmonie pratique* (Paris, ?1816–18; Ger. trans. in Czerny, 1834; Eng. trans., 1854/*R*1977)

——: *Traité de haute composition musicale* (Paris, 1824–6; Ger. trans. in Czerny, 1834; It. trans., 1850; Eng. trans., 1850)

——: *Art du compositeur dramatique ou cours complet de composition vocale* (Paris, 1833; Ger. trans. by Czerny, 1835 as *Die Kunst der dramatischen Komposition*)

E. Bücken: 'Anton Reicha als Theoretiker', *ZMw*, ii (1919–20), 156

See also Bent (1980), Cole (1969), Groth (1983), Moyer (1969), Ritzel (1969), Schmalzriedt (1984) and Stevens (1974)

B. Reimer: 'Information Theory and the Analysis of Musical Meaning', *Council of Research in Music Education Bulletin*, no.2 (1964), 14

R. Réti: *The Thematic Process in Music* (New York, 1951)

——: 'The Role of Duothematicism in the Evolution of Sonata Form', *MR*, xvii (1956), 110; Ger. trans. in *ÖMz*, xi (1956), 306

——: *Tonality, Atonality, Pantonality: a Study of some Trends in Twentieth Century Music* (London, 1958/*R*1978)

——: *Thematic Patterns in Sonatas of Beethoven*, ed. D. Cooke (London, 1967)

D. M. Schwejda: *An Investigation of the Analytical Techniques used by Rudolph Réti in the 'Thematic Process in Music'* (diss., Indiana U., 1967)

See also Beeson (1971) and Dahlhaus (1977)

W. H. Reynolds: 'Unity in Music', *JMT*, ii (1958), 97 [see also exchange with W. Gettel, ii (1958), 240, and iii (1959), 140]

E. F. E. Richter: *Die Grundzüge der musikalischen Formen und ihre Analyse* (Leipzig, 1852)

H. Riemann: *Über das musikalische Hören* (diss., U. of Göttingen, 1873; Leipzig, 1874) [also pubd as *Musikalische Logik* (Leipzig, 1873)]

——: *Musikalische Syntaxis: Grundriss einer harmonischen Satzbildungslehre* (Leipzig, 1877/*R*1971)

——: *Der Ausdruck in der Musik* (Leipzig, 1883)

——: *Musikalische Dynamik und Agogik: Lehrbuch der musikalischen Phrasierung* (Hamburg and St Petersburg, 1884)

——: *Systematische Modulationslehre als Grundlage der musikalischen Formenlehre* (Hamburg, 1887)

——: *Katechismus der Kompositionslehre (Musikalische Formenlehre)* (Leipzig, 1889, 3/1905 as *Grundriss der Kompositionslehre*; Eng. trans., n.d.)

——: *Katechismus des Generalbass-Spiels* (Leipzig, 1889, 2/1903; 4/1917 as *Anleitung zum Generalbass-Spielen (Harmonie-Übungen am Klavier)*, some later edns. as *Handbuch des Generalbass-Spiels)*

——: *Handbuch der Fugen-Komposition (Analyse von J. S. Bachs 'Wohltemperiertem Klavier' und 'Kunst der Fuge')* (Leipzig, 1890, 2/1906; partial Eng. trans. by J. S. Shedlock, 1925 as *Analysis of J. S. Bach's Wohltemperirtes Clavier (48 Preludes and Fugues))*

——: *Katechismus der Harmonie- und Modulationslehre* (Leipzig, 1890, 9/1923–4 as *Handbuch der Harmonielehre*)

——: *Vereinfachte Harmonielehre oder die Lehre von den tonalen Funktionen der Akkorde* (London and New York, 1893, 2/1903; Eng. trans. by H. Bewerunge, 1896)

——: *Präludien und Studien: gesammelte Aufsätze zur Ästhetik, Theorie und Geschichte der Musik* (Leipzig, 1895–1901/*R*1967)

——: *Geschichte der Musiktheorie im IX.–XIX. Jahrhundert*, iii: *Die Harmonielehre* (Leipzig, 1898, 2/1921; Eng. trans., ed. W. C. Mickelsen, 1977)

——: *Vademecum der Phrasierung* (Leipzig, 1900, 8/1912 as *Handbuch der Phrasierung*)

——: *Grosse Kompositionslehre*, i: *Der homophone Satz* (Berlin and Stuttgart, 1902, 2/1912); ii: *Der polyphone Satz* (Berlin and Stuttgart, 1903, 2/1912); iii: *Der Orchestersatz und der dramatische Gesangstil* (Berlin and Stuttgart, 1913)

——: *Beethovens Streichquartette* (Berlin, 1903)

——: *System der musikalischen Rhythmik und Metrik* (Leipzig, 1903/*R*1971)

——: *Ludwig van Beethovens sämtliche Klavier-Solosonaten: ästhetische und formal-technische Analyse* (Berlin, 1918–19, 4/1920)

——: see also Marx (1837–47)

166

Bibliography

—— and C. Fuchs: *Katechismus der Phrasierung (Praktische Anleitung zum Phrasieren)* (Leipzig, 1890)

G. Becking: ' "Hören" und "Analysieren" (über Riemanns Beethoven-Analysen)', *ZMw*, i (1918–19), 587

T. Christenson: 'The Schichtenlehre of Hugo Riemann', *ITO*, vi/4 (1982), 37

H. Grabner: *Die Funktionstheorie H. Riemanns und ihre Bedeutung für die praktische Analyse* (Munich, 1923, 2/1930)

E. Seidel: 'Die Harmonielehre Hugo Riemanns', *Beiträge zur Musiktheorie des 19. Jahrhunderts*, ed. M. Vogel (Regensburg, 1966), 39–92

See also Federhofer (1958, 1981)

J. Riepel: *Anfangsgründe zur musikalischen Setzkunst*, i: *De Rhythmopoeia* (Regensburg, 1752, 2/1754); ii: *Grundregeln zur Tonkunst insgemein* (Frankfurt am Main, 1755); iii: *Gründliche Erklaerung der Tonordnung* (Frankfurt am Main, 1757); iv: *Erlaeuterung der betrueglichen Tonordnung* (Augsburg, 1765); v: *Unentbehrliche Anmerkungen zum Contrapunct* (Regensburg, 1768)

E. Schwarzmaier: *Die Takt- und Tonordnung Joseph Riepels* (Wolfenbüttel, 1936)

W. Twittenhoff: *Die musiktheoretischen Schriften Joseph Riepels (1709–1782) als Beispiel einer anschaulichen Musiklehre* (Halle and Berlin, 1935/R1971)

See also Feil (1955)

N.-E. Ringbom: *Über die Deutbarkeit der Tonkunst* (Turku, 1955)

F. Ritzel: *Die Entwicklung der Sonatenform im musiktheoretischen Schrifttum des 18. und 19. Jahrhunderts* (Wiesbaden, 1969)

B. V. Rivera: 'Harmonic Theory in Musical Treatises of the Late Fifteenth and Early Sixteenth Centuries', *MTS*, i (1979), 80

——: 'The Seventeenth-century Theory of Triadic Generation and Invertibility and its Application in Contemporaneous Rules of Composition', *MTS*, vi (1984), 63

C. Roads: 'An Overview of Music Representations', *Musical Grammars and Computer Analysis: Modena 1982*, 7–37

T. D. Robison: '*IML–MIR*: a Data-processing System for the Analysis of Music', *Elektronische Datenverarbeitung in der Musikwissenschaft*, ed. H. Heckmann (Regensburg, 1967), 103

G. Rochberg: *The Hexachord and its Relation to the Twelve-tone Row* (Bryn Mawr, Penn., 1955)

——: 'The Harmonic Tendency of the Hexachord', *JMT*, iii (1959), 208

——: 'Set Structure as a Compositional Determinant', *JMT*, v (1961), 72

M. R. Rogers: 'Chopin, Prelude in A Minor, op.28, no.2', *19th Century Music*, iv (1980–81), 244

H. G. Rohrer: *Musikalische Stylanalyse auf der Grundlage eines Modelles für Lernprozesse* (Berlin and Munich, 1970)

J. Rohwer: 'Zur Analyse neuer Musik', *Mf*, xxi (1968), 69

——: *Die harmonischen Grundlagen der Musik* (Kassel, 1970)

Roland-Manuel: 'L'analyse musicale: langage, styles et formes', *Précis de musicologie*, ed. J. Chailley (Paris, 1958), 332

G. H. Roller: *The Development of the Methods for Analysis of Musical Composition and for the Formation of a Symmetrical Twelve-tone Row using the Electronic Digital Computer* (diss., Michigan State U., 1964)

——: 'Development of a Method for Analysis of Musical Compositions using an Electronic Digital Computer', *JRME*, xii (1965), 249

C. Rosen: *The Classical Style: Haydn, Mozart, Beethoven* (New York, 1971, 2/1972)

——: *Sonata Forms* (New York, 1980)

H. Rösing: *Probleme und neue Wege der Analyse von Instrumenten- und Orchesterklängen* (Vienna, 1970)

D. Rostan: 'Set Design and Formal Symmetry in Stravinsky's "The Flood" ', *Sonus*, ii/2 (1982), 26

J. Rothgeb: 'Some Uses of Mathematical Concepts in Theories of Music', *JMT*, x (1966), 200

——: 'Some Ordering Relationships in the Twelve-tone System', *JMT*, xi (1967), 176

——: see also Schenker (ii)

Bibliography

J. Rufer: *Die Komposition mit zwölf Tönen* (Berlin, 1952; Eng. trans. by H. Searle, 1969)

P. Rummenhöller: *Musiktheoretisches Denken im 19. Jahrhundert: versuch einer Interpretation erkenntnistheoretischer Zeugnisse in der Musiktheorie* (Regensburg, 1967)

——: 'Anmerkungen zur musikalischen Analyse', *Zeitschrift für Musiktheorie*, iii/1 (1972), 2

J. Rushton: 'The Overture to "Les Troyens" ', *MusA*, iv (1985), 119

N. Ruwet: 'Contradictions du langage sériel', *RBM*, xiii (1959), 83; repr. in *Langage, musique, poésie* (Paris, 1972), 23

——: 'Fonction de la parole dans la musique vocale', *RBM*, xv (1961), 8; repr. in *Langage, musique, poésie* (Paris, 1972), 41

——: 'Méthodes d'analyse en musicologie', *RBM*, xx (1966), 65; repr. in *Langage, musique, poésie* (Paris, 1972); Eng. trans. in *MusA*, v (1986)

——: 'Musicologie et linguistique', *Revue internationale des sciences sociales*, xix (1967), 85

——: 'Quelques remarques sur le rôle de la répétition dans la syntaxe musicale', *To Honor Roman Jakobson* (The Hague, 1967), 1693

——: *Langage, musique, poésie* (Paris, 1972) [incl. articles on music written 1959–67]

——: 'Théorie et méthodes dans les études musicales', *Mj*, no.17 (1974), 11

K. J. Sachs and C. Dahlhaus: 'Counterpoint', *Grove 6*

G. de Saint-Foix: *Les symphonies de Mozart* (Paris, 1932; Eng. trans., 1946)

G. Saint-Guirons: 'Quelques aspects de la musique considérée d'un point de vue linguistique (recherche d'une analyse musicale distinctive)', *Etudes de linguistique appliquée*, iii (1964), 12

A. Salop: *Studies in the History of Musical Style* (Chicago, 1971)

F. Salzer: see Schenker (i) and (ii)

E. Sanders: 'The Early Motets of Philippe de Vitry', *JAMS*, xxviii (1975), 24

M. V. Sandresky: 'The Continuing Concept of the Platonic-Pythagorean System and its Application to the Analysis of Fifteenth-century Music', *MTS*, i (1979), 107

E. Sapir: 'Representative Music', *MQ*, iv (1918), 161

C. Schachter: see Schenker (ii) and (iv)

P. Schaeffer: *Traité des objets musicaux: essai interdisciplines* (Paris, 1966)

——: *Guide des objets sonores* (Paris, 1983)

J. Schalk: 'Das Gesetz der Tonalität', *BB*, xi (1888), 192, 381; xii (1889), 191; xiii (1890), 65

J. A. Scheibe: *Der critische Musikus* (Hamburg, 1737–40, 2/1745)

SCHENKER: *(i) primary*

H. Schenker: *Ein Beitrag zur Ornamentik, als Einführung zu Ph. Em. Bachs Klavierwerken, mitumfassend auch die Ornamentik Haydns, Mozarts u. Beethovens etc.* (Vienna, 1904, 2/1908/ R1954; Eng. trans. by H. Siegel in *Music Forum*, iv (1976), 1–139)

——: [orig. anon.]: *Harmonielehre*, Neue musikalische Theorien und Phantasien, i (Berlin and Stuttgart, 1906/R1978; Eng. trans. by E. M. Borgese, 1954/R1973 as *Harmony*)

——: *Chromatische Fantasia und Fuge D moll von Joh. Seb. Bach: kritische Ausgabe mit Anhang:* (Vienna, 1910, rev. 1970 ed. O. Jonas; Eng. trans. by H. Siegel, 1984)

——: *Kontrapunkt I: Cantus firmus und zweistimmiger Satz*, Neue musikalische Theorien und Phantasien, ii/1 (Vienna, 1910); *Kontrapunkt II: Drei- und mehrstimmiger Satz*, Neue musikalische Theorien und Phantasien, ii/2 (Vienna, 1922)

——: *Beethovens Neunte Sinfonie: eine Darstellung des musikalischen Inhaltes unter fortlaufender Berücksichtigung auch des Vortrages und der Literatur* (Vienna, 1912/R1969)

——: *Die letzten fünf Sonaten von Beethoven: kritische Ausgabe mit Einführung und Erläuterung* ['Erläuterungsausgabe'] (Vienna, 1913–21, 2/1971–2): *Sonate E dur Op.109* (1913); *Sonate As dur Op.110* (1915); *Sonate C moll Op.111* (1916); *Sonate A dur Op.101* (1921) [that of op.106 unpubd] [review by W. Drabkin, *PNM*, xii/1–2 (1973–4), 319]

——: *Der Tonwille: Flugblätter zum Zeugnis unwandelbarer Gesetze der Tonkunst* (Vienna, 1921–4) [in 10 issues]; Eng. trans. of essay on Schubert in *Sonus*, vi (1986), 31

——: *Beethoven: Fünfte Sinfonie: eine Darstellung des musikalischen Inhaltes nach der Handschrift unter fortlaufender Berücksichtigung des Vortrages und der Literatur* (Vienna, 1925/ R1969) [orig. in *Der Tonwille*, i, v, vii]

——: *Das Meisterwerk in der Musik: ein Jahrbuch* (Munich, Vienna and Berlin, 1925–30/

*R*1974) [essays and analyses, incl. analyses of Mozart: Symphony no.40 in G minor, ii, 105–59 and Beethoven: Symphony no.3 in E♭, iii, 25–99] [Eng. trans. by J. Rothgeb of i, 61 in *Music Forum*, iv (1976), 141 as 'The Largo of J. S. Bach's Sonata no.3 for Unaccompanied Violin (BWV 1005)'; Eng. trans. by O. Grossman of ii, 45 in *JMT*, xii (1968), 164, repr. in Yeston (1977), 38 as 'Organic Structure in Sonata Form'; Eng. trans. by H. Siegel of ii, 97 in *Music Forum*, ii (1970), 274 as 'The Sarabande of J. S. Bach's Suite no.3 for Unaccompanied Violoncello (BWV 1009)']

——: *Fünf Urlinie Tafeln* (Vienna, 1932; New York, 1933 as *Fünf Urlinie-Tafeln: Five Analyses in Sketch Form*; Eng. version with glossary by F. Salzer, 1969 as *Five Graphic Music Analyses (Fünf Urlinie-Tafeln)*)

——: *Der freie Satz*, Neue musikalische Theorien und Phantasien, iii (Vienna, 1935, 2/1956; Eng. trans. by E. Oster, New York, 1979 as *Free Composition*)

(ii) Schenkerian theory by other writers and extensions of Schenkerian theory

Anon.: 'A Glossary of the Elements of Graphic Analysis', *Music Forum*, i (1967), 260

J. M. Baker: 'Schenkerian Analysis and Post-tonal Music', *Aspects of Schenkerian Theory*, ed. D. W. Beach (New Haven, 1983)

D. W. Beach: [Analysis of Beethoven, op.53], *JMT*, xiii (1969), 188; repr. in Yeston (1977), 202

——: 'A Recurring Pattern in Mozart's Music', *JMT*, xxvii (1983), 1

——, ed.: *Aspects of Schenkerian Theory* (New Haven, 1983), esp. 1–38

——: 'Motive and Structure in the Andante Movement of Mozart's Piano Sonata K.545', *MusA*, iii (1984), 227

P. Bergquist: 'Mode and Polyphony around 1500: Theory and Practice', *Music Forum*, i (1967), 99–161

——: 'The First Movement of Mahler's Tenth Symphony: an Analysis and Examination of the Sketches', *Music Forum*, v (1980), 235–94

C. Burkhart: 'Schenker's "Motivic Parallelisms"', *JMT*, xxii (1978), 145–75

——: 'Schenker's Theory of Levels and Musical Performance', *Aspects of Schenkerian Theory*, ed. D. W. Beach (New Haven, 1983), 95

A. Cadwallader: 'Schenker's Unpublished Graphic Analysis of Brahms's Intermezzo op.117, no.2: Tonal Structure and Concealed Motivic Repetition', *MTS*, vi (1984), 1

A. Forte: *Contemporary Tone Structures* (New York, 1955)

——: *The Compositional Matrix* (New York, 1961/*R*1974)

—— and S. E. Gilbert: *Introduction to Schenkerian Analysis* (New York, 1982) [see also companion volume *Instructors Manual for Introduction to Schenkerian Analysis* (New York, 1982)]

M. Hughes and others: 'Analysis Symposium: Moments musicals op.94, Franz Schubert', *JMT*, xii (1968), 184–239; see also xiii (1969), 129, 218; repr. in Yeston (1977), 141–201

O. Jonas: *Das Wesen des musikalischen Kunstwerks: eine Einführung in die Lehre Heinrich Schenkers* (Vienna, 1934, rev. 2/1972 as *Einführung in die Lehre Heinrich Schenkers*; Eng. trans., 1982 as *Introduction to the Theory of Heinrich Schenker*)

——: 'Ein Bach Präludium: ein Weg zum organischen Hören', *Der Dreiklang* (1937), April, p.13; repr. in *Musikerziehung*, xx (1967), 205

——: 'Mozarts ewige Melodie, I–II', *Der Dreiklang* (1937), June, p.84; repr. in *Musikerziehung*, xxx (1977), 118

R. Kamien: 'Aspects of Motivic Elaboration in the Opening Movement of Haydn's Piano Sonata in C♯ Minor [Hob.XVI:36]', *Aspects of Schenkerian Theory*, ed. D. W. Beach (New Haven, 1983), 77

A. T. Katz: *Challenge to Musical Tradition: a New Concept of Tonality* (London, 1945)

L. Laskowski: 'Context and Voice Leading: Influence on Thematic and Tonal Structure', *TP*, iv/1 (1979), 15 [response by R. Gauldin: 'Further Thoughts on Some Bach Preludes', 38; reply by Laskowski: 'Symmetrical Design and its Relationship to Voice Leading', 57]

Bibliography

E. Laufer: [Analysis of Brahms op.105 no.1], *JMT*, xv (1971), 34

J. Lester: *A Theory of Atonal Prolongations as Used in an Analysis of the Serenade, op.24, by Arnold Schoenberg* (diss., U. of Michigan, Ann Arbor, 1971)

D. Loeb: 'An Analytic Study of Japanese Koto Music', *Music Forum*, iv (1976), 335–93

A. McNamee: 'The Introduction in Schubert's *Lieder*', *MusA*, iv (1985), 95

W. J. Mitchell: 'The Tristan Prelude: Techniques and Structure', *Music Forum*, i (1967), 162

S. Novack: 'The Analysis of Pre-Baroque Music', *Aspects of Schenkerian Theory*, ed. D. W. Beach (New Haven, 1983), 113

E. Oster: 'The Fantaisie-Impromptu: a Tribute to Beethoven', *Musicology*, i (1947), 407; repr. in Beach (1983), 189

——: 'The Dramatic Character of the Egmont Overture', *Musicology*, ii (1949), 269; repr. in Beach (1983), 209

——: 'Register and the Large-scale Connection', *JMT*, v (1961), 54; repr. in Yeston (1977), 54

——: [Analysis of Mozart, K355], *JMT*, x (1966), 32

J. Rothgeb: 'Design as a Key to Structure in Tonal Music', *JMT*, xv (1971), 230; repr. in Yeston (1977), 72

——: 'Chopin's C-minor Nocturne, op.48, no.1, First Part: Voice Leading and Motivic Content', *TP*, v/2 (1980), 26

——: 'Thematic Content: a Schenkerian View', *Aspects of Schenkerian Analysis*, ed. D. W. Beach (New Haven, 1983), 39

F. Salzer: *Sinn und Wesen der abendländischen Mehrstimmigkeit* (Vienna, 1935)

——: *Structural Hearing* (New York, 1952, 2/1962) [review by M. Babbitt in *JAMS*, v (1952), 260]

——: 'Tonality in Early Medieval Polyphony: toward a History of Tonality', *Music Forum*, i (1967), 35

——: 'Heinrich Schenker and Historical Research: Monteverdi's Madrigal "Oimè, se tanto amate" ', *Aspects of Schenkerian Analysis*, ed. D. W. Beach (New Haven, 1983), 135

—— and C. Schachter: *Counterpoint in Composition: the Study of Voice Leading* (New York, 1969)

C. Schachter: 'Landini's Treatment of Consonance and Dissonance: a Study of Fourteenth-century Counterpoint', *Music Forum*, ii (1970), 130–87

——: 'Rhythm and Linear Analysis: a Preliminary Study', *Music Forum*, iv (1976), 281–334; 'Rhythm and Linear Analysis: Durational Reduction', *Music Forum*, v (1980), 197–232

——: 'Motive and Text in Four Schubert Songs', *Aspects of Schenkerian Analysis*, ed. D. W. Beach (New Haven, 1983), 61

——: 'The First Movement of Brahms's Second Symphony: the First Theme and its Consequences', *MusA*, ii (1983), 55

J. Straus: 'A Principle of Voice Leading in the Music of Stravinsky', *MTS*, iv (1982), 106

R. Travis: 'Towards a New Concept of Tonality', *JMT*, iii (1959), 257

——: 'Directed Motion in Two Brief Pieces by Schoenberg and Webern', *PNM*, iv/2 (1966), 85

——: 'Tonal Coherence in the First Movement of Bartók's Fourth String Quartet', *Music Forum*, ii (1970), 298–371

——: 'J. S. Bach, Invention no.1 in C major: Reduction and Graph', *ITO*, ii/7 (1976), 3; 'J. S. Bach, Invention no.13 in A minor: Reduction and Graph', *ITO*, ii/8 (1976), 29

—— and A. Forte: 'Analysis Symposium: Webern, Orchestral Pieces (1913) Movement I ("bewegt")', *JMT*, xvii (1974), 2–43

C. Wintle: 'Kontra-Schenker: *Largo e mesto* from Beethoven's op.10 no.3', *MusA*, iv (1985), 145–82

M. Yeston: 'Rubato and the Middleground', *JMT*, xix (1975), 286; repr. in Yeston (1977), 94

Bibliography

——: *The Stratification of Musical Rhythm* (New Haven and London, 1976)

——, ed.: *Readings in Schenker Analysis and Other Approaches* (New Haven, 1977)

See also Baker (1980), Dunsby and Stopford (1981), Kassler (1967), Komar (1971) and Morgan (1976, 1978)

(iii) bibliography

D. W. Beach: 'A Schenker Bibliography', *JMT*, xiii (1969), 1–37; repr. in *Readings in Schenker Analysis and Other Approaches*, ed. M. Yeston (New Haven, 1977), 273–311; continued in *JMT*, xxiii (1979), 275

L. Laskowsky, ed.: *Heinrich Schenker: an Annotated Index to his Analyses of Musical Works* (New York, 1978) [incl. list of Schenker's writings and bibliography of Schenkerian theory]

(iv) secondary

D. W. Beach: 'The Current State of Schenkerian Research', *AcM*, lvii (1985), 275–307

H. Federhofer: 'Die Musiktheorie Heinrich Schenkers', *SMz*, lxxxvii (1947), 265

——: *Heinrich Schenker, nach Tagebücher und Briefen in der Oswald Jonas Memorial Collection* (Hildesheim, 1985)

A. Forte: 'Schenker's Conception of Musical Structure', *JMT*, v (1959), 1–30; repr. in Yeston (1977), 3–37

H. Kaufmann: 'Fortschritt und Reaktion in der Lehre Heinrich Schenkers', *NZM*, Jg.126 (1965), 5; also in *Das Orchester*, xiii (1965), 44

W. Keller: 'Heinrich Schenkers Harmonielehre', *Beiträge zur Musiktheorie des 19. Jahrhunderts*, ed. M. Vogel (Regensburg, 1966), 203

M. Mann: 'Schenker's Contribution to Music Theory', *MR*, x (1949), 3

R. P. Morgan: 'Schenker and the Theoretical Tradition', *College Music Symposium*, xviii (1978), 88

W. Pastille: 'Heinrich Schenker, Anti-organicist', *19th Century Music*, viii (1984–5), 28

——: *Ursatz: the Musical Philosophy of Heinrich Schenker* (diss., Cornell U., 1985)

K. O. Plum: *Untersuchungen zu Heinrich Schenkers Stimmführungsanalyse* (Regensburg, 1979)

W. Riezler: 'Die Urlinie', *Die Musik*, xxii (1929–30), 502

C. Schachter, D. Epstein and W. E. Benjamin: 'Review Symposium: Schenker, "Free Composition"', *JMT*, xxv (1981), 115–73

S. Slatin: *The Theories of Heinrich Schenker in Perspective* (diss., Columbia U., 1967)

C. J. Smith: 'Beethoven via Schenker: a Review' [of *Ludwig van Beethoven: Complete Piano Sonatas*, ed. H. Schenker (New York, *R*1975)], *ITO*, iv/1 (1978), 37

S. W. Smoliar and others: 'A LISP-based System for the Study of Schenkerian Analysis', *CHum*, x (1976–7), 21

J. Snell: *Design for a Formal System for Deriving Tonal Music* (diss., MIT, 1979)

R. Travis: 'Towards a New Concept of Tonality?', *JMT*, iii (1959), 257

G. Warfield: *Layer Analysis: a Primer of Elementary Tonal Structures* (New York, 1976)

M. Yeston, ed.: *Readings in Schenker Analysis and other Approaches* (New Haven, 1977)

See also Dahlhaus (1973–4), Dunsby (1977–8), Federhofer (1950, 1958, 1981, 1982) and Narmour (1977)

W. Schenkman: 'Fixed Ideas and Recurring Patterns in Berlioz's Melody', *MR*, xl (1979), 25

——: 'Rhythmic Motifs as Key to Beethoven's Characteristic Phrase Structure', *MR*, xliv (1983), 186

A. Schering: 'Die Lehre von der musikalischen Figuren', *KJb*, xxi (1908), 106

——: *Musikalische Bildung und Erziehung zum musikalischen Hören* (Leipzig, 1911, 4/1924)

——: 'Das kolorierte Orgelmadrigal des Trecento', *SIMG*, xiii (1911–12), 172

——: 'Zur Grundlegung der musikalischen Hermeneutik', *Zeitschrift für Ästhetik und allgemeine Kunstwissenschaft*, ix (1914), 168

——: 'Bach und das Symbol', *BJb*, xxii (1925), 40; xxv (1928), 119

——: 'Musikalische Analyse und Wertidee', *JbMP 1929*, 9

171

Bibliography

——: *Beethoven in neuer Deutung* (Leipzig, 1934)
——: *Beethoven und die Dichtung* (Berlin, 1936)
——: *Das Symbol in der Musik* (Leipzig, 1941)
——: *Vom Wesen der Musik: ausgewählte Aufsätze*, ed. K. M. Komma (Stuttgart, 1974)
    A. Forchert: 'Scherings Beethovendeutung und ihre methodischen Voraussetzungen', *Beiträge zur musikalischen Hermeneutik*, ed. C. Dahlhaus (Regensburg, 1975), 41
L. Schiedermair: *Der junge Beethoven* (Leipzig, 1925, 3/1951)
J. Schillinger: *The Schillinger System of Musical Composition* (New York, 1946/R1977)
N. Schiødt and B. Svejgaard: 'Application of Computer Techniques to the Analysis of Byzantine Sticherarion Melodies', *Elektronische Datenverarbeitung in der Musikwissenschaft*, ed. H. Heckmann (Regensburg, 1967), 187
R. Schlösser: 'Der Stufenweg rechts und das Umrahmungsmotiv', *BB*, xliii (1920), 28
J. Schmalfeldt: *Berg's "Wozzeck": Pitch-class Set Structures and the Dramatic Design* (diss., Yale U., 1979; New York and London, 1983 as *Berg's "Wozzeck": Harmonic Language and Dramatic Design*)
——: 'On the Relation of Analysis to Performance: Beethoven's Bagatelles op.126, nos.2 and 5', *JMT*, xxix (1985), 1–31
S. Schmalzriedt: 'Durchführen, Durchführung', 'Exposition', 'Reprise/ripresa', *HMT*
——: 'Charakter und Drama: zur historischen Analyse von Haydnschen und Beethovenschen Sonatensätzen', *AMw*, xli (1984), 37
A. Schmitz: *Beethovens 'zwei Prinzipe'* (Berlin and Bonn, 1923)
——: *Die Bildlichkeit der wortgebundenen Musik J. S. Bachs* (Mainz, 1950)
——: 'Figuren, musikalisch-rhetorische', *MGG*
R. Schneider: *Semiotik der Musik: Darstellung und Kritik* (Munich, 1980)
A. Schoenberg: *Harmonielehre* (Vienna, 1911/R1978; Eng. trans. by R. D. W. Adams, 1948 as *Theory of Harmony*; Eng. trans. by R. E. Carter, 1978 as *Theory of Harmony*)
——: *Models for Beginners in Composition* (Los Angeles, 1942, enlarged 2/1943, rev. 3/1972 by L. Stein)
——: *Style and Idea* (New York, 1950) [15 essays]
——: *Structural Functions of Harmony* (London, 1954, rev. 2/1969)
——: *Preliminary Exercises in Counterpoint*, ed. L. Stein (London, 1963)
——: *Fundamentals of Musical Composition*, ed. G. Strang and L. Stein (London, 1967; Ger. trans., 1979)
——: *Style and Idea: Selected Writings*, ed. L. Stein (London, 1975) [104 essays]
    M. Beiche: 'Grundgestalt', *HMT*
    P. Carpenter: ' "Grundgestalt" as Tonal Function', *MTS*, v (1983), 15
    J. Dunsby: 'Schoenberg on Cadence', *JASI*, iv (1980), 35
    W. Frisch: 'Brahms, Developing Variation, and the Schoenberg Critical Tradition', *19th Century Music*, v (1981–2), 215
    ——: *Brahms and the Principle of Developing Variation* (Berkeley and Los Angeles, 1984)
    A. Goehr: 'The Theoretical Writings of Arnold Schoenberg', *PRMA*, c (1973–4), 85
    ——: 'Schoenberg's "Gedanke" Manuscript', *JASI*, ii (1977), 4
    ——: 'Schoenberg and Karl Kraus: the Idea behind the Music', *MusA*, iv (1985), 59
    M. Musgrave: 'Schoenberg and Theory', *JASI*, iv (1980), 34
    C. Parmentola: 'La "Harmonielehre" di Schoenberg nella crisi del pensiero moderno', *NRMI*, ii (1968), 81
    D. Rexroth: *Arnold Schönberg als Theoretiker der tonalen Harmonik* (Bonn, 1971)
    L. Richter: 'Schoenbergs Harmonielehre und die freie Atonalität', *DJbM*, xiii (1968), 43
    J. Spratt: 'The Speculative Content of Schoenberg's "Harmonielehre" ', *CMc*, no.11 (1971), 83
    E. Stein: *Praktischer Leitfaden zu Schönbergs Harmonielehre* (Vienna, 1923)
    See also Beeson (1971), Dahlhaus (1973–4), Dunsby (1977–8) and Epstein (1979)
W.-A. Schultz: *Die freien Formen in der Musik des Expressionismus und Impressionismus* (Hamburg, 1974)
——: 'Anmerkungen zur Stilanalyse', *Mf*, xxvi (1973), 241
J. A. P. Schulz: see Kirnberger (1773) and Sulzer (1771–4)

Bibliography

E. Schwebsch: *J. S. Bach und die Kunst der Fuge* (Stuttgart, 1931)

S. Sechter: *Die Grundsätze der musikalischen Komposition* (Leipzig, 1853–4)
> W. E. Caplin: 'Harmony and Meter in the Theories of Simon Sechter', *MTS*, ii (1980), 74
> See also Wason (1981, 1983)

C. Seeger: 'Factorial Analysis of the Song as an Approach to the Formation of a Unitary Field of Theory', *JIFMC*, xx (1968), 33

W. Seidl: *Über Rhythmustheorien der Neuzeit* (Berne and Munich, 1975)
——: *Rhythmus: ein Begriffsbestimmung* (Darmstadt, 1976)

J. Selleck and R. Bakeman: 'Procedures for the Analysis of Form: Two Computer Applications', *JMT*, ix (1965), 281

B. Shamgar: 'On Locating the Retransition in Classic Sonata Form', *MR*, xlii (1981), 130

U. Siegele: *Kompositionsweise und Bearbeitungstechnik in der Instrumentalmusik Johann Sebastian Bachs* (Neuhausen, 1975)
——: *Bachs theologischer Formbegriff, dargestellt an das Duett F-dur* (Neuhausen, 1978)

N. Slonimsky: *Thesaurus of Scales and Melodic Patterns* (New York, 1947)

F. Smend: *Johann Sebastian Bach bei seinem Namen gerufen* (Kassel and Basle, 1950)

C. J. Smith: 'Prolongation and Progression as Musical Syntax', *Music Theory: Special Topics*, ed. R. Browne (New York, 1981), 139–74

F. J. Smith: 'Vers une phénoménologie du son', *Revue de métaphysique et de morale*, iii (1968), 328
——: *The Experience of Sound: Prelude to a Phenomenology of Music* (New York, 1979)

R. Smith: 'The Sorry Scheme of Things', *MR*, xxii (1961), 212

H. E. Smither: *Theories of Rhythm in the Nineteenth and Twentieth Centuries, with a Contribution to the Theory of Rhythm for the Study of Twentieth-century Music* (diss., Cornell U., 1960)
——: 'The Rhythmic Analysis of 20th-century Music', *JMT*, viii (1964), 54–88

S. W. Smoliar: *A Parallel Processing Model of Music Structures* (diss., MIT, 1972)
——: 'Process Structuring and Music Theory', *JMT*, xviii (1974), 309
——: 'Music Programs: an Approach to Music Theory through Computational Linguistics', *JMT*, xx (1976), 105

R. Solie: 'The Living Work: Organicism and Musical Analysis', *19th Century Music*, iv (1980–81), 147

W. R. Spalding: *Music: an Art and a Language* (Boston and New York, 1920)

I. Spink: *An Historical Approach to Musical Form* (London, 1967)

G. P. Springer: 'Language and Music: Parallels and Divergences', *For Roman Jakobson: Essays on … his Sixtieth Birthday* (The Hague, 1956), 504–13; Fr. trans. in *Mj*, no.5 (1971), 31

M. J. Steedman: 'The Perception of Musical Rhythm and Metre', *Perception*, vi (1977), 555

G. Stefani: 'Analisi, semiosi, semiotica', *RIM*, xi (1976), 106

R. Steglich: 'Das c-moll-Präludium aus dem ersten Teil des Wohltemperierten Klaviers J. S. Bachs', *BJb*, xx (1923), 1
——: *Die elementare Dynamik des musikalischen Rhythmus* (Leipzig, 1930)

L. Stein: *Structure and Style: the Study and Analysis of Musical Forms* (Evanston, 1962, 2/1965, rev., enlarged 3/1979) [see also companion book *Anthology of Musical Forms* (Evanston, 1962)]

W. Steinbeck: '"Ein wahres Spiel mit musikalischen Form": zum Scherzo Ludwig van Beethoven', *AMw*, xxxviii (1981), 194

R. Stephan, ed.: *Neue Wege der musikalischen Analyse: acht Beiträge von Lars Ulrich Abraham, Jürg Baur, Carl Dahlhaus, Harald Kaufmann und Rudolf Stephan* (Berlin, 1967)
——: *Probleme des musiktheoretischen Unterrichts: sieben Beiträge von Frédérique Baecker, Siegfried Borris, Carl Dahlhaus, Diether de la Motte, Erhard Karkoschka und Rudolf Stephan* (Berlin, 1967)
——: *Versuche musikalischer Analysen: sieben Beiträge von P. Benary, S. Borris, D. de la Motte, H. Enke, H.-P. Raiss und R. Stephan* (Berlin, 1967)

J. R. Stevens: 'Theme, Harmony and Texture in Classic–Romantic Descriptions of Concerto First-movement Form', *JAMS*, xxvii (1974), 26–60

K. Stockhausen: *Texte*, ed. D. Schnebel, i: *Texte zur elektronischen und instrumentalen Musik*; ii:

Bibliography

Texte zu eigenen Werken, zur Kunst anderer Aktuelles; iii: *Texte zur Musik, 1963–70*; iv: *Texte zur Musik, 1970–77* (Cologne, 1963–78)

W. Stockmeier: *Musikalische Formprinzipien, Formenlehre* (Cologne, 1967)

R. Stöhr, H. Gol and A. Orel: *Formenlehre der Musik* (Leipzig, 1933, 2/1954)

J. G. Sulzer: *Allgemeine Theorie der schönen Künste* (Leipzig, 1771–4, rev. 2/1778–9, 3/1786–7 ed. F. von Blankenburg, 4/1792–9/R1967) [articles on musical subjects by Sulzer, Kirnberger and Schulz]

I. Supičić: *La musique expressive* (Paris, 1957)

——: 'Matter and Form in Music', *IRASM*, i (1970), 149

——: 'Expression and Meaning in Music', *IRASM*, ii (1971), 194

R. Swift: '1–XII–99: Tonal Relations in Schoenberg's "Verklärte Nacht"', *19th Century Music*, i (1977–8), 3

A. Sychra: 'La chanson folkloristique du point de vue sémiologique', *Slovo a slovesnost* (Prague, 1949), 7; repr. in *Mj*, no.10 (1973), 12

V. H. Talley: 'A Critique of Musical Analysis', *JAMS*, vi (1953), 87

E. Tarasti: *Myth and Music: a Semiotic Approach to the Aesthetics of Myth in Music, especially that of Wagner, Sibelius and Stravinsky* (The Hague, 1979)

——: 'Pour une narratologie de Chopin', *IRASM*, xiv (1983), 53

R. Teitelbaum: 'Intervallic Relations in Atonal Music', *JMT*, ix (1965), 72–127

J. Tenney: *Meta (+) Hodos: a Phenomenology of Twentieth Century Musical Materials and an Approach to the Study of Form* (New Orleans, 1964)

—— and L. Polansky: 'Temporal Gestalt Perception in Music', *JMT*, xxiii (1979), 205–41

W. Thomson: 'The Problem of Music Analysis and Universals', *College Music Symposium*, vi (1966), 89

——: 'Style Analysis: or the Perils of Pigeonholes', *JMT*, xiv (1970), 192

J. Thym: 'Text-music Relationships in Schumann's "Frühlingsfahrt"', *TP*, v/2 (1980), 7

R. von Tobel: *Die Formenwelt der klassischen Instrumentalmusik* (Berne and Leipzig, 1935)

R. L. Todd: 'Liszt, Fantasy and Fugue for Organ on "Ad nos, ad salutarem undam"', *19th Century Music*, iv (1980–81), 250

P. A. Tove, L. Ejdesjö and A. Svärdström: 'Frequency and Time Analysis of Polyphonic Music', *Journal of the Acoustical Society of America*, xli (1967), 1265

D. F. Tovey: *A Companion to Beethoven's Pianoforte Sonatas (Bar-to-Bar Analysis)* (London, 1931/R1976, 2/1948)

——: *Essays in Musical Analysis*, i: *Symphonies*; ii: *Symphonies (II), Variations and Orchestral Polyphony*; iii: *Concertos*; iv: *Illustrative Music*; v: *Vocal Music*; vi: *Supplementary Essays, Glossary, and Index* (London, 1935–9/R1972; most essays repr. in 2 vols., 1981)

——: *A Musician Talks* (London, 1941/R1977)

——: *Essays in Musical Analysis*, vii: *Chamber Music* (London, 1944)

——: *Musical Articles from the Encyclopaedia Britannica* [14th edn.], ed. H. J. Foss (London, 1944)

    J. Kerman: 'Counsel for the Defense [of Tovey]', *Hudson Review*, iii (1950), 438

    ——: 'Tovey's Beethoven', *American Scholar* (1975–6), winter, 795; repubd in *Beethoven Studies*, ii, ed. A. Tyson (London, 1977), 172

    C. Wintle: 'Humpty Dumpty's Complaint: Tovey Revalued', *Soundings*, no.11 (1983–4), 14–45

R. Traimer: 'Zum Problem der musikalischen Werkanalyse', *NZM*, Jg.117 (1956), 621

R. Travis: see Schenker (ii) and (iv)

—— and A. Forte: 'Analysis Symposium: Webern, Orchestral Pieces (1913) Movement I ("bewegt")', *JMT*, xvii (1974), 2–43

C. H. Treibitz: 'Substance and Function in Concepts of Musical Structure', *MQ*, lxix (1983), 209

L. Treitler: 'Harmonic Procedure in the Fourth Quartet of Bela Bartók', *JMT*, iii (1959), 292

——: 'Music Analysis in an Historical Context', *College Music Symposium*, vi (1966), 75

——: 'The Present as History', *PNM*, vii/2 (1969), 1–58

——: 'Methods, Style, Analysis', *IMSCR*, xi *Copenhagen 1972*, i, 61

——: 'Homer and Gregory: the Transmission of Epic Poetry and Plainchant', *MQ*, ix

(1974), 333–72

——: 'History, Criticism, and Beethoven's Ninth Symphony', *19th Century Music*, iii (1979–80), 193

——: ' "To Worship that Celestial Sound": Motives for Analysis', *JMus*, i (1982), 153

B. Trowell: 'Proportion in the Music of Dunstable', *PRMA*, cv (1978–9), 100–41

V. Tsukkerman: 'Vidï tselostnovo anliza' [Aspects of integrated musical analysis], *SovM* (1967), no.4, p.100

P. Tunstall: 'Structuralism and Musicology', *CMc*, no.27 (1979), 51

R. E. Tyndall: *Musical Form* (Boston, 1964/*R*1977)

A. D. Ulïbïshev [Oulibicheff]: *Nouvelle biographie de Mozart suivie ... de l'analyse des principales oeuvres de Mozart* (Moscow, 1843)

——: *Beethoven: ses critiques et ses glossateurs* (Leipzig and Paris, 1857)

J.-M. Vaccaro: 'Proposition d'analyse pour une polyphonie vocale', *RdM*, lxi (1975), 35

B. Vermazen: 'Information Theory and Musical Value', *Journal of Aesthetics and Art Criticism*, xxix (1970–71), 367

J. A. Vertrees: 'Mozart's String Quartet K465: the History of a Controversy', *CMc*, no.17 (1974), 96

M. Vetter: *Untersuchungen zu den in der deutschen musikalischen Fachliteratur von 1918 bis 1964 enthaltenen Methoden der musikalischen Werkanalyse* (diss., Institut Greifswald, 1966)

J. Viret: 'Mélodie und "Gestalt": pour une nouvelle approche de l'analyse mélodique', *IRASM*, xiii (1982), 39

M. Vogel, ed.: *Beiträge zur Musiktheorie des 19. Jahrhunderts* (Regensburg, 1966)

G. J. Vogler: *Tonwissenschaft und Tonsetzkunst* (Mannheim, 1776/*R*1970)

——: *System für Fugenbau als Einleitung zur harmonischen Gesang-Verbindungs-Lehre* (Offenbach, ?1811)

    F. K. Grave: 'Abbé Vogler and the Study of Fugue', *MTS*, i (1979), 43

    ——: 'Abbé Vogler's Theory of Reduction', *CMc*, no.29 (1980), 41

    J. R. Stevens: 'Georg Joseph Vogler and the "Second Theme" in Sonata Form', *JMus*, ii (1983), 278

M. Wagner: *Die Harmonielehren der ersten Hälfte des 19. Jahrhunderts* (Regensburg, 1974)

A. Walker: 'Unconscious Motivation in the Composing Process', *MR*, xx (1959), 277

——: *A Study in Musical Analysis* (London, 1962)

——: *An Anatomy of Musical Criticism* (London, 1966)

    See also Beeson (1971)

R. Wallace: *Contemporaneous Criticism of Beethoven: a Case Study in Musical Aesthetics* (diss., Yale U., 1984; Cambridge, 1986 as *Beethoven's Critics*)

G. Warfield: see Schenker (iv)

R. Wason: *Fundamental Bass Theory in Nineteenth-century Vienna* (diss., Yale U., 1981; Ann Arbor, 1983 as *Viennese Harmonic Theory from Albrechtsberger to Schenker and Schoenberg*)

——: 'Schenker's Notion of Scale-step in Historical Perspective: Non-essential Harmonies in Viennese Fundamental Bass Theory', *JMT*, xxvii (1983), 49

G. Weber: *Versuch einer geordneten Theorie der Tonsetzkunst* (Mainz, 1817–21, 3/1830–32; Eng. trans. by J. Warner as *The Theory of Musical Composition*, 1842, rev. 2/1851 ed. J. Bishop)

    See Vertrees (1974)

A. Webern: *Der Weg zur neuen Musik* (Vienna, 1960; Eng. trans., 1963)

J. Webster: 'Schubert's Sonata Form and Brahms's First Maturity', *19th Century Music*, ii (1978–9), 18; iii (1979–80), 52

——: 'Sonata Form', *Grove 6*

M. Weingart: 'Etude du langage parlé suivi du point de vue musical avec considération particulière du tchèque', *Travaux du Cercle Linguistique de Copenhague*, i (1945), 172

E. Wen: 'A Disguised Reminiscence in the First Movement of Mozart's G minor Symphony', *MusA*, i (1982), 55

A. B. Wenk: *Analyses of Twentieth-century Music, 1940–1970* (Ann Arbor, 1975)

——: 'The Composer as Poet in "Das Lied von der Erde"', *19th Century Music*, i (1977–8), 33

M. H. Wennerstrom: *Parametric Analysis of Contemporary Musical Form* (diss., Indiana U., 1967)

175

Bibliography

W. Werker: *Studien über Symmetrie im Bau der Fugen ... des 'Wohltemperierten Klaviers'* (Leipzig, 1922)

——: *Bach-Studien*, ii: *Die Matthäuspassion* (Leipzig, 1923)

P. Westergaard: 'Some Problems in Rhythmic Theory and Analysis', *PNM*, i/1 (1962), 180

——: 'On the Notion of Style', *IMSCR*, xi *Copenhagen 1972*, i, 71

K. Westphal: 'Analyse und Interpretation', *Die Musik*, xxiv (1931–2), 5

——: 'Barockes und Klassisches Formhören', *SMz*, lxxv (1935), 365

——: *Der Begriff der musikalischen Form in der Wiener Klassik* (Leipzig, 1935)

J. D. White: *The Analysis of Music* (Englewood Cliffs, 1976)

A. Whittall: 'Post-twelve-note Analysis', *PRMA*, xciv (1967–8), 1

——: 'Tonality and the Whole-tone Scale in the Music of Debussy', *MR*, xxxvi (1975), 261

——: 'Musicology in Great Britain since 1945: III Analysis', *AcM*, lii (1980), 57

——: 'Music Analysis as Human Science?: "Le sacre du printemps" in Theory and Practice', *MusA*, i (1982), 33

——: 'Wagner's Great Transition?: from "Lohengrin" to "Das Rheingold"', *MusA*, ii (1983), 269

H. Wilcox and Pozzi Escot: 'A Musical Set Theory', *TP*, iv/2 (1979), 17

P. Wilson: 'Concepts of Prolongation in Bartók's Opus 20', *MTS*, vi (1984), 79

F. Winckel: 'Die informationstheoretische Analyse musikalischer Strukturen', *Mf*, xvii (1964), 1

S. D. Winnick: *Rhythm: an Annotated Bibliography* (Metuchen, 1974)

T. Winograd: 'Linguistics and the Computer Analysis of Tonal Harmony', *JMT*, xii (1968), 2–49

R. S. Winter: *Compositional Origins of Beethoven's String Quartet in C sharp Minor, op.131* (Ann Arbor, 1982)

C. Wintle: 'Schoenberg's Harmony: Theory and Practice', *JASI*, iv (1980), 50

——: 'Analysis and Performance: Webern's Concerto op.24/II', *MusA*, i (1982), 73

——: see also Dahlhaus, Schenker (ii) and Tovey

G. E. Wittlich: *An Examination of some Set-theoretic Applications in the Analysis of Non-serial Music* (diss., U. of Iowa, 1969)

——: 'Interval Set Structure in Schoenberg's op.11, no.1', *PNM*, xiii/1 (1974), 41

——: 'Sets and Ordering Procedures in Twentieth-century Music', *Aspects in Twentieth-century Music*, ed. G. E. Wittlich (Englewood Cliffs, 1975), 388–476

——: 'Compositional Premises in Schubert's Opus 94, Number 6', *ITO*, v/8 (1981), 31

C. Wolff: 'Towards a Methodology of Dialectic Style Consideration: Preliminary Terminological and Historical Considerations', *IMSCR*, xi *Copenhagen 1972*, i, 74

H. von Wolzogen: *Thematischer Leitfaden durch die Musik zu Richard Wagner's Festspiel 'Der Ring des Nibelungen'* (Leipzig, 1876)

——: *Thematischer Leitfaden durch die Musik von Richard Wagner's 'Tristan und Isolde'* (Leipzig, 1880)

——: *Thematischer Leitfaden durch die Musik von Richard Wagner's 'Parsifal'* (Leipzig, 1882)

K. H. Wörner: *Die Zeitalter der thematischen Prozess in der Geschichte der Musik* (Regensburg, 1969)

Y. Xenakis: *Musiques formelles: nouveaux principes formels de composition musicale* (Paris, 1963; Eng. trans., 1971 as *Formalized Music: Thought and Mathematics in Composition*)

——: *Musique, architecture* (Paris, 1971)

J. Yasser: *A Theory of Evolving Tonality* (New York, 1932/R1975)

M. Yeston, ed.: *Readings in Schenker Analysis and other Approaches* (New Haven, 1977)

——: see also Schenker (ii)

J. E. Youngblood: 'Style as Information', *JMT*, ii (1958), 24

R. Zaripov: *Kibernetika i muzïka* (Moscow, 1963; Eng. trans. in *PNM*, vii/2 (1969), 115–54)

V. Zuckerkandl: *Sound and Symbol*, i: *Music and the External World*, ii: *Man the Musician* (Princeton, 1956–73)

Index

179

Illustration Acknowledgments

We are grateful to the following for permission to reproduce illustrative material: British Library, London (fig.8); Schott & Co. Ltd, London (fig.23); Belmont Music Publishers, Los Angeles (figs.24 and 45); Faber & Faber Ltd, London (figs.24 and 31–4); Harvard University Press, Cambridge, Mass. (fig.25); The MIT Press, Cambridge, Mass. (figs.26–7); Universal Edition (Alfred A. Kalmus Ltd), Vienna (fig.28); Dover Publications Inc., New York (figs.29–30); Macmillan Publishing Company, New York (© 1967 by Rudolph Réti) (figs.31–4); Cornell University Press, Ithaca, NY (© 1970 by Cornell University) (fig.38); Société Belge de Musicologie, Brussels (fig.39); Union Générale d'Editions, Paris (figs.40–42); Edition Wilhelm Hansen A/S, Copenhagen (fig.43).

Analysis
Ian Bent
with William Drabkin

When *The New Grove Dictionary of Music and Musicians* was published in 1980 the article on analysis by Ian Bent was considered by Carl Dahlhaus, writing in *Music and Letters*, to be "one of the most outstanding contributions" to the dictionary. It has become a seminal work recommended to all students of the subject. In this volume, the author has revised the text and greatly extended the bibliography to take account of the intense theoretical activity of recent years, and his colleague, William Drabkin, has added an invaluable glossary of analytical terms in current use.

The textual material is presented in four sections, the first of which considers the place of analysis in the study of music. This is followed by an unparalleled and extensive survey of the history and development of analysis from its beginnings in the Middle Ages to the present day, as well as a new discussion of set theory. The final section is devoted to the various analytical methods, from the Schenkerian approach to Information Theory.

"*Analysis* by Ian D. Bent...is a tour de force, lucid, informative, and authoritative."
—Allen Forte, *The Musical Quarterly*